Typhoon: The Other Enemy

THE THIRD FLEET AND THE PACIFIC STORM
OF DECEMBER 1944

By Captain C. Raymond Calhoun,
U.S. Navy (Retired)

NAVAL INSTITUTE PRESS
Annapolis, Maryland

Copyright © 1981
by the United States Naval Institute
Annapolis, Maryland

Fourth printing, 1988

Library of Congress Cataloging in Publication Data
Calhoun, C. Raymond, 1913 –
    Typhoon, the other enemy.
    Bibliography: p.
    Includes index.
    1. World War, 1939–1945 – Naval operations,
American. 2. Philippine Sea, Battles of the, 1944.
3. World War, 1939–1945 – Personal narratives,
American. 4. Calhoun, C. Raymond, 1913 –
5. United States. Navy. Task Force 38 – History.
6. Typhoons – History – 20th century. 7. Destroyers
(Warships) – History – 20th century. I. Title.
D774.P5C34   940.54'5973   81-38384
ISBN 0-87021-510-8   AACR 2

Printed in the United States of America

This book is dedicated to the officers and men
of the United States Third Fleet
who lost their lives
during the typhoon of 18 December 1944.

Contents

Preface

This is the story of the U.S. Third Fleet's battle with a devastating typhoon in the Philippine Sea on 18 December 1944. It is about men and ships under conditions of extreme adversity, and tells of their desperate, often heroic, sometimes tragic struggle to survive. The account describes the loss of seven hundred and ninety officers and men, three destroyers, and well over a hundred aircraft. It notes that two of the three ships lost were *Farragut*-class destroyers, long known to have low margins of stability. Included is an eyewitness account of the experience of the *Dewey*, a destroyer of the same class, which rolled to the limit of its capacity to recover—in the words of Hanson Baldwin, "perhaps the first vessel in the history of the sea to survive such a roll."[1] Some of these events raised questions about destroyer stability and the responsibility of the Bureau of Ships for destroyer design. This book addresses those questions.

While many factors contributed to the fleet's entrapment, the most significant were failures in command. A number of errors at both the fleet and task force commander levels were crucial and contributed to the disaster. These and many other facts—dealing with operational considerations, weather, and ship design—provide the framework for a detailed account of what happened when the most powerful fleet in the world was allowed to blunder into one of the most destructive storms in modern naval history.

The book draws heavily on the personal experience of the author. It is undergirded with data taken from action reports, ships' logs, war diaries, official messages, and the record of proceedings of the court of inquiry that investigated the circumstances. Letters from and interviews with some of the individuals who survived have added a number of interesting details. In order to be precise about the role of the principal commanders, the account includes extracts from their testimony taken at the court of inquiry. Selected portions of the testimony of survivors of the lost ships, their rescuers, and the expert witnesses who were called by the court, also have been included. The story should provide a fuller appreciation of the risks and sacrifices that are always a part of life at sea.

For the small, wet, and bedraggled group of men who clung for their lives to the gale-ravaged bridge of the *Dewey*, the typhoon was a traumatic, soul-searing, and humbling experience. It left its indelible imprint on each of them. Just before deliverance was assured, when every giant roll appeared to be their last, and the wind's roar was almost deafening, there came a stillness as the tempest drew its breath. In that moment of silence the voices of those men were heard intoning the words of the Navy Hymn:

Oh hear us when we cry to Thee
For those in peril on the sea.

Typhoon:
The Other Enemy

PART I

Prelude to a Typhoon

CHAPTER 1

Symptoms of Instability

Her throttle wide open, the destroyer knifed her way through the calm waters of Puget Sound. She headed into the Straits of Juan de Fuca and a wider expanse of open water. As she surged ahead, the steady vibration of her turbines told me that her engineering plant was in excellent condition. I noted the light brown wisps of smoke that roiled up from her stacks. It quickly dissipated, so that only fifty or sixty feet of trailing haze was visible. It was clear that her engineers had the forced draft under perfect control. Too much air would have caused white smoke, and too little would have produced billowing black clouds instead of a light haze. The immense bow wave signaled speed and power. With her stern low in the water, her huge wake churned up beautiful white swirls behind each propeller. Her halyards whistled. She was a living thing, and I realized that despite her age she was still a vigorous and powerful warship. With a bright sun, a blue sky, a very light breeze, and almost no traffic, it was a perfect day for postrepair trials, including the four hours at full power that we had just begun.

The date was 27 September 1944, and the ship was the USS *Dewey* (DD349), a *Farragut*-class destroyer built by the Bath Iron Works at Bath, Maine, and commissioned on 4 October 1934. Now assigned to Destroyer Squadron One, she and her seven sister ships were the first modern destroyers built for the United States Navy since the four-stackers of World War I. One, the *Worden*, had been lost in the Aleutians. A total of only seven now remained. The *Farragut*s were dubbed "the gold-platers" because they were so plush compared to their predecessors. These were two-stackers. They were armed with four semiautomatic, five-inch, thirty-eight-caliber guns, numerous smaller antiaircraft weapons, and two centerline-mounted clusters of four torpedo tubes each. Their main propulsion systems were capable of developing close to fifty thousand horsepower. Designated as 1,500-tonners, the addition of radar and antiaircraft armament during the war years had pushed their total weight to well over the designed tonnage. Such modifications were supposed to be

The USS *Dewey*, at Puget Sound Navy Yard on 26 September 1944, shifts to a new berth preparatory to her postrepair trials the next day.

offset by compensating weight reduction, but tight scheduling of time in shipyards often resulted in failure to remove the designated weight. Sometimes it was postponed, to be accomplished "next time." The Bureau of Ships recognized that destroyers were "frequently operated at displacements greatly in excess of those for which the ships were designed,"[1] (although they attributed it to the overloading of provisions, stores, and ammunition) and established new overload limits. For the *Farragut* class the maximum loading was set in May, 1944, at 2,255 tons, and commanding officers were directed to observe the established limitations unless specifically authorized to exceed them.[2]

The *Dewey* was my second wartime command, and I had reported aboard only four days earlier. I had come directly from duty as commanding officer of a high-speed minesweeper, the *Lamberton* (DMS2), and had been her skipper during the preceding nine months. Most of that time was spent operating in the Hawaiian area, towing targets for gunnery exercises conducted by major fleet units of all types as they prepared for deployment to the Western Pacific.

That first command had permitted a great deal of independence and operating flexibility. I enjoyed the responsibilities that accompanied a single-ship operational assignment. Lessons in command-level seamanship came with the job—lessons that included a new appreciation for the use of the ship's anchor, ship-handling, towing, and forecasting the weather on the basis of local indicators. These were fundamental skills, to be sure, but opportunities to learn them as a lieutenant, or a junior lieutenant commander, were usually somewhat hard to come by. Normally it would have taken a couple of years of destroyer command experience to encounter all of these learning situations. Nevertheless, while I understood and appreciated the benefits of that first command, I did not relish the thought of spending the rest of the war towing targets. A chance at-sea encounter with my former destroyer commanding officer, now a squadron commander, to whom I expressed my sentiments, generated a request to the Bureau of Personnel to assign me to a destroyer command. Dispatch orders and a quick flight back to San Francisco provided just enough time to collect my wife and youngster from San Diego and drive to Seattle to take command of the *Dewey*.

The ship was in the final throes of a much needed shipyard overhaul. It was my responsibility to tidy her up, get her ready for sea in all respects, and within a very few days, sail her back to the Western Pacific. Fleet commanders, then and now, never seem to have enough destroyers. Although the *Farragut*s were not up to the newer and more glamorous *Fletcher*s and *Sumner*s in their armament, communications, or appearance, they were still dependable performers and their services were needed.

The *Dewey* was at Pearl Harbor undergoing tender overhaul when the Japanese attacked. Since then she had taken part in the Battles of the Coral Sea and Midway, the invasion of Guadalcanal, the Aleutian Campaign, where she had rescued many of the *Worden*'s survivors, the landings on Eniwetok and Hollandia, the raids on Palua, Yap, Ulithi, Tinian, and Saipan, and the invasion of Guam. During those actions she also had rescued 112 survivors from the carrier *Lexington*, and 40 from the transport *George F. Elliot*. She had joined in the antiaircraft fire against many Japanese air attacks, bombarded shore installations, and recovered numerous downed aviators from the water. The officers and crew were seasoned in the ways of the sea and had been tested in combat.

Standing on the port wing of the bridge, I noted with satisfaction that we were finally in an area that afforded enough sea room for a few changes of course. Anxious to learn how the ship handled at full power, I turned to the helmsman and ordered, "Right, ten degrees rudder!" At once the *Dewey* lurched awkwardly and heeled over to about fifteen degrees. She didn't snap back, but hung over to the port side for what seemed like a long time before she slowly righted herself. Five years of destroyer experience told me that something was wrong. As soon as we were able to do so without interfering with our full-power trial, I put the ship through a series of turns, maneuvering her at various speeds with various amounts of rudder.

She heeled over more than the normal amount and was consistently slow in returning to an even keel whenever any significant amount of rudder was applied. I commented about it to Lieutenant Commander Frank Bampton, the veteran executive officer of the *Dewey*, a knowledgeable and competent seaman who had ridden her for more than two years. He agreed that she was behaving badly, and although he noted that she had always had a lazy roll, he confirmed that her handling characteristics now appeared more sluggish than they were when she first entered the shipyard in August. I was bothered, and found myself wondering how she would behave in bad weather. Further maneuvering had to be abandoned when a heavy fog suddenly appeared, and we had to return to port. As soon as we moored to the pier at Puget Sound Naval Shipyard, I called my squadron commander, Captain Preston V. Mercer, at his hotel in Bremerton. The *Dewey* was designated as his flagship, and I invited him to come with me the next day, when we would resume our full-power trial and provide a demonstration of how his new floating home was going to behave at sea. Having joined the squadron in the shipyard only a few weeks earlier, he had not had any opportunity to ride the *Dewey*. He accepted my invitation.

The next day we went to sea again. This time we completed our full-power trial successfully. Then, with the commodore's concurrence, I put the *Dewey* through a more extensive test of her maneuvering characteristics. We turned her in tight turns and in wide turns; with full rudder and both engines full-ahead (twenty knots); with one engine full-ahead and the other full-astern; with five, ten, fifteen, and then with twenty degrees of rudder. We did not execute radical turns at speeds in excess of twenty knots, because we considered it imprudent to do so. In all of it we remained dissatisfied. Something was amiss. It wasn't that I felt the ship was in any danger of capsizing. That thought never occurred to me, nor do I suppose that it did to Mercer. But we agreed that the *Dewey* did appear to have some kind of a serious stability problem. We returned to our berth at the shipyard.

As Preston Mercer left the ship to go ashore that afternoon, he directed me to concentrate on getting the ship ready for sea. He said that he considered it his responsibility to present the *Dewey*'s problem to the appropriate authorities at the shipyard, because her stability characteristics obviously had implications for all of Destroyer Squadron One. He added that he would initiate whatever corrective action might be indicated.

Although I was not aware of it at the time, I later learned that only a few days prior to the *Dewey*'s postrepair trials, Puget Sound Naval

Shipyard had conducted an inclining test on a sister ship and squadron mate, the *Aylwin*. The results of that test disclosed that the *Aylwin*'s stability, like that of many other destroyers, had been substantially reduced during the war years.

For reasons that still are not clear to me, the shipyard's report of the *Aylwin*'s stability test had not generated any signs of concern on the part of the Bureau of Ships, despite that Bureau's assigned responsibility for ship design. Awareness of the fact that BuShips had not evidenced any alarm over the *Aylwin* report may have minimized any serious concerns by the shipyard concerning the stability of the *Dewey*. The two ships were figuratively cast from the same mold. Perhaps it appeared unlikely that there would have been any significant difference in their stability characteristics. Armament changes and other alterations to ships during the war were undertaken on an entire class at a time. Theoretically, whatever had been done to alter the characteristics of one *Farragut*-class destroyer during the past three years had been done to all of them. In reality, of course, there were significant differences between the ships of any class.

The commodore spent all of the next morning at shipyard headquarters. After lunch he returned to the *Dewey* to tell me that while the shipyard staff understood our concerns, the question of scheduling a formal inclining experiment was beyond the scope of local authority. Accordingly, he had placed a call to the Bureau of Ships in Washington to explain the situation and propose that the *Dewey* be delayed for a few days to do a full-scale stability analysis. The Bureau's response was that although the ship's stability might have undergone some reduction, she was still basically stable, and that in the light of pressures from the operating forces to deploy all available destroyers to the Western Pacific as a matter of urgency, no delay in the *Dewey*'s completion date was feasible. Captain Mercer noted that BuShips had assured him they would do a full stability analysis of a sister ship, the *Macdonough*, when she had her overhaul the following spring. We were disappointed, but we considered that the Bureau of Ships staff knew what they were doing (in my mind, at least, they were the experts on the subject), accepted their statement that *Farragut*-class destroyers were stable, and went about the business of getting ready for sea. I concluded that we would have to accept something less than optimum stability, but we had the assurance of BuShips that there was no cause for serious concern. At worst we might suffer some discomfort. Since that was consistent with the "Can do" philosophy of destroyer duty, it appeared to be completely in order, and I filed the whole business in the back of my mind. Had I had any conception of how much difference the *Dewey*'s margin of stability was going to make in just a little over two months, I would have made noises clearly audible in Washington, D.C., and I am confident that Preston Mercer would have done the same. As it was, we turned our full attention to getting ready in all respects for our departure and deployment. At least a new awareness that the *Dewey*'s stability was somewhat touchy had entered our consciousness.

CHAPTER 2

Typhoon Warning at Ulithi

On 1 October 1944, eight days after I had assumed command of the *Dewey*, we departed from Seattle, and in company with the *Monaghan*, set a course for Honolulu on the first leg of our voyage to the Western Pacific.¹ The transit to Pearl Harbor gave me a good opportunity to get acquainted with my new squadron commander. Preston Mercer was about six feet one. Scholarly and intellectual in appearance, he looked more like a professor or a well-to-do banker than a naval officer. He wore impeccably tailored uniforms and carried himself with an air of self-assurance and pride. My initial impression of him was that he was coldly impersonal, aloof, and somewhat condescending. As the days passed, however, it became apparent that he was intelligent, articulate, knowledgeable about the Navy in general and destroyers in particular, and a thoroughly seasoned professional. He also was demanding, precise, and set a high standard of performance for the squadron. He intended to improve Destroyer Squadron One, and he made clear to us what he expected. I soon found myself admiring and liking the man. Certainly I couldn't quarrel with his objectives. He had an excellent sense of humor and a bag full of sea stories. I determined that I would do my best to produce the kind of performance he expected and to listen carefully and learn from him. We developed a good rapport.

The ten days from Seattle to Pearl Harbor also provided time to observe some of the ship's key officers in an at-sea environment. It was one thing to be a popular young junior officer in port, but it was something else to deliver a consistent and dependable performance at sea. In addition to myself there were eighteen officers assigned to the *Dewey*, two of whom were graduates of the Naval Academy; the rest were reservists. Seven had joined the ship just a few months earlier, and the others had been aboard more than a year. Four additional officers rode the *Dewey* as members of the squadron staff, so that our wardroom mess included a total of twenty-three. Although the squadron commander took his meals in his own cabin, usually with two of three wardroom officers as his guests, I frequently invited him to join us in the wardroom for lunch or dinner and found him to be excellent company. He enjoyed the chance to talk to the junior officers, and they often made the suggestion that I invite him to be our guest.

The executive officer was Lieutenant Commander Frank Bampton, a regular officer who had integrated into the regular Navy from the Reserve after receiving a commission from the NROTC. Prior to my arrival, he had been the acting commanding officer for two or three months when the former CO had been hospitalized. Frank was a rugged six-footer, with light hair and an open countenance. He impressed me as someone who was serious and steady. I concluded that he had hoped, and perhaps even expected, to be ordered as the permanent commanding officer. I sensed his disappointment and frustration when I arrived, with a date of rank only a few weeks senior to him, and he had to revert to the job of executive officer, an assignment normally filled by a senior-grade lieutenant. Under the circumstances it would have been understandable had he evidenced some element of resentment, directed not only at the situation, but at the new commanding officer. I detected no sign of personal animosity, and he proved to be most cooperative; he was always entirely correct in his dealings with me. I found him especially adept in handling personnel. When first commissioned in 1938 he had been assigned to a Civilian Conservation Corps unit, and I attributed his mature judgment to be a consequence, at least in part, of that challenging experience. I considered myself fortunate to have Frank Bampton as my exec. He knew the *Dewey*, and he knew her men. I grew to respect his advice and to depend upon his superior performance.

Lieutenant Don Weed, a career officer and Naval Academy graduate who was enthusiastic about the *Dewey* and about his job, fleeted up from assistant gunnery officer to gunnery officer on 21 October. Tall, good-looking, and a natural athlete, he had a quick wit and a contagious smile. He also had a low boiling point, but there were times when that appeared to be an asset. Don was the senior watch officer. He was especially well informed in communications and tactics. I thought he was inclined to be impulsive, but I realized that his reactions were excellent, and that he could be trusted to respond effectively in any emergency.

Don's assistant and understudy, clearly one of the most outstanding young officers on the ship, was Lieutenant (j.g.) W. A. (Bill) Buzick. Also a qualified officer of the deck under way, Bill was one of those to whom relative motion was never a problem. Whenever a signal was received directing a change in the *Dewey*'s station, he could visualize the speed vectors of the guide and his own ship, and immediately set a course and speed that would take him where he wanted to go. After settling on that first course and speed he would check his solution with the maneuvering board diagram. Inevitably his first guess was within a few degrees and a knot or two of being correct. He was completely "unflappable" in a crisis. Bill was of medium height and build. Like most of us at that time he wore his black hair in a crewcut that stood straight up in the air. He had a high forehead, a strong chin, and piercing blue eyes. He had a great sense of humor, and often told stories at the wardroom table that were entertaining and sometimes hilariously funny. It was a pleasure to have him aboard.

The other Naval Academy graduate was Lieutenant (j.g.) Bob Gibson, one of the assistant engineers. He was tall and slender, dark-haired, with dark eyes, straight features, and a toothy smile. He impressed me as a thoroughly nice guy, who had a special knack for getting along with people. He also appeared to be quite intelligent. The present chief engineer was Lieutenant Paul Uhl, an outstanding performer. Paul, however, was expecting orders to new construction, and I expected that within a matter of a few weeks I would lose him. I considered Bob Gibson to be his most logical replacement, despite the fact that he was not the senior assistant in the department. I suspected that except for Uhl, Gibson understood the basic theory of the engineering plant better than any other officer then serving in the black gang. We had several officers and chief petty officers with a greater depth of practical operating experience and more familiarity with the specific machinery of that particular ship. Nevertheless, I felt that the leadership of the engineering department should be in the hands of a knowledgeable engineer, who understood the complex physical properties of steam and could better comprehend and trouble-shoot the several elements of the plant. I determined to verify my opinion about this, and if it remained unchanged, to make Bob Gibson the next chief engineer—hopefully without ruffling too many feathers. He would quickly become familiar with the details of the system, and in the meantime we had a wealth of people with competence in the "hands-on" practical operational aspects.

The paymaster and supply officer was a Supply Corps reserve officer named Roscoe D. McMillan. "Pay's" rank was lieutenant, junior grade. Older than most of the other wardroom officers, he soon proved himself to be an outstanding performer in his specialty. A typical southern gentleman from North Carolina, and a graduate of the university at Chapel Hill, his slow drawl was a pleasure to hear. My wife, Ginny, was also a Tar Heel, and we found much in common. "Pay" was about six feet tall, slender in build, and had a thin face and sharp nose, sandy hair, and a ruddy complexion. He was very personable and was obviously one of the most popular officers on the *Dewey*, well liked by the crew as well as by his colleagues in the wardroom. He was always a step ahead of all supply problems, and the ship benefited from his foresight. The food in the general mess was exceptionally good, largely as a result of his close supervision. There could hardly have been any more important factor in establishing and maintaining high morale.

One of the most likeable characters in the *Dewey* wardroom was the warrant boatswain, a former Connecticut tobacco farmer and World War I veteran named Miller, who had enlisted after Pearl Harbor. "Boats" must have been in his late fifties. He was of medium height, with a stocky build and a round, almost cherubic face except for a broken nose, which suggested that he was no stranger to violence. He was almost completely bald, with a fringe of gray hair around the sides and back of his head. He was well weathered, active, and spry. I found him to be very knowledgeable about marlinspike seamanship and sought his advice as to how we could improve our line-handling when mooring. Probably his greatest contribution to the *Dewey* was his mature wisdom and his effectiveness in counseling our young sailors. They went to him with their problems and he listened, questioned, and suggested. He reminded me of a modern-day Friar Tuck, and I considered him to be a fine shipmate and valuable asset.

While the foregoing descriptions cover less than half of the officer complement of the *Dewey*, the individuals mentioned were the principal participants in the events covered by this narrative. Among the remaining eleven the majority were excellent, and one or two were outstanding in their performance of duty. Lest it appear that things were too good to be true, however, during the course of the next year I found it necessary to submit fitness reports in the "unsatisfactory" category for two *Dewey* officers. They were both good men, but they simply were miscast as naval officers and were unable to adapt to their circumstances. I have little doubt that they "found themselves" and were successful in civilian life. In any case, I felt then—and have never changed my mind since—that that group of officers, about 90 percent of them reservists, were a fine example of the remarkably high caliber of the junior officers who manned the ships of the United States Navy during World War II.

Checking recently through a collection of my letters to Ginny, in search of comments about conditions aboard the *Dewey* at that time, we discovered that on 7 October 1944 I had written a letter telling her of the "first serious casualty" that had occurred since my departure. The squadron commander's and commanding officer's cabins on *Farragut*-class destroyers were separated by a single "head." In civilian lingo, these officers shared a bathroom. On the date in question we held various routine drills, including general quarters. My steward's mate was responsible for closing the ports and dogging them tightly closed. In the process he dropped the heavy dog wrench. It fell "kerplunk" into the toilet bowl, and put a hole right through it. For the next three days, until a replacement was obtained in Pearl Harbor, Preston Mercer and I had to use the wardroom facilities one deck below. The situation was made to order for some good-natured ribbing about our "holy head." I was pleased to observe that our new squadron commander not only took it in good humor, but also was quick with a witty response. The dropped wrench had not only broken the bowl, it had also broken the ice. No contrived strategy could have served so well to establish a comfortable relationship between the commodore and the wardroom officers.

We reached Pearl Harbor on 10 October. As we came into the harbor we passed the *Lamberton* at one of the piers, and I received a nice message of welcome from my old shipmates. It was the day after my thirty-first birthday. The wardroom had risen to the occasion with a special menu and a decorated cake complete with candles. We moored alongside the destroyer tender *Yosemite*, and remained there until the 18th. This interval provided a welcome opportunity to conduct upkeep and maintenance routines and complete the overhaul work that had not been finished prior to our departure from Puget Sound.

The first week in Pearl Harbor enabled me to see another side of Preston Mercer. He had a keen sense of Navy politics and deliberately focused a significant amount of his attention on developing friendly relations with a number of flag officers. I viewed his efforts to cultivate senior officers as a natural consequence of his past duty assignments. His most recent duty had been as assistant chief of staff for administration on the staff of Admiral Nimitz (his second tour of duty with him), where he had developed a close working relationship with many of the two- and three-star admirals in subordinate commands. While some of his contemporaries appeared to consider him an apple-polisher, I saw no evidence of that trait. In any event, his contacts with the top echelon of command provided a number of bonus benefits for the ship's officers, one of which was the privilege of playing host to Admirals Nimitz, Spruance, Hill,

Calhoun, and others, for lunch aboard the *Dewey*. In my case, it resulted in an interesting exchange, which was to continue after the war, with Vice Admiral Bill Calhoun, who was interested in genealogy and advanced the theory that we were related. (As it turned out we were, in his words, "Not of the same tree, but from the same garden.") While none of these contacts ever appeared to be of any direct help to the *Dewey*, they did serve to put the ship's officers at ease in dealing with senior officers. That in itself was worthwhile.

Shortly after our arrival in Pearl Harbor, the commodore indicated that there was a continuing concern on the part of Admiral Nimitz over the lack of naval personnel available, especially in the commissioned categories, to man the fleet. Mercer explained that this puzzled Nimitz because the statistics indicated that the Navy's manning level was adequate, yet from time to time there didn't seem to be enough experienced people to go around. As he spoke about this, I recalled that when I was hospitalized for nine months after being wounded in the South Pacific, I had encountered quite a few convalescents who were fully recovered and fit for duty, but were being held in the hospital because of an administrative backlog in processing their papers. Mercer, very interested in this information, vowed that he would look into it. A few days later, upon his return from a visit to CinCPac Headquarters, he told me that he had told Admiral Nimitz about the potential manpower pool among hospital patients, and that his (Nimitz's) staff had located more than two thousand officers and men in various hospitals who were fit for duty. Immediate action by Admiral Nimitz resulted in the establishment of new guidelines covering retention and release of ambulatory patients. The effect of this action was to make available several hundred officers and men for immediate assignment to active duty. I was duly impressed with Mercer's capacity to get things done. My respect for him increased.

Several of the squadron's commanding officers had graduated from the Naval Academy with me in 1938. The opportunity to go ashore with them now provided an important element of team spirit and enabled me to renew many old acquaintances. Promoted to lieutenant commander within the past year, we now were the most junior destroyer skippers in the Navy. Bill Rogers of the *Aylwin*, Jim Marks in the *Hull*, and Connie Hartigan in the *Farragut* were classmates. I counted all of them as friends and on the basis of their service reputations, considered them to be outstanding destroyer officers. Bruce Garrett later raised our number to five when he took command of the *Monaghan* in December.

We enjoyed several evenings ashore with Preston Mercer, discussing plans for working together in the months ahead. On one memorable evening at the home of one of his friends in Honolulu, we had an interesting discussion with Fletcher Pratt, noted author and war correspondent, who intrigued me from the outset by constantly balancing a highball glass on his knee. A thin, bony man, he was seated on the floor with his knees drawn up in front of him. It appeared to me that his kneecaps came to sharp points, yet throughout the evening I marveled at the sight of a glass perched solidly and unmovingly on one or the other of those twin peaks. The subject of a destroyer "sweep" of the South China Sea was discussed at some length. It was a concept for which the commodore actively lobbied with CinCPac's staff, and I believe every one of us would have welcomed the chance to go in harm's way, seeking action with the enemy. The logic of sending destroyers of our vintage on such a mission, where heavy enemy air action could be anticipated, raised some questions in my mind, but I figured that the fleet commander would weigh the risks and we wouldn't be given orders to do anything that did not appear warranted. Months later the *Farragut* participated in such a sweep with good results, but the *Dewey*, *Aylwin*, *Monaghan*, and *Hull* were all engaged elsewhere.

From 18 October to 10 December the ships of Destroyer Squadron One never operated together as a squadron. Based part of the time in Pearl Harbor and part in Ulithi, all of us were given assignments

The USS *Monaghan* at Puget Sound Navy Yard on 26 September 1944. Note the tall and slender forward stack, and the four 5-inch guns, typical of *Farragut*-class destroyers at that time.

that provided ample opportunity to shake down, tidy up the work of the shipyard overhaul, conduct destroyer tactical exercises, upgrade our communications, and educate watch-standers.

During this period we frequently found ourselves in company with the *Monaghan*, and with her we conducted a number of destroyer training exercises. She had been built in Boston Navy Yard, where she was commissioned in 1935. On 7 December 1941 at Pearl Harbor, she had rammed, depth-charged, and sunk a Japanese midget submarine. Like the *Dewey*, she also had participated in the Battles of the Coral Sea and Midway, the Aleutians Campaign, actions in the Marshalls and Gilberts, the Hollandia landings, and the Battle of the Philippine Sea in June of 1944. During the months of October and November of 1944, her skipper was Commander Wally Wendt, USNA '34, a veteran destroyerman, who handled his ship exceptionally well.[2]

On 25 October, in company with a group of escort carriers and three other destroyers (one of which was the *Spence*), the *Dewey* departed Pearl Harbor and proceeded to Ulithi, fueling en route at Eniwetok. We arrived at Ulithi on 5 November. This large atoll in the western Caroline Islands had been occupied by U.S. forces without opposition less than two months earlier. Elliptical in shape, with its long axis extending north-south for about twenty miles, it provided a splendid anchorage large enough to accommodate the entire Third Fleet.

The first news to greet us on arrival was a message indicating that all ships in Ulithi Lagoon were in Typhoon Condition II. This required that all fleet units hold themselves in a high degree of readiness to encounter a typhoon that might strike Ulithi in the next day or two. The alert period lasted for three full days. On 8 November we were directed to reduce the degree of readiness to Typhoon Condition III, which meant that while the storm's arrival was no longer imminent, there was still a possibility that it might strike Ulithi.

Although the typhoon in question did not materialize in the vicinity of the fleet anchorage, the three days spent in Typhoon Condition II served a useful purpose. It impressed upon us the fact that we would be operating in an area where we had to be prepared to deal with typhoon weather conditions. I feel certain that many other officers aboard ships then anchored in Ulithi Lagoon sought, as I did, to reacquaint themselves with those sections of Knight's *Modern Seamanship*[3] and *The American Practical Navigator*[4] by Bowditch that dealt with cyclonic storms.

The tenth edition of Knight's *Modern Seamanship* contained only two pages covering indications of the approach of a hurricane. Apparently the officers of the Department of Seamanship and Navigation at the Naval Academy, who had revised the book for that edition, placed their emphasis on the Rules of the Road and the avoidance of collision. The eleventh edition, published in March of 1945, included a much more detailed discussion of tropical cyclones, no doubt prompted by the Third Fleet's typhoon experience. Therefore, Knight's *Modern Seamanship* wasn't of much help to us, but the information contained in Bowditch in November 1944 was of great value to the uninitiated destroyer skipper, and so far as typhoons were concerned, almost all of us were in the "uninitiated" category.

Fortunately, I had one unique advantage. I had commissioned and served four years aboard the destroyer *Sterett*. During the first two of those exciting years, I had as a shipmate Lieutenant Watson T. Singer, U.S. Navy, the *Sterett's* first executive officer, whose knowledge of seamanship and the lore of the sea was remarkable. His previous duties included several years on the China station and a tour in command of a fleet tug. "Watso" was a tough and durable character who never minced words. He had often discussed typhoons with us and had left me with a legacy of advice, which included the knowledge that in any typhoon, some structural damage to any ship caught in its path is almost inevitable. I also recalled hearing him quote "Singer's Law," an approximate translation of which would be, "When the barometer drops .10 inch or more in three hours or less, you're in the path of a typhoon, and you'd better haul ass!" Bowditch confirmed this counsel with the sentence: "If the wind remains steady in direction and increases in force in heavy squalls while the barometer falls rapidly, say, at a greater rate than .03 of an inch per hour, the vessel is probably on or near the track of the storm and in advance of the center."[5] It then recommended, "putting as much distance as possible between the ship and the storm center."[6] I preferred the brevity, emphasis, and color of Singer's Law.

Fully developed hurricanes/typhoons are elliptical, and normally cover an area about three hundred miles in diameter with a calm center, called the eye of the storm, ten to twenty miles in diameter, where the pressure is low and the seas violent and confused. The strongest winds occur near the center, often attaining velocities in excess of 125 knots, with gusts to twice that velocity! They become less violent farther from the center, and the direction of their rotation around the eye is counterclockwise in the Northern Hemisphere and clockwise in the Southern Hemisphere.

Of special interest to me were the thumb rules regarding local indicators of a typhoon's approach. One of the first signs that may become apparent is a cross swell. Also, unusual barometric readings provide some of the earliest and most dependable warnings. Bowditch noted that each tropical cyclone (the term is synonymous with hurricanes and typhoons) is surrounded by a "territory of large extent"[7] in which the barometer reads a tenth of an inch below average. As the storm center grows nearer, the wind increases, the barometer falls, and torrential rains are present.

The rule of thumb for locating such a storm in the Northern Hemisphere is to face the wind and look 90° to 135° to the right. The storm center will be within that 45° arc. The rule governing avoiding action is almost as simple. Vessels to the right of the storm's track, facing in the direction of its travel, are said to be in the dangerous semicircle, and should put the wind on the starboard bow and attempt to run out of it. Ships in the direct path, or to the left of the storm's track, in the so-called "navigable" semicircle, should put the wind on the starboard quarter and run.

Most of the officers of the *Dewey* reviewed these rules during that three-day period of Typhoon Condition II in Ulithi. In the course of the next few days I frequently heard the subject discussed. On a few occasions I engaged in those discussions, and answered questions about my own heavy-weather experience, most of which had occurred in the North Atlantic. I had never had any direct involvement with typhoons and so indicated. One officer and one chief petty officer had gone through one, but neither volunteered that information when it might have helped, and we didn't learn of their previous experience until our own ordeal was behind us. The rest of us had no conception of the overwhelming destructiveness of such a storm. It occurred to me that at least the *Dewey*'s watch officers would recognize the approach of a typhoon if ever we had the bad luck to encounter one. I discounted the likelihood of that ever happening as long as we were in company with the fleet. Only if we were operating independently did it seem necessary to concern ourselves with avoiding bad weather.

CHAPTER 3

DesRon One Joins the Third Fleet

The war in the Pacific in November of 1944 was marked by repeated carrier aircraft attacks against a widening range of targets. The focus of the effort was in the Philippines. The U.S. Sixth Army had landed on the island of Leyte on 23 October. The fighting continued without pause. Carrier aircraft from the Third Fleet (Task Force 38, under command of Vice Admiral John S. McCain), attacked Luzon on the 5th and 6th of November. On the 8th the *Dewey* departed Ulithi and proceeded to join the logistic support group (TG 30.8) under the command of Captain Jasper Acuff. The replenishment area was about three hundred miles east of Luzon. The mission of TG 30.8 was to provide the fuel oil, aviation gasoline, aircraft, replacement parts, consumable supplies, ammunition, food, personnel, and anything else it needed, to Task Force 38. When the carrier force joined with the oilers for replenishment on the 10th, it was heavily committed to sustain pressure on the enemy's air and surface units in the Philippines.

During this initial week of operations with the logistic support group, the *Dewey* was stationed in the screen of escorts, which protected both the replenishment units and the carrier forces they were replenishing. We welcomed the opportunity to break into the routine and learn the procedures and techniques then in use for at-sea underway replenishment. We found ourselves quite familiar with the Third Fleet's standard operating procedures, since they all conformed to fleetwide tactical instructions that had been in use for several years.

The ships of Task Force 38, about ninety in number, were organized at that time into four task groups, each with two attack carriers (CVs), one or two light carriers (CVLs), two battleships (BBs), three light cruisers (CLs), one antiaircraft cruiser (CL(AA)), and thirteen destroyers (DDs). As the four task groups of TF 38 approached the logistic support group, which had fourteen oilers as its core element, Captain Acuff split his task group into four corresponding task units of three or four oilers each, with accompanying

19

escort carriers, tugs, and escorts on a line of bearing. Each of the four groups from Task Force 38 approached a predesignated unit belonging to Task Group 30.8, and on a carefully arranged schedule went alongside those logistic support ships assigned to deliver their particular needs. Normally, during one daylight period all ninety carrier task force ships would refuel, and if necessary, reprovision. Since each major ship of TF 38 might have to go alongside more than one ship of TG 30.8 to obtain what it needed, the complexity of replenishment operations should be apparent. They required a great deal of careful organization, full cooperation, and precise execution. Superior seamanship and shiphandling skills were required on the part of every commanding officer. It was not exactly child's play to maneuver a carrier, battleship, cruiser, or even a destroyer—especially in rough weather—to within about 50 feet of a fleet oiler or an ammunition ship. Once in position, it was necessary to steam along with her, side by side, at a speed of 7 to 12 knots, never getting too close and never getting farther away than 100 feet. That was the limit of the span of fuel hoses. Beyond that distance the hoses simply broke, with consequences that were not only unpleasant but also often dangerous.

Replenishment operations were essential to the accomplishment of the fleet's mission. They enabled the Third Fleet to remain on station and conduct air strikes in support of the land battle over periods as long as several weeks. The attack carriers would proceed to a launch point close to the objective area, conduct strike operations around the clock for two or three days, retire to a rendezvous point about 200 miles farther away, refuel and replenish, and be back at the launch point after a two- or three-day absence. While the officers and men on the oilers and other support ships (and their escorts) did not have as frequent direct contact with enemy aircraft as did the ships of Task Force 38, they were always vulnerable to submarine and suicide air attack. Occasionally they were called upon to run in to the objective area and remain for two or three days at a time. Anything could happen then and often did. In any case, the morale of TG 30.8 was extremely good. All hands took great pride in doing their jobs in seamanlike fashion, and the men of the *Dewey* quickly developed the feeling that their ship was privileged to serve on such a professional team.

On 19 November the *Dewey* was detached from TG 30.8 to escort two empty fleet oilers back to Ulithi. As we approached the southern entrance in the very early morning of the 20th, we gained a sonar contact. Quickly evaluating it as non-sub because of its mushy echo quality, we dropped one depth charge as a precautionary measure.

Unable to regain contact, we entered the lagoon at 0800 and by 0950 we were anchored in the northern anchorage. The next morning a midget sub torpedoed one of our tankers in the southern anchorage. Apparently the torpedo was defective, because the ship did not explode and its cargo did not ignite. The *Dewey* and several other destroyers got under way to search out any additional midgets that might have slipped into the lagoon, with negative results. We couldn't help but recall our contact from the day before, but we were certain that what we had heard was not a submarine, and we dismissed any further speculation on the subject. Nevertheless, because of the submarine threat, a continuing antisubmarine patrol was established off the harbor entrance, and on 21–22 November the *Dewey* spent two largely uneventful days as the A/S patrol ship. There was one cheerful development. On the 21st we were delighted to see our squadron mates the *Aylwin*, *Monaghan*, and *Dale* arrive at Ulithi. I viewed this as a happy omen and looked forward to operating with our own "family" again.

When we returned to the lagoon we moored alongside the *Aylwin*. Built by the Philadelphia Navy Yard, she had been commissioned on 1 March 1935. Like the *Dewey* she had lived a charmed life, and so far had suffered no battle damage. Bill Rogers had assumed command of her on 13 May 1944. He was of medium build, with thinning light hair and a poker-faced countenance, marked by a sharp and prominent nose. Formal and serious in his manner, he appeared

The USS *Aylwin* at Puget Sound, 29 September 1944. Just a few days before, the Navy Yard had conducted an inclining test that showed the *Aylwin*'s stability to be lower than it had been prior to overhaul.

to be deliberate and prudent. I had always had the impression that he lacked a sense of humor, but I learned otherwise as we became better acquainted. I had observed the performance of Bill's ship several times over the past two months and considered him to be a good seaman and an excellent shiphandler. We established a good relationship, which was enhanced by a low-key sense of competition between us concerning the performance of our ships. I respected him and was happy to have him as a squadron mate.

Shore leave in Ulithi consisted of a visit to Mog-Mog Island, on the western side of the lagoon, where the SeaBees had constructed a thatched-hut recreational area. Fleet personnel (both officer and enlisted) could get their feet on dry land there, enjoy barbecued steaks and picnic fare, and have a beer or two. Preston Mercer remarked that it was a good place to maintain contacts with senior officers. Since I didn't know any, the advice wasn't of much use. In any case, although it was anything but plush, it provided a great place to relax and have a convivial cocktail hour. We all enjoyed it, and it had a marked impact on morale. The *Dewey*'s sailors blew off a lot of steam on Mog-Mog, and they appeared to benefit from it, despite a few black eyes and an occasional puffed lip.

On 30 November the *Dewey* escorted three fleet tugs to an at-sea rendezvous with TG 30.8. We returned on 3 December, and were pleased to find that another squadron mate, the *Hull*, had arrived in Ulithi on the 1st. The commodore directed me to moor alongside her so that he could confer with the commanding officer and brief him regarding operations with the logistic support group. Mercer was aware that the *Hull* would now be operating with TG 30.8 for the first time, and would not be familiar with the group's operating style.

Jim Marks had been the skipper of the *Hull* since 1 October 1944, about one week later than my reporting date on the *Dewey*. He had been in the Fourth Battalion with me at the Naval Academy, but I had never had more than a casual acquaintance with him. Short, slight, with dark hair, dark eyes, and an olive complexion, he impressed me as one who was very serious and very regulation. We visited back and forth and compared notes on our ships, to our mutual advantage.

I had visited aboard the *Hull* during the Guadalcanal Campaign in the fall of 1942, when I was gunnery officer of the destroyer *Sterett*. Like her squadron mates, the *Hull* had been in the thick of it and was credited with shooting down several enemy planes and sinking a small schooner near Guadalcanal. The Aleutians Campaign, the Marshall and Gilbert Island operations, and "The Great

The USS *Hull* under way in Puget Sound on 10 October 1944. The photograph provides an indication of the power and grace of the *Farragut*-class destroyers.

Marianas Turkey Shoot" of 19 June 1944 were among her many engagements, and she had picked up her fair share of downed aviators and returned them to their carriers to fight another day.

One of the bright spots in Destroyer Squadron One was in the person of Lieutenant Commander Conway C. Hartigan, the commanding officer of the *Farragut*. Decorated for heroism for his rescue of survivors from the carrier *Yorktown* during the Battle of Midway, Connie was one of the most respected and beloved members of the Naval Academy Class of '38. An excellent athlete, he was about an inch short of six feet, of medium to stocky build, sandy-haired, and handsome. He was very popular with the opposite sex and always seemed to be relaxed. He was a natural leader and a very competent professional and the officers and men of the *Farragut* loved him. I enjoyed a close friendship with Connie and spent many hours of shore leave in his company. A born story teller, he was one of our main sources of entertainment. I still recall the tale about Herman, the Gilbert Islands chicken, which was mysteriously acquired by the *Farragut* during the course of the island-hopping campaign and soon became the ship's mascot. We heard many stories about Herman, but the best involved Connie's division commander. The *Farragut* was designated as the flagship of Commander J. F. Walsh (brother of the Naval Academy crew coach) who commanded the second division of Destroyer Squadron One. Apparently Commodore Walsh frequently found Herman sitting on his bunk, and whenever he did, regardless of where Connie was—on the bridge or in the engine room—he would hear Walsh's voice yelling "Hartigan!". On those occasions a rescue squad, already organized specifically for the purpose, rushed to the commodore's cabin to rescue Herman from certain annihilation. One day just before we left Ulithi, Connie met me on Mog-Mog and immediately proposed a toast to Herman, bidding him farewell. That morning Connie had been conducting an inspection in the forward fireroom, when he heard "Hartigan!". This time he thought he detected a special note of urgency in Walsh's voice. He dashed up the ladder to the main deck, and then up to the commodore's cabin, where a livid Walsh pointed to Herman, sitting on his bunk, and said, "That damned rooster just laid an egg on my bunk! He's a hen! You know Navy Regulations prohibit women aboard ship at sea! Get rid of her!" Connie refused to disclose what disposition had been made of Herman. I suspected that she was still aboard the *Farragut* somewhere, perhaps in the boatswain's locker or the torpedo shack, but alive and well, wherever she was. We drank our toast to Herman with great feeling, as if we'd just lost one of our best friends, and her fate remains a closely guarded military secret to this day!

We remained alongside the *Hull* until the 6th, when the *Dewey*, *Hull*, *Monaghan*, and *Macdonough* went to sea together for one day to conduct antiaircraft gunnery training exercises. Each time that we were in company with the *Hull*, I was favorably impressed with the appearance of Jim's ship and the quality of her underway performance.

There was no opportunity to work with Bruce Garrett before getting under way for fleet operations on the 10th, since he didn't take over as commanding officer of the *Monaghan* until 9 December. Among the smallest of my classmates, and probably one of the youngest looking, he had a quiet dignity and a winning smile; I am sure that he was well liked by his officers and crew. Since there could hardly have been another commanding officer in the entire Third Fleet with less time in command than Bruce had on 10 December 1944, I can imagine the great pride he felt as he got the *Monaghan* under way and took her out of Ulithi for his first tour as a destroyer skipper.

CHAPTER 4

Fleet Operations, 10–16 December

As the Third Fleet sortied from Ulithi on 10 December 1944, the pace of combat in the Pacific had in no way diminished. The Fleet's primary task continued to be the support of General MacArthur's campaign in the Philippines. He had decided to land on Mindoro on the 15th. The purpose of the landing was to establish U.S. air bases within supporting distance of Luzon, so that when the impending invasion of that island took place, control of the air would be assured. Admiral Halsey had assumed responsibility for the destruction or suppression of enemy land-based air power in the Luzon area.

To help conceal the target date of the Mindoro landing and enhance the element of surprise, on 7 December Halsey sent the antiaircraft cruiser *San Juan* to a remote position to transmit urgent dummy messages that might create the impression that the Third Fleet was where it wasn't.[1] Communications deception had also been used to conceal the departure of Task Force 38 from Ulithi on the 10th, by directing the forces remaining there to continue radio broadcasts of the same urgency and type as would have been transmitted had none of the ships departed.[2] Task Force 38 proceeded directly to a scheduled rendezvous with TG 30.8 to refuel on the 13th.

The *Dewey* departed Ulithi on 10 December, in company with the *Aylwin, Monaghan,* and *Hull.* We joined TG 30.8 and proceeded to the fueling rendezvous. On the 12th we transferred Paul Uhl, now on his way home to commission a new destroyer. I was very sorry to lose him, but I felt fortunate to have an officer so well qualified to relieve him. Bob Gibson immediately took over as the chief engineer.

When Task Force 38 joined for replenishment we noted at once that the force had been reorganized since we were last in company with it. The new organization was one of four special measures designed to cope with the serious threat now posed by Japanese suicide air attacks.[3] Kamikaze hits on the carriers *Intrepid, Essex,*

The USS *Dewey*, at anchor in Ulithi on 7 December 1944, airs her bunting.

Hancock, and *Cabot* on 25 November had inflicted an unacceptable level of damage. The Third Fleet commander decided to initiate extraordinary countermeasures, which he believed would reduce the degree of risk to a more acceptable level.

Instead of four task groups of carriers and supporting combatants as before, there now were only three. Therefore, each of the three carrier groups was stronger and could concentrate its defensive firepower with greater effectiveness. The composition of each group was four or five attack carriers (CVs and CVLs), two or three battleships, four or five cruisers, and from sixteen to twenty destroyers.[4]

This structure was intended to provide maximum available antiaircraft gun protection to the carriers and still permit ample space for air operations. The increased number of destroyers in each group provided more flexibility for meeting the demands for picket ships, plane guards (rescue ships), the delivery of mail, and for duty as "Tom Cats."

The use of destroyers as "Tom Cats" was the second special defensive measure.[5] This consisted of stationing destroyers equipped with aircraft homing devices on each side of the target bearing line on strike days. The Tom Cats were to assist in controlling our own strike aircraft and in providing early warning of enemy aircraft as they approached the carrier force. Aircraft returning from strikes were directed to make a full turn around one of the Tom Cats before returning to the carriers. Combat air patrols over these destroyers would inspect the returning planes to be sure they were friendly. This was intended to prevent enemy aircraft from following our strike planes so as to locate and attack the carriers to which they were returning.

The third special defensive measure was a substantial increase in the fighter aircraft complement aboard the attack carriers.[6] The former complement of thirty-six VF (fighters), thirty-six VB (dive bombers), and eighteen VT (torpedo planes), was changed to seventy-three VF, fifteen VB, and fifteen VT.

The final special countermeasure was the use of "Air Blanket" operations.[7] This involved establishing combat air patrols over the area of enemy operations in sufficient strength, day and night, to discourage the takeoff or landing of any enemy aircraft during the stipulated period.

Responding to the new Task Force 38 organization, Captain Acuff formed three logistic support units to match the three carrier task groups. The replenishment on the 13th proceeded very expeditiously. The combatant ships were still fresh and needed little more than a topping-off of fuel. They finished with the oilers and disappeared over the horizon for their launch point. Our logistic support ships would remain in the same general vicinity and hold themselves in readiness for the return of the attack carriers. The next replenishment was set for the morning of the 17th.

On 14 December the escorts of TG 30.8 refueled from their own oilers, and the *Dewey* topped off her tanks. The *Aylwin, Monaghan,* and *Hull* did likewise. In the next two days the ships of TG 30.8 did practically nothing but mark time in an effort to conserve fuel, so that we wouldn't deplete the stocks available for Task Force 38 or interfere in any way with their replenishment schedule. We burned about 6 percent of capacity per day from the time of departure of TF 38 on the 13th until they returned on the 17th.

During fueling operations on the 14th, the oiler *Patuxent* also delivered to us a number of replacement personnel by highline. This method of transfer is not for the faint-hearted. The oiler, or other delivering ship, rigs a heavy manila line from high in its superstructure (hence the term "highline"). It then fires a shot, with a small messenger line attached, to the receiving ship, which hauls in the other end of the manila line and secures it high in its superstructure. The individual awaiting transfer then takes his seat in a small boatswain's chair that hangs from a pulley-wheel mounted on the manila line. Another small manila line attached to the chair is then passed to the receiving ship, and a group of line-handlers—perhaps twenty-five or more—heave-in or run away with the smaller line and haul the passenger across the highline, (and hopefully above the gulf of water that intervenes between the two ships) until he is safely on the deck of the receiving ship. What makes this somewhat more than a stroll in the park is the fact that the ship's superstructures are moving with the motion of the waves. Sometimes they lean toward each other, and sometimes they sway apart. The manila highline must be kept taut throughout the process, or else the passenger is apt to be dunked in the water—or worse, dropped in when the line becomes too taut and breaks from the sudden strain. Although it is possible that some poor soul has actually been lost by highline transfer mishap, it has never happened that way in my experience, and most Navy men seem to enjoy it—like a ride on a roller coaster.

Among the replacements transferred to us on the 14th was Frank Bampton's relief. Frank had orders to command his own destroyer, the *Conyngham*, and after a few days for turning over his duties he would leave the *Dewey*.

The new executive officer was Lieutenant David S. Bate, USNR. Dave had had two years at Harvard Law School before reporting for active duty. By 1944 he had three years of wartime destroyer experience to his credit. He was tall, probably 6 feet 3 inches in height, slender, but with square shoulders and an erect posture. He had regular features, a high forehead, straight dark hair, a large head, blue eyes, fair complexion, a strong chin, and a pleasant manner. My first impression was that he was intelligent, quiet, and unassuming, and I liked him immediately. He busied himself with Frank, trying to pick his brain for details about the *Dewey* before he got away from him.

On the 14th of December, while Task Group 30.8 was refueling, Task Force 38 began intensive air-strike operations from a launch point about 200 miles northeast of Manila. Heavy attacks were launched over a three-day period against Japanese air installations on and in the vicinity of Luzon. The Mindoro landing took place as scheduled. During that period Third Fleet pilots reportedly shot down 64 enemy planes and destroyed 208 more on the ground.[8] They also reportedly sank 18 Japanese ships and damaged 37, most of them small and medium-sized oilers and freighters.[9] These achievements did not come cheaply. In the course of that three-day period, Task Force 38 lost fifty-four aircraft. Of these, twenty-seven were from antiaircraft fire, four ran out of fuel, seven suffered mechanical failures, three had mid-air collisions, eleven were operational crashes, and two were from unknown causes.[10] These figures provide a measure of the need for Task Group 30.8 to include replenishment carriers loaded with replenishment planes. The loss data also should convey some appreciation of the risk factors, both enemy and operational, that confronted attack carrier pilots even at that phase of the Pacific War, when Japanese air strength had been mortally wounded.

The high-speed steaming required by continuous flight operations during this three-day period resulted in very high expenditures of fuel by the destroyers in Task Force 38. Escorting a carrier task force when it is engaged in a heavy schedule of air operations always requires the destroyers to make frequent changes in station, from plane guard position, ready to rescue a downed aviator, to screening station, prepared to provide air or submarine defense. Furthermore, because it facilitates the launching and landing of aircraft, carrier flight operations are conducted into the wind at high speed, to create the maximum relative wind over the flight deck. During World War II, carriers seldom slowed below thirty knots when conducting air operations. Most of the time the escorting destroyers therefore had to steam at speeds in excess of thirty knots. Fuel consumption of any conventionally powered ship at that speed is very high.

As air operations came to a halt on 16 December, Admiral Halsey withdrew the entire carrier strike force to the east to join Task Group 30.8 for the next day's replenishment. It was his intention to return to the launch point and resume the attacks on Luzon as soon as practicable, but in any event no later than the 19th. Aboard the *Dewey*, Dave Bate relieved Frank Bampton as executive officer on the 16th.

Several Task Force 38 destroyers were critically low on fuel. With strike operations scheduled to resume in two days, it was imperative that all ships be refueled as soon as possible. The fueling rendezvous was selected close enough to the launch position to enable the carriers to get back to it in time to meet their strike schedule.

The Philippines Campaign appeared to be at a critical juncture. The Third Fleet was heavily committed to the resumption of their supporting strikes. This overriding sense of commitment was to be a major factor in command decisions concerned with the handling of the fleet during the next two harrowing days.

CHAPTER 5

The Storm Approaches, 17 December

Local weather indicators for individual ships of the Third Fleet on 17 December were markedly different, depending upon their geographical locations. On board the battleship *New Jersey*, Third Fleet flagship, the entry in the deck log for one o'clock in the morning shows a barometer reading of 29.88 (normal pressure at sea level is 29.92), temperature 81°, and wind 23 knots from 065° T.¹ At that time on the *Dewey*, located more than 200 miles to the east southeast, the barometer reading was 29.72, temperature 81°, and wind 6 knots from 060° T.² Recalling the Bowditch description of the structure of a typhoon, which notes that surrounding the actual storm there is a large area in which the barometer reads a tenth of an inch or more below the average, it appears that the *Dewey* may already have come into the outer fringes of the storm as early as 170100. Although we were aware of a lower than normal barometer reading on the *Dewey*, and paid special attention to it, we were not yet alarmed by it.

Meanwhile, on the *New Jersey* ComThirdFleet was copying a number of radio weather broadcasts that the smaller ships were not able to monitor. These included broadcasts by radio Kwajalein every six hours, containing complete weather reports from land stations in the Western Pacific; broadcasts every three hours from Manus, Admiralty Islands, Southwest Pacific, of reports covering the South and Southwest Pacific and the Philippines; twice daily broadcasts from Saipan, of search-plane weather reports submitted by planes operating out of Saipan, Guam, Ulithi, Kossol Roads, and Peleliu; reports four times a day from Oahu, giving ship, land, and selected aircraft reports from the Central and North Pacific, and finally weather map analyses broadcast four times a day by Fleet Weather Central, Pearl Harbor.

Aboard the destroyers, the available weather forecasting tools were the barometer and the thermometer. Perhaps because they were all we had, we paid a lot of attention to them. We also had some elementary knowledge of the laws of storms, varying degrees

The Third Fleet battleship *New Jersey* (BB 62) takes a heavy sea during operations in the Pacific. These rugged giants provided remarkably steady gun platforms and endured severe weather with a minimum of difficulty.

of intuition, awareness, and common sense, and the habit of observing closely the look of the sky, the direction and force of the wind, and direction and size of the swells.

At 170100 the *Dewey* was steaming in company with Task Group 30.8 on course 180° T, at 12 knots. The main body, with twelve oilers, five escort carriers, and three fleet tugs, was in a compact rectangle of five columns. The escorts (five destroyers and ten destroyer escorts) were in a circular screen around the main body. The *Dewey* was stationed 3.5 miles from the formation center and dead ahead of the oilers. Commander Task Group 30.8, in the *Aylwin*, was the OTC (officer in tactical command) and Commander Destroyer Squadron One, in the *Dewey*, was the screen commander. At 0400 formation course was changed to 240° T. At 0659 formation speed was changed to 10 knots. The three replenishment units, TU 30.8.2, TU 30.8.3, and TU 30.8.4, each consisting of four oilers, one destroyer, and two destroyer escorts, now were directed to proceed independently to take station for replenishment operations. TU 30.8.3 took station to the north, TU 30.8.4 held the center position, and TU 30.8.2 took station to the south. The units were separated by about 10 miles. The *Dewey* took station in the center of the three-ship screen of TU 30.8.4. CTG 30.8 had designated the *Aylwin* and three fleet tugs to operate under his direct operational control. Task Units 30.8.12 (two CVEs and two DEs), and 30.8.14 (three CVEs, one DD, and two DEs), organized as replenishment carrier units, were assigned to operate independently, conducting such flight operations as were necessary for the fly-aboard delivery of replacement aircraft for the attack carriers. Task Group 30.7, comprising one CVE, three DDs, and two DEs, was designated as the antisubmarine group, and had been directed to provide A/S surveillance for the entire Third Fleet during replenishment operations. Task Group 30.7 stationed itself in an operating area about ten miles to the east of TG 30.8, where it was least likely to interfere with the maneuvers of other units. Thus the logistic support group, not including the antisubmarine group, was composed of a total of thirty-five ships. The approaching units of Task Force 38 numbered ninety-seven ships. As they joined forces in new groupings tailored to the replenishment process, they totaled 132 vessels of all types, steaming in close proximity to each other. It was a congested area, to say the least.

When the carrier forces approached for replenishment at about 1000, they found the logistic support group deployed on a line of bearing from 330° to 150° T, with the three oiler units waiting in readiness. At 1025 the formation course was changed to 040° T. This was to be the course for fueling, and the *Dewey* adjusted position so as to be 7,000 yards directly ahead of the *Cache*, a fleet oiler that had been designated formation guide. At 1049 speed was changed to 8 knots, and the ships of TF 38 took station astern of their designated replenishment units. Task Group 38.3 was to the north with TU 30.8.3., TG 38.2 in the center joined TU 30.8.4; and TG 38.1 was to the south with TU 30.8.2.

On the *Dewey* we observed that the wind had picked up to a sustained 20 knots from 060° T. Gusts were about 35 knots, and the seas were rough. Our barometer at 1000 was 29.70.[3] The *New Jersey*, then no more than 30 miles to the northwest, logged a 1000 barometer reading of 29.85[4] with the wind 25 knots from 034° T.

On the smaller ships, where weather took on a distinctly more personal dimension than it did on the carriers and battleships, there was some considerable doubt as to whether or not the scheduled fueling operations could be conducted. The weather was deteriorating rapidly. Aboard the *Dewey* we recorded nine-tenths cloud cover at 1000 and by 1100 a completely overcast sky. The ship was pitching heavily, and we were experiencing a lot of slamming.

On the *New Jersey*, the quartermaster noted, "1107 USS *Spence* came along starboard side to fuel."[5] The *Spence* was one of the several TF 38 destroyers that were critically low on fuel. We had been shocked to learn that many of them had as little as 15 percent of capacity aboard. It seemed incredible to me that they had been allowed to deplete their fuel to such a low level. I could only conclude that the refueling of destroyers had for some unknown reason been deemed inconsistent with the primary objective. In spite of that rationalization, the officers on the *Dewey*, including the skipper and the squadron commander, had the unhappy impression that the fleet and force commanders had been remiss in permitting this critical fuel situation to develop. I had never known destroyers to be that low on fuel before, and Preston Mercer commented that he wouldn't be surprised if some of them ran out of gas before the weather allowed them to refuel.

From numerous voice radio transmissions, it soon became apparent that the fleet commander also was concerned about the status of the escorts, and that he considered their refueling to be a top priority task. We viewed the assignment of the *Spence* to refuel from the *New Jersey* as evidence of his concern. Fueling a destroyer from a battleship in rough weather is often somewhat less difficult than fueling from a fleet oiler, since the high freeboard, mass, and maneuverability of the battleship create a lee and provide a steadier platform. As we watched, however, we could see that the conditions for fueling were just as unfavorable as we had guessed they would be. All of the destroyers within our range of vision were having great difficulty in maintaining station alongside their assigned refueling ships. As they yawed away, and the distance became too great, fuel hoses lashed and whipped until they were unmanageable. Fueling from alongside was so hazardous that several attempts were made to fuel from positions astern of the delivering ships, but all oilers were not rigged for fueling by the astern method, and in any case it proved next to impossible to take an oiler's trailing hose onto the pitching forecastle deck of any destroyer and then haul it back and secure it into the forward fuel oil trunk just below the pilot house. On those few occasions when a fuel hose was successfully manhandled into a destroyer fuel trunk, station-keeping within the usual limits of tolerance was not possible, and the hose either parted or was cut adrift, usually gushing hundreds of gallons of black oil onto the destroyer's deck and superstructure. It was dirty work, and it was dangerous.

Aboard the *New Jersey*, Admiral Halsey sat down to lunch in his flag mess. By looking through the open door he could see the mast and upperworks of the *Spence* alongside to starboard as she attempted to fuel. The destroyer's excessive rolling and radical course changes as she strove to maintain station made it obvious that the weather conditions were worsening. Several times it appeared to those on the *New Jersey* that the *Spence* was going to collide with them.[6]

The *New Jersey*'s log at 1100 recorded the wind at 32 knots from 020° T, gusting to 45 knots.[7]

The heaving and pitching destroyers began to report their difficulties to the fleet commander. At 1208 the *Collett* reported that conditions for fueling alongside the battleship *Wisconsin* were very bad, and that both fuel hoses had carried away. At 1220 the *Stephen Potter* reported that she had just parted a fuel hose. In the next half hour, the *Mansfield*, *Lyman K. Swenson*, *Preston*, *Thatcher*, and *Hunt* parted their fuel hoses and had to clear the side.[8]

At 1300, for the second straight hour, the barometer on the *New Jersey* dropped radically, this time to a reading of 29.73, a change of .10 inch in two hours.[9] Now perhaps the fleet flagship also had come into the "territory of large extent" surrounding the storm.[10]

At 1310 Admiral Halsey, concerned over the safety of the ships fueling, ordered that fueling operations be suspended at the earliest time practicable. The individual task group and task unit commanders, now clearly worried about the critically low level of their oil, continued the attempt to fuel destroyers for another several hours. Destroyers were directed to remain alongside the ships from which they were then receiving fuel until they had enough to reach the next morning's rendezvous, located at 17° N, 128° E. This point was about 160 miles northwest of the original fueling rendezvous, and later proved to be about 120 miles north of the typhoon's actual track.[11] CTU 38.2.3 recommended that attempts to refuel the *Hickox*, *Maddox*, and *Spence* be continued, but noted that the rest of his destroyers could make it to the rendezvous without refueling. The *Spence* remained alongside the *New Jersey* until 1339, when she cast off, having received only 6,000 gallons of oil. Admiral Halsey recommended that she then attempt fueling from an oiler. Leaving the thirstiest of the escorts behind with the oilers, Task Force 38 now departed, heading generally to the northwest for the next morning's rendezvous.

The 1400 barometer reading on the *New Jersey* was 29.70. In an interval of three hours the barometric pressure had dropped .13 inch. With an average diurnal change of .03 to .04 inch in the same period, the drop was enough to signal the possible approach of a typhoon. Based only on primitive local indicators, there was reason to suspect that the fleet might be threatened. Up until this point the *New Jersey* had been steaming on a fueling course of 040° T, with the wind on the port bow. A storm approaching from the southeast would have been closing the distance, bringing with it a falling barometer. An old table from Piddington's *Horn Book*, which is quoted in Bowditch, suggests that the distance to the center of a

A Third Fleet destroyer, as seen from the *New Jersey* as she comes alongside during steadily worsening weather on 17 December 1944.

cyclonic storm can be determined by observing the average hourly fall of the barometer. It shows that an average drop of .02 to .06 inch per hour indicates the storm center to be from 250 to 150 miles distant. [12] On that basis, the center was about 200 miles away at 1400. We now know that it was much closer; only 120 miles distant.

Aboard the *Dewey*, we had changed course from 240° T to 040° T at 1025. We now watched with growing concern as the barometer dropped from 29.70 at 1100 to 29.58 at 1400.[13] Here was a drop in barometric pressure of .12 inch in three hours. While we knew that some portion of that change could be attributed to the diurnal variation, I considered it to be within the category of a .10 inch fall in three hours. It could signal the approach of a typhoon. We decided that the *Dewey* was then on the outer edge of a tropical cyclone whose center was located to the east-southeast.

Dave Bate's recollection of these events notes that "On the 17th we thought we might well be in the path of a typhoon, which we believed to be somewhere to the southeast of us. I remember the attempts to fuel on the 17th. . . . I know that we lashed down everything that we could, because on the 17th we believed we were going to be in trouble."[14]

At 1533 Admiral Halsey directed that the rendezvous point for fueling the next morning be changed to 14° N and 127°30′ E.[15] The new rendezvous was about 180 miles south of that which had been ordered just a couple of hours earlier. It later proved to be about 55 miles south of the typhoon's actual track.

At about 1600, Captain Acuff called Captain Mercer to ask him his opinion as to whether it was advisable to continue efforts to fuel the *Hickox*, *Maddox*, and *Spence*, or to abandon those efforts and proceed to the next day's rendezvous. Mercer suggested that the *Dewey* attempt to take fueling station alongside one of the oilers so that he could observe conditions at first hand. I maneuvered alongside the designated oiler. Although I was able to bring the ship into position and maintain station within the maximum distance for fueling, the wind and sea made it impossible to hold a steady course. Each heavy swell caused the *Dewey* to yaw about twenty degrees, and then we had to apply full rudder to bring her back on the base course. On those occasions we often closed the distance to as little as five yards. A superb performance by our helmsman, and a large measure of good luck, bolstered by many silent prayers, enabled us to avoid collision. We continued to maintain station abreast of the oiler for about twenty minutes. It appeared to me that we would not be able to keep a fuel hose rigged under those conditions. I commented to Preston Mercer that in my judgment it was useless to continue the effort to refuel destroyers by the alongside method. He concurred and so reported to CTG 30.8. A few minutes later the task group commander signaled that he was abandoning any further attempts to fuel that day. Task Unit 30.8.4 then proceeded to steam independently on course 240° T, heading for the rendezvous point scheduled for 0600 on the 18th, where another attempt would be made to refuel the destroyers. At last we were on a course more to our liking. Now the *Dewey* was also running ahead of the storm.

All of us on the bridge of the *Dewey*, including Preston Mercer, were concerned over the fleet commander's signaled intentions to undertake fueling operations again beginning at daybreak on the 18th. We simply did not consider such a plan to be realistic. At 1855 formation course was changed to 248° T, an adjustment that more nearly paralleled the projected track of the storm as we estimated it.

The destroyers *Spence*, *Hickox*, and *Maddox*, which were deemed to be in the most urgent need of fuel, had remained with the logistic support force. Now Acuff directed them to join TU 30.8.4, which was our task unit. The hope was that if they remained in company with the oilers, Preston Mercer, in his dual capacity as task unit and screen commander, might find a way to refuel them. Mercer had assigned them to appropriate stations in our screen, and immediately concerned himself with their need to obtain fuel. We discussed their situation and tried to devise some solution to it. We could think of no way to ensure that they could be fueled the next day, but recalling our low expenditure during the preceding three days, we figured that with luck the *Spence*, *Hickox*, and *Maddox* should be able to hold out for another thirty-six hours. By that time we thought it would be possible to find a fueling area where the weather conditions would permit replenishment.

At about 2000, Preston Mercer asked me if I knew the skipper of the *Spence*. I told him that I did, that Lieutenant Commander Jimmy Andrea and I had been in the same battalion while midshipmen at Annapolis, that he had graduated in '37 and I had not seen him since. I also said that I thought he had only recently taken command of the *Spence* (Andrea had taken command on 8 July 1944), and that I did not know how much destroyer experience he had had. Mercer asked me if I thought he had ballasted. I replied that I thought it likely that he had, since it was a general practice in destroyers to ballast whenever the fuel load fell below about 70 percent of capacity, but I added that the only way to be sure was to ask him. A conversation then ensued over voice radio, in which the subject of ballasting was discussed. Captain Acuff, Captain Bill Kenny (Commander Destroyer Division 104 in the *Hickox*) and the skippers of the *Spence* and *Maddox* all were asked to comment on the subject. When asked, Jim Andrea noted that the *Spence* had not been ballasted during that day's operations, and that "it would have been helpful."[16] Preston Mercer ended the conference by directing the three ships (*Hickox*, *Maddox*, and *Spence*) to ballast immediately to 50 percent of their total fuel capacity. The intention of the directive was that they ballast with sufficient seawater to give added stability through the night, but keep their tanks sufficiently clear to be able to receive fuel in the morning if conditions permitted. Both the *Hickox* and *Maddox* complied with these instructions. So far as can be determined from the available records, the *Spence* did not take ballast aboard at all during the night of 17–18 December. There appears to be no documented explanation as to why the *Spence* did not comply, although destroyer engineering officers frequently resist putting seawater into their fuel tanks because of their fear of contamination.

At 2200 the *Dewey*'s barometer reading dropped to 29.54.[17] The wind was blowing at about 36 knots from 026° T, and in addition to the normal swell caused by the wind, there were long cross swells

The USS *Spence* increases speed as she proceeds to a new station.

from about 110° T.[18] The sea was very rough, and it seemed to me that the weather indicators were now ominous.

At 2220 the fleet commander directed Task Force 38 to change the rendezvous for fueling to 15°30′ N and 127°40′ E at 0700 on the 18th.[19] This change moved it about 90 miles north of the position that had last been designated at 1533, and later proved to be about 40 miles north of the typhoon's actual track. At 2247 formation course was changed to 298° T. We thought the new course might be to the right of the storm's track. Under no circumstances did we want to cross over to the right side of its projected path. To do so would put us in the dangerous semicircle, where the speed of the storm's movement over the surface would be added to the speed of the wind's counterclockwise rotation. We trusted the fleet commander's orders and raised no question about the course. The *Dewey* deck log entry reads, "2247 Changed course to 298° T. High wind and heavy seas made it very difficult to maintain station and even more difficult to regain station when screen reoriented on the 50° course change to the right."[20]

By 2300 the *Dewey* barometric reading was 29.50, a drop of .07 inch in two hours.[21] The storm was definitely closing in on us, despite the fact that we were now running ahead of it at 14 knots.

Preston Mercer remained on the bridge of the *Dewey* until shortly after midnight. We discussed the storm situation in detail, and reviewed the several local weather signs that seemed to us to indicate the approach of a typhoon. When I commented that even the most junior officers of the *Dewey* had deduced that there was a typhoon to the southeast of us and that the Third Fleet seemed to be directly in its path, he replied, "I know. I'm really tempted to call the fleet commander and tell him of my concerns, but then I remember that he has a big staff, including an aerologist, and is getting analyses from Pearl Harbor. I can only conclude that it would be presumptuous of me to offer advice under those circumstances." I agreed that they certainly had a lot more information than we did and said I was sure that Admiral Halsey knew what he was doing.

By the time Mercer was ready to turn in, I had organized a special inspection party composed of the first lieutenant, the warrant boatswain, and the chief boatswain's mate, for the purpose of conducting a thorough inspection of the ship to check the status of our heavy-weather preparations. Although I knew that Frank Bampton had already made an inspection for the same purpose, I wanted to see for myself that no reasonable precautionary measure had been overlooked. The commodore wished us well and retired to his cabin.

It was a somber little group that faced me as I explained the vital importance of our inspection. In the dark of the pilot house, with no light except the glow of illuminated instrument dials, their faces took on an eery quality. I could see their serious expressions and was impressed by their calm determination. Boatswain Miller commented that he didn't relish going through a typhoon, but that if he had to do it he was glad that he was on the *Dewey*. I could see his rugged countenance beneath his cap visor and was touched by his expression of confidence. He was old enough to be my father. I felt very fortunate to have such men under my command.

Our inspection disclosed that the deck force had done a superb job in securing for the storm. Lifelines had been rigged on the entire topside, and all loose gear on the weather decks had either been lashed down or struck below. We paid particular attention to the storage of depth charges, the tight closure of hatches, the transfer of boiler feed water into the lowest feed tanks, and the removal and transfer of 5-inch gun ammunition from ready-service racks and upper handling rooms to the magazines. One item we were unable to do anything about was our motor whaleboat. In our preoccupation with other precautions, we had allowed the boat to remain in its outboard position, in readiness for use. The point where we could have put the boat safely into the sea had long since passed, and now it was entirely too rough to attempt to swing it in; to try to do so would involve unacceptable risk to those engaged in the task. I decided that the boat would just have to take its chances. If we lost it, we lost it!

I returned to the bridge at about 0230, feeling that we had done all we could to make the *Dewey* ready. It now appeared certain that we were going to be battling a typhoon in a matter of hours. I had written very detailed night orders, and after a few words with the officer of the deck (Lieutenant (j.g.) S. H. Harrison, USNR), I went back to my sea cabin, just abaft the pilot house.

Once again I reviewed our situation. We had about 78 percent fuel capacity aboard, and would still have more than 76 percent by 0800, so I did not consider the ship's stability to be in jeopardy. We had a veteran crew. They had secured for heavy weather in expert fashion. The officers were completely dependable and competent. The factor of the ship's age I listed on the credit side of the ledger. The *Dewey* herself was a veteran. She was in good material condition, her engineering plant was in excellent working order, and her engineers seemed to know exactly what they were doing. I was confident that we could deal successfully with any storm we might encounter, but my thoughts turned to Admiral Halsey, and again I wondered why he wasn't taking drastic action to avoid the storm. I recalled my meeting with him in November of '42, when as the gunnery officer of the *Sterett* I had conducted him on a tour to inspect our battle damage following the Third Battle of Savo Island. I remembered his expressions of admiration that a destroyer could absorb three 14″ and eight 5″ shell hits, and still steam away under her own power. I also recalled how he stood with us at the gangway as he was leaving the ship and extended his heartfelt sympathy for the loss of thirty-two of our shipmates killed and another twenty-four severely wounded in the action. Tears had streamed down his cheeks as he spoke of their sacrifice, and I had said to myself, with great respect, "God, what a leader!" Ever since then I would have followed Admiral Halsey anywhere. Now as I reflected on the storm situation, I put my doubts aside. I concluded again that he knew more than we did, and that the fleet's movements were deliberately planned to deal with problems still unknown to us.

PART II

The Struggle for Survival

CHAPTER 6

The Fleet Is Overtaken

When Admiral Halsey decided at 1400 on the 17th to head for a new rendezvous 200 miles to the west, the move was based on the conclusion that there was a tropical disturbance to the eastward of the fleet's position. Commander George F. Kosco, his staff aerologist, had received radio weather reports from Ulithi and Guam on the 16th that indicated the possibility that a tropical storm was forming somewhere between those two stations. He reported to Halsey that he estimated the disturbance to be a weak low, and that he expected it to move off to the northeast. Later in the evening of the 16th, coded reports from Pearl Harbor also indicated the existence of a tropical storm in about the same location.[1] By noon of the 17th, with local weather conditions deteriorating rapidly, Halsey became concerned over the safety of the destroyers as they endeavored to fuel. At about 1400 Kosco prepared a message, addressed for action to all task force and task group commanders of the Third Fleet, giving the fleet position at 1300 as "14°59'N, 130°08'E." The dispatch further stated, "Barometer 1006 mb falling steadily, strong northeast winds backing to north, heavy seas and moderate rain squalls. Tropical disturbance of increasing intensity located 15°00'N, 138°00'E, moving north-northwest 12–15 knots; estimate it will move into calm front and recurve to northeast as extratropical storm."[2] To the best of my knowledge, this message was never readdressed to the individual ships of the Third Fleet. In any event, we did not receive it on the *Dewey*, and it is fortunate that we didn't, since it would have been confusing. As the afternoon of the 17th wore on, Kosco decided that the storm was increasing in intensity. He also revised his estimate of its location, deciding that it probably was as far west as 134 or 135 degrees east, about 200 miles closer than indicated in his message. For some reason he never sent a correction to that effect. Consideration then was given to the desirability of going south. Kosco recommended that "the place to go would be to the southwest."[3] However, at about 1400 or 1500 a report from the *Chandeleur*, a seaplane tender whose planes sent reports on weather encountered during their patrol flights, stated they had a report of a "definite storm center" at 13 degrees north and 132 degrees east, with winds "to 60 knots."[4] Since winds of 65 knots by definition are categorized to be of hurricane force, this report appears to have been of great significance. Halsey and his staff decided that to go south would encounter the storm reported by the *Chandeleur*. Accordingly, the next morning's rendezvous was chosen at a point generally to the west instead of to the southwest. At about 2230, Halsey's chief of staff (Rear Admiral Robert B. Carney), the staff operations officer (Captain Ralph E. Wilson), and Commander Kosco met in the admiral's mess and decided that their avoiding action up to that point was the best that could be taken for the rest of the night. Kosco then apparently went to bed, since he was scheduled to have the morning watch (from 0400 to 0800) and would have to get up early.

The deck log of the *New Jersey* for the 18th of December, 1944, shows barometer readings at 0100 of 29.76, and at 0300 of 29.65.[5] Again the barometer had provided the fleet staff with a warning, this time a drop of .11 inch in two hours.

Kosco woke up at 0230 with the feeling, as he later expressed it, that "something was wrong."[6] He went to his office and checked all the reports. He decided that, "Things didn't look bad," the barometer was "going up and down as normal," and the wind was hauling around to the west, which he attributed to the passage of a tropical storm.[7] In retrospect one has to wonder why a drop of .11 inch in two hours, even discounting the diurnal variation, would have appeared to be "normal"!

At about 0345, Kosco learned that Admiral Halsey was up. The aerologist went in to see him. He told Halsey that from all indications the storm was increasing in intensity and was likely to hit the fleet if they continued on a northwesterly course. Halsey sent for the chief of staff and operations officer. With Kosco they met in the wardroom, where they discussed the storm. Kosco was asked for his recommendation. He said he thought they should immediately turn south. At that point (shortly before 0420) Kosco took over the staff watch. Admiral Halsey asked Kosco to call CTF 38 (Vice Admiral McCain) on the TBS, and ask him where he thought the storm was. McCain's response was that he wouldn't be able to fuel. Frustrated by the task force commander's failure to answer the question, Kosco then called CTG 38.2 (Rear Admiral Gerald F. Bogan) and asked him for his estimate of the storm's position. Bogan replied that he thought it was at 17 degrees north and 131 degrees east, about 190 miles northeast of its actual position. Kosco thought it was at 15 degrees north and 131 degrees east, about 100 miles east of its actual position. Meanwhile, Admiral McCain, apparently overhearing this conversation and realizing that he had not provided the requested information, called back and gave his estimate, which placed the center 12½ degrees north and 131 degrees east, about 190 miles southeast of its actual position. Both McCain and Bogan said they thought the storm's movement was to the northwest at 12 knots. Kosco told Halsey and Carney that he thought his estimate of the storm's location was the best, and that the southerly course they were then steering should be continued.

The following paraphrased extracts from Admiral Halsey's report of the typhoon provide an idea of how the events of the 18th appeared from the fleet commander's viewpoint.[9] It is obvious that although Halsey was besieged with reports of events, none of them conveyed to him a full appreciation of the gravity of the situation that existed on many of his ships over a period of about twelve hours.

At 0500 the *New Jersey* clocked the wind at 38 knots from 355° T.[10] The Third Fleet was just about 100 miles ahead of the storm, about 25 miles to the north of its track, and some 18 miles to the southwest of the rendezvous point. Admiral Halsey now canceled the rendezvous, and directed all groups to come to course 180° T at present speed (15 knots), and to commence fueling as soon as practicable. These two directives simply were not compatible. With the wind and sea from the north, it was impossible to fuel on a southerly course. He also suggested that needy destroyers fuel from astern of the oilers if necessary. That this was not a feasible alternative had been clearly demonstrated the day before.

CTG 30.8 reported at 0538 that the destroyers *Maddox*, *Hickox*, and *Spence*, which had been left with TG 30.8.4 on the 17th, had not been able to fuel and that he had advised them to ballast and plan to fuel in two separate fueling operations.

At 0616, Commander Task Force 38 changed fleet course to 150 degrees T. The reason for this thirty-degree change to the left is not apparent from the record. Obviously, it moved the entire disposition closer to the center of the storm.

At 0710, Commander Task Force 38 directed the force to come to 060° T, speed 10 knots, and to commence fueling. McCain was doing what he had to do in order to fuel. Halsey was aware of this course change, but he did not interfere with it. According to the *New Jersey* log, the wind was 39 knots from 002° T. By now it was obvious that fueling from alongside the oilers was impossible. McCain tried the only alternative that was left, to fuel destroyers from the lee side of the large carriers.

The 0730 fuel reports from the destroyers low in fuel were *Stockham* and *Welles* 22 percent, *Yarnall* 20 percent, *Moore* 21 percent, *Taussig* 18 percent, *Wedderburn, Colahan, Bush, Franks, Cushing,* 15 percent, and *Maddox, Hickox,* and *Spence* all 10 to 15 percent.

At 0743 CTG 38.2 reported to CTF 38 that under present conditions fueling the destroyers from the carriers was not possible. Also at this same time, the escort carrier *Nehenta Bay* reported that the CVEs could not take the sea. The *Cape Esperance* and *Rudyerd Bay* reported that they were pounding heavily. CTF 38 directed the CVEs to select a course and speed at their own discretion, but to remain together. CTG 30.8 designated the commanding officer of the *Nehenta Bay* to take tactical command of the CVEs, and they immediately turned to a southerly course at a speed of 10 knots.

At 0803, an hour after the fleet had turned to the fueling course, Admiral Halsey directed that fueling be discontinued and the fleet continue to the south. The task force commander complied by issuing the order to change course to 180° at 0809. The flagship *New Jersey* was now encountering very heavy seas, with the wind at 43 knots from 025° T. At 0818 Halsey sent a message to General MacArthur, stating that he had been unable to dodge the storm and would not be able to strike targets on Luzon on the 19th.

At 0845 the fleet tug *Jicarilla* reported having engine trouble.

At 0907 the carrier *Independence* reported a man overboard.

At 0911 the *Monterey* reported that excessive rolls had caused the aircraft on her hangar deck to break loose and that they had caught fire.

At 0915 Admiral Halsey sent a message to the Commander in Chief Pacific Fleet estimating the 0830 position of the "tropical disturbance" as 15 degrees north, 130 degrees east, moving northwest at 12 knots. He still did not diagnose it as a typhoon.

At 0920 the fleet turned to course 220° T.

At 0924 the *Monterey* reported she could only make 5 knots and was losing speed. Now the staff of the Third Fleet finally concluded that the fleet was encountering a typhoon. The numerous messages received from ships of all types made it clear that conditions were extreme. The light carriers and the escort carriers were reporting alarming experiences, rolling very heavily and suffering extensive damage to their embarked aircraft. The fleet staff had lost control of the picture. They were unable to plot accurately the location of individual units, and their radar failed to provide an accurate visual presentation of present ship positions.

At 0925 CTG 38.2 directed one cruiser and two completely fueled destroyers to remain with the *Monterey*. The *Monterey* reported she had lost steerageway. The cruiser *New Orleans* and the destroyers *Brush*, *Miller*, *Twining*, and *McCord* were directed to remain with her. Admiral Halsey directed that two fleet tugs join the ships standing by to help the *Monterey*.

At 0930 CTF 38 directed a change of course to 140° T, speed 12 knots. He also told Commander Task Group 38.1 (the southernmost carrier task group) to operate independently.

At 0931 the *Independence* reported two men overboard.

At about 0941 the escort carriers *Cape Esperance* and *Kwajalein* reported trouble with their steering systems. Both ships continued to experience difficulty and were unable to keep up with their task unit (30.8.3). The destroyer *Thorn* was designated to turn back and screen them.

At 0945 the *Monterey* reported her fire under control, but proposed to remain stopped until she was able to make the formation speed.

At 0959 the *Monterey* reported her hangar deck fire was out and that she expected to have power soon.

At 1002 the *New Jersey* changed course to 220° T to avoid an unidentified escort carrier that was stopped.

At 1005 CTG 38.1 reported to Commander Third Fleet that he had directed the *New Orleans* to take charge of the *Monterey* and the escorting destroyers and proceed to Ulithi.

At 1007 Admiral Halsey directed CTG 38.1 to cancel his orders to the *New Orleans* and to hold the *Monterey* group with the fleet insofar as possible.

At 1010 the *Dewey* was heard reporting that she was turning hard left to avoid collision.

At 1012 the *Wisconsin* reported the loss of one Kingfisher aircraft overboard. In the next 12 minutes the cruisers *Boston* and *Miami* also lost their planes.

At 1025 the *Dewey* reported she was behind the formation and heading into the wind, trying to come around to the formation course.

At 1051 the *Cowpens* reported a fire on her hangar deck. Fourteen minutes later she reported the fire to be under control.

At 1149 Admiral Halsey directed Commander Task Force 38 to take the most comfortable course with the wind on the port quarter.

The USS *Monterey* proceeds down the Delaware River after completing overhaul at Philadelphia Navy Yard, 24 July 1943.

(No such message was directed to the ships of TG 30.8, but it would have been too late to have been of assistance in any case.)

At 1156 CTF 38 directed TF 38 to come to course 120° T. In the vicinity of the fleet flagship the wind was 51 knots from 345° T, with a barometer reading of 29.55. Compared to the weather then being encountered by the destroyers of TG 30.8.4, the *New Jersey* was in a mild breeze!

At 1201 the *Langley* reported that she was rolling consistently to 35 degrees on both sides.

At 1203 CTG 38.3 came to a new course of 150° T.

At 1228 the *Cape Esperance* reported a fire on the flight deck. Seven minutes later she reported the fire was out. Admiral Halsey directed that a cruiser be sent to stand by her. The *Miami* was directed to comply.

At 1236 the *San Jacinto* reported that four planes were still adrift on her hangar deck and that every effort was being made to secure them.

At 1243 CTF 38.1 reported that the fire on the *Cowpens* had been extinguished.

At 1310 the wind velocity in the vicinity of the *New Jersey* increased from 75 to 83 knots with gusts to 93 knots. Her barometer reading was 29.23, a drop of .07 inch in ten minutes.[11] Now at last the fleet flagship also was beginning to taste the fury of the storm.

At 1345 Admiral Halsey reported to the Commander in Chief, Pacific Fleet, Commander in Chief Southwest Pacific, and to the Third Fleet, giving his 1300 position as 14°10′N, 127°48′E, and reporting heavy confused seas, ragged ceiling, heavy rains, wind west-northwest 70 knots, barometer 991 mb, *typhoon* of increasing intensity, lower than 900 mb, center located at 14°54′N, 128°00′E, moving west at 12 knots. This was the first message sent from any source that indicated the presence of a typhoon!

At 1358 CTF 38 reported the center of the typhoon was showing clearly on his surface search radar at 000° T, distant about 35 miles.

At 1418 the *San Jacinto* reported all fires out except one small electrical fire, and that her planes had all been secured on deck.

At 1420 the *Buchanan* reported her gyro compass out of commission.

At 1425 the cruiser *Baltimore* and destroyers *Halsey Powell* and *Benham* joined the *Cowpens* to assist her as might be necessary.

At 1500 wind on the fleet flagship had fallen off to 56 knots from 255° T. The barometer was up to 29.40.[12] The *New Jersey* had experienced less than two hours of severe weather.

At 1520 Admiral Halsey directed that at 1800 the fleet should come to a comfortable southerly course in search of fueling weather. CTG 30.8 and so-called "stragglers" were to be advised if possible.

At 1545 CTG 30.8 reported his flagship, the *Aylwin*, was dead in the water and that he could receive only on TBS. (Obviously the storm must still be severe where he was!)

At 1600 the *New Jersey* recorded wind 35 knots from 235° T, barometer 29.46.[13]

At 1718 Admiral Halsey directed that all Third Fleet ships rendezvous for fueling at 12°N, 129°E, at 0700 on the 19th.

At 1745 Halsey sent another message to the Third Fleet, requesting prompt reports of storm damage and deficiencies.

At 1800 the fleet course was changed to 200° T, speed 11 knots.

At 1848 Halsey directed CTF 38 to conduct a thorough search of the area through which the fleet had passed to try to locate any men lost overboard. He suggested that search planes carry extra life rafts for rescue purposes, and that any straggling ships be reported by high frequency voice transmission. The loss of the *Hull*, *Monaghan*, and *Spence* had not yet been discovered.

At about 2000 several carriers reported seeing lights in the water and hearing the sound of pocket whistles. Their screening destroyers were alerted to listen for whistles and effect rescues whenever possible. Unfortunately, the destroyers were unable to locate the source of any of these signals.

At 2247 CTU 30.8.2 was directed to take charge of all TG 30.8 units and to prepare for fueling in the morning.

At 2330 CTG 30.8 reported his position at 14°N, 128°29'E, and noted that the tug *Jicarilla* was disabled and the *Mataco*, another fleet tug, was standing by.

As the 18th of December passed into history, the Commander Third Fleet could not possibly have had any real appreciation of the magnitude of the disaster that had just befallen his ships. Not until the 19th did the tragic picture begin to unfold.

CHAPTER 7

The Dewey's Ordeal[1]

It was early in the morning of 18 December. Aboard the *Dewey*, sleep had been impossible. She was rolling and pitching with a violence that left no doubt about the severity of the storm whose outer fringes now touched us. If typhoons, like ships, were female, this one was going to be a real bitch!

At 0500 a tremendous roll to starboard hurled me from my bunk. A whole barrage of books from my bookshelf bombarded my head and shoulders. I reacted with a few choice expletives, but then I decided that perhaps Fate was telling me to get up and take a look at the weather. As I dressed, the messenger opened the door to report a formation course change to 180° T. It hadn't helped make life any easier. The *Dewey* had been heaving and pitching violently before, but now she had added a new dimension of movement. The dominating motion was rolling, and she creaked and groaned anew as her frames twisted from the buffeting of the sea. She sounded as though she were in pain. In any case, I now understood what had pitched me out of my bunk. The change of course to 180° T had turned us to a heading almost at right angles to the track of the storm. The long cross swell now was coming at us from a point or two forward of the port beam. No wonder we were rolling! We could expect the barometer to drop rapidly now as the eye of the storm grew closer.

Out on the open bridge a few minutes later I was greeted by Bill Buzick, who had the morning watch as the officer of the deck. With his usual good humor and a wide smile he commented that the weather was great for building character. I chuckled and observed that if that was so I thought we were going to build a lot of it in the next few hours. I asked about the barometer, and was not surprised to learn that it had been almost steady since midnight. The 0500 reading was 29.50. We had been running ahead of the storm on a parallel course, maintaining our distance from the center. The dawn was gray and overcast. The wind was at gale force (28–33 knots) from east-northeast.[2]

Only two or three ships in our task unit were visible. I had observed mountainous seas many times before in the North Atlantic, but none to match those through which we now were wallowing. The northerly wind was producing huge waves, the tops of which were blowing off and driving across the wind-streaked sea like a torrential horizontal rain. The water was slate gray, and the sky was almost as dark. The heavy cross swell from the east made the sea confused. Not until I watched the destroyer *Maddox*—only 1,500 yards from the *Dewey*—disappear from sight in the trough, did I realize that these waves were indeed tremendous. I estimated that they were more than 60 feet high—above our eye level on the bridge. I called down to the commodore and briefed him on the situation. In a few minutes he joined us on the bridge. There wasn't much conversation, but there was complete agreement on the fact that the typhoon was almost upon us.

At 0605 formation speed was changed to 8 knots, and the ships of Task Force 38 again joined us. At 0616 formation course was changed to 150° T. The wind by now was at whole gale strength (48–55 knots) from the northeast. It seemed obvious that fueling operations would be impossible, yet at 0710 formation course was changed to 060° T, and speed was changed to 10 knots. To our disbelief, fueling was going to be attempted despite the worsening weather. The 0710 entry in the *Dewey*'s deck log read, "Found it impossible to countermarch to new station because of unfavorable conditions of wind and sea." I found myself wondering how in the hell the fleet commander could think that fueling was possible. When I posed that question to Preston Mercer he just shook his head.

Visibility now was about two miles and lowering. The mountainous seas and strong winds soon began to take their toll of lives as the sailors of 132 ships worked on deck, struggling to secure hoses and lines, either in preparation for fueling or in battening down for heavy weather. The chilling report, "Man overboard!" came by voice radio from first one ship and then another. I must have heard it at least a dozen times in an hour. The microphone of our public address system was on the starboard side of the pilot house. I slid and lurched over to it to warn all hands: "Rescue in these seas would be impossible. Every man who is not performing an essential job topside must stay below."

In addition to an extensive system of lifelines over all the weather decks, we had stationed a special four-man life buoy watch at the after conning station. Lashed to the ship's structure, their duty was to keep a sharp lookout for men overboard, and to heave a life ring to such unfortunates as might be sighted in the water. Lifejackets were made the mandatory uniform of the day for all hands.

Dave Bate's recent letter to me noted, "Frank and I cooperated in the duties of Executive Officer and Navigator on the 17th, but the approaching storm had created conditions bad enough by very early morning of the 18th, so that you and Frank and Captain Mercer all agreed that Frank had better 'act' as Executive Officer and Navigator throughout the storm."[3] (Dave's recollection is correct. I thought it was in the best interest of the *Dewey* to avail ourselves of Frank Bampton's knowledge and experience, as well as his established authority and relationship with the other officers and men. This decision had nothing to do with Dave Bate's competence or my confidence in him, for I had no doubts on either score.)

At 0745 Bill Buzick was relieved as officer of the deck by Don Weed. Don's first comment was "What did we do to deserve this?" I told him that the commodore had arranged it in order to test our Heavy Weather Preparation Bill! Buzick went below for a cup of coffee and a piece of toast, but he was back on the bridge in a few minutes, anxious to be of some help.

By 0800 the barometer had dropped from 29.49 an hour earlier, to 29.42.[4] The savage fury of the storm now was overtaking us.

At 0820 the formation course was changed to south. It had taken the task force commander an hour and ten minutes to decide that fueling operations were impossible. It was a costly delay.

As we struggled and pounded our way around to a course of 180° T again, we lost steering control from the bridge.[5] Control was shifted to the steering motor room. Our helmsman now steered by turning a little knob that sent signals to the steering motor room, showing the crew there how to place the rudder. We had rehearsed this emergency procedure many times in our underway drills. It posed no serious problem.

Radio transmissions crackled and squawked with reports that all ships were wallowing and riding very heavily. The rain and blown spray drove at us with terrific force. The roar of the storm grew with every passing minute. Visibility continued to lower. The change of course put the *Dewey* in the rear of the formation. The heavy seas made it very difficult to regain station ahead.

The surface search radar went out of commission. In extremely poor visibility we lost track of the formation guide. Steering control was regained on the bridge. At 0849 formation course was changed to 150° T in order to avoid an adjacent task group. Visibility was reduced to 300 yards.

The chief gunner's mate reported completion of special securing measures in all the ship's magazines, to ensure that 5-inch powder cases and projectiles could not break adrift.[6] I directed that all gun and other topside watches, except the bridge watch and the lookouts, secure from their assigned stations and seek shelter inside the ship. Again I warned all hands to wear lifejackets, and directed them not to come topside unless it was absolutely necessary. Formation course was shifted back to 180° T. The surface search radar became operational again. We now were able to locate the guide, and discovered ourselves to be 5,000 yards on her starboard beam. Since our assigned station now was 5,000 yards dead-ahead of her, we increased speed to 12 knots in an attempt to get back to where we belonged. Even at that speed we were pitching and pounding badly. At 0910 several ships were heard reporting the loss of more men overboard. Even the attack carriers had men swept off or blown into the sea.

On the *Dewey* we set condition "Affirm," and buttoned her up as tightly as we could, with all watertight doors and hatches closed.[7] At 0911 our voice radio went out of commission. Electrical failures now became a recurring problem. Everything was being short-circuited by the driving rain and spray. Our helmsman was having to use from 20 to 25 degrees of right rudder to maintain a heading of 160° T, the course necessary to regain station in the van of the formation. At 0928, with the ship rolling 40 degrees to starboard (and about 30 degrees to port), the *Dewey* lost suction on the port main lubricating oil pump. We had to stop the port engine in order to prevent wiping the main bearings. Lube-oil suction was soon regained. We went ahead with standard speed (15 knots) in order to turn back to 160° T. The ship's head had fallen off to 110° T while we were stopped. It was necessary to use hard right rudder to turn her back through that 50-degree arc. We pounded very heavily in the process. At 0933 the TBS radio was back in commission.

On the bridge we were engaged in hand-to-hand combat with the storm. We had to struggle constantly to remain upright. The helmsman had to fight the ship's wheel to stay on course, not because the wheel itself was any harder to turn, but because his footing was so unsteady that he often found himself unable to exert any leverage. The wheel became his anchor, but at the same time he had to spin it rapidly in order to steer. It became an exhausting task.

It was so difficult to stand that I looked for some part of the ship's structure against which I could brace myself. I discovered that I could wedge my body between the annunciator (or RPM indicator) and the engine-order telegraph. From that vantage point I could turn and look forward through the bridge windows and see what lay ahead, or face aft and observe everyone and everything in the pilot house, including an inclinometer that measured the magnitude of every roll. Increasingly I was facing aft. The lowering visibility prevented my being able to see ahead, while the degree to which we were rolling had become a matter of serious concern. I found myself constantly reviewing our preparations for heavy weather, wondering if there was anything more that we could do.

By 0930 the visibility was less than 300 yards and steadily diminishing. The *Dewey* was corkscrewing and writhing like a wounded animal. The wind was about 65 knots sustained, from 030° T. I estimated that it must be gusting to 90 or 100 knots. The steering motor room reported that a leak through a mushroom ventilator on the main deck was causing the space to flood. I directed that they stuff the leak with rags and form a bucket brigade to bail out the water.

At 0942 the light carrier *Monterey* reported that several of her aircraft had broken loose and started a fire on her hangar deck. She indicated that she had stopped, was dead in the water, and requested that a fleet tug stand by to render assistance if necessary. At 0950 we observed an unidentified carrier dead ahead of us. I slowed to one-third (5 knots) and attempted to identify her. If it was the *Monterey* I knew that she was stopped, and I could avoid her by turning either way. If it was some other carrier, she probably was going ahead, and we would have to go astern of her. In the reduced visibility we couldn't tell whether this one was headed across to the right or to the left. We were abeam of her, but we couldn't tell which beam. Bearings remained steady. I concluded that she must be stopped. At a range of less than 300 yards I ordered, "Hard left rudder, come to course 130° T." The *Dewey*'s head swung around and we passed clear. As we went by close under her stern we could see her name very clearly. It was the *Monterey*, and I noted a heavy pall of smoke low over the sea on her lee side.

We increased speed to 10 knots. After we had avoided the *Monterey*, I ordered "Right full rudder, return to course 180° T." Watching the gyro repeater, I noticed that we were changing our heading very slowly. The quartermaster said, "She's not answering, Cap'n." I ordered, "Port ahead full." Still the *Dewey* wouldn't turn. I had never known a destroyer to fail to respond when sufficient power was applied to provide adequate headway. I now ordered, "Left full rudder. Port stop. Starboard ahead full!" If she wouldn't turn to the right, perhaps we could go around to the left. This time the *Dewey* came left about 20 degrees, then refused to budge one more degree. She was in the trough, struggling to twist herself out of the grip of wind and sea, but she couldn't do it. The *Dewey* was "in irons."

Visibility was now down to zero. Most of the time I couldn't even see the jackstaff. I thought of stopping, but couldn't be sure of where the heavies were. Our surface search radar was too cluttered with sea return to show them. I decided to keep going.

I addressed TG 30.8 on TBS and, using the *Dewey*'s voice call, told the support group, "This is Achilles. I am out of control, crossing through the formation from starboard to port. Keep clear!" The next few minutes seemed like an eternity. The *Dewey* staggered across into the formation. I knew that even if they could see us, there wasn't much they could do to avoid running us down. They couldn't change course without the risk of colliding with one of their own group, and with the visibility down as low as it was, by the time they saw us we'd be so close they couldn't stop.

Suddenly a huge black hull loomed up in front of us. As we were lifted high on the cross swell, it seemed to me that we were going to coast right down on top of her, but as we descended into the trough, the oiler was picked up by the next crest. Towering above us now, her own momentum, plus the force of the wind and sea coming from behind her, were overpowering. She lumbered across ahead of us. I said to Bill Buzick, "I could have thrown a spud at her," and I knew I could have hit her with it. We couldn't be sure how many more heavies we would encounter, but we were certain that there were more. The radar was useless now for any short-range targets. It didn't seem possible that we could miss hitting, or worse, being hit by one of those huge ships. It would be "curtains" for us if we collided, but by some miracle the others also slid safely past, one of them so close that I felt I could reach out and touch her.

Safely through the formation of heavies, I realized we were hopelessly out of position. I knew that it would take a lot more power than we could apply in those seas to turn the *Dewey* back to the formation course. I abandoned all efforts to rejoin. The safety of the ship was the paramount concern. I told Preston Mercer that I was going to give up trying to stay with the formation until we were out of the storm. He agreed. I felt relieved that we didn't have to fight our way back to our assigned station.

We had begun to lose lubricating oil suction on the port engine every few minutes. Every time we did, the engineers stopped the port shaft and rang up "Stop" on the engine-order telegraph. As soon as they were able to go ahead, they would notify us by sound-powered telephone. I would then ring up one-third ahead on the port engine. I decided to keep the starboard engine at "Stop" except as might be necessary to turn the shaft in order to prevent warping it. The ship was rolling a consistent 50 degrees to starboard and as much as 40 degrees to port, although the rolls to port decreased as those to starboard grew in magnitude. It became apparent that every roll to starboard in excess of 40 degrees would cause the loss of lube oil suction. Chief Machinist's Mate Dorwin Hill was in charge of that problem, and I knew that he could handle it if anyone could. It seemed to me that somewhere in the engineering design process someone had dropped the bricks!

At 1006 Preston Mercer directed me to fill the *Dewey*'s port side fuel tanks to capacity. I complied at once. I figured that with the wind steadily backing to the west, we must be in the navigable semicircle. I didn't anticipate that we had to worry about going through the eye of the storm, or that there might be a sudden reversal of the wind that would make us roll to port. I welcomed Mercer's suggestion and considered it sound advice. Within the next hour we pumped 21,500 gallons of oil and 5,300 gallons of water from the starboard to the port and centerline tanks.

At about 1015 we lost voice radio and radar contact with most of the formation. Nevertheless, we did continue to hold radar contact on another ship 3,000 yards distant, bearing almost due east of the *Dewey*. We suspected that this might be the *Monaghan*, since we had heard Bruce Garrett report that he too was "in irons." I had called him and assured him that we were in the same predicament. The range and bearing to this unidentified contact remained steady for the next hour or so. Whoever she was, it appeared that the unknown contact was also "in irons," unable to maneuver.

We were taking very heavy rolls to starboard. Quickly and alarmingly, they became more severe. No sooner would the ship struggle back to an upright position than she would roll again. For the first time, the thought of capsizing occurred to me as a possibility. Facing aft from between my supporting pillars, I watched the inclinometer. It registered 55–56–57—then 60 degrees. I tried to recall the stability curves that I had examined back in the shipyard. To my recollection they had shown that the *Dewey* could recover from a roll of 70 degrees. I called Frank Bampton over and quietly asked him whether my memory served me correctly. He confirmed the maximum roll to be 72 degrees. But that inclining data had been prepared a couple of years ago. Major alterations had been made in her armament and radar installations since then, and those stability characteristics had certainly undergone some significant changes. I recalled my concerns during our postrepair trials, but took comfort from the recollection that BuShips had not shared those concerns. I told myself that no modern destroyer could capsize. On the other hand, I had never rolled more than 50 degrees in all the rough weather encountered by the *Sterett* in three years of operating in the North Atlantic. The *Dewey* already had substantially beaten that record, and even as I watched, the rolls to starboard went beyond the 60° mark.

The wind had increased to a force I had never before experienced. It drove spray and spume with the force of a sand-blaster. Capillary bleeding was etched on any face exposed directly to it. When the lookouts and signalmen turned away from it their cheeks and foreheads were pocked with a bloody tattoo. It sanded the paint from patches of hull and superstructure. It drove into every crevice. "Watertight" instruments were not watertight. Even the tightly sealed case of our gun director admitted the high-velocity spray. I couldn't tell where the ocean ended and the sky began. Sound-powered telephone circuits became electrically grounded. First one and then another of our remote-control stations became isolated from us on the bridge.

At 1020 we lost steering control from the bridge again, and shifted control to the steering motor room. The radars continued to deteriorate. We turned off our main gyroscope as a precautionary measure and shifted to the magnetic compass for steering. In the words of my prep school roommate, "Things were going to hell in a handbasket!" I wondered what would happen next.

The 1100 barometer reading was 28.84, a drop of .50 inch in one hour.[8] At about 1102 our surface search radar became inoperative. The unidentified "pip" that we thought might be the *Monaghan* was therefore no longer visible. We made a final effort to remove a small amount of additional topside weight, and succeeded in jettisoning a few hundred pounds of consumable supplies. The doctor reported that several men had been injured by falling, but so far the worst casualty involved possible fractured ribs.

The wind's voice had become a wild howl. Above the din of the main gale were the higher-pitched sounds of the frequent and prolonged gusts. They were raging and overwhelming in their intensity. An octave or two higher were the screeching notes of our rigging and guy wires. It was hell's chorus, and we had to yell to each other at the top of our lungs to make ourselves heard above it.

At 1130 all controls and communications were lost from the bridge. Our isolation brought a new feeling of helplessness. I was desperately searching my mind now for some new idea that might help our situation. I refused to envision what it would be like to roll over. Somehow I had the feeling that if I allowed myself to picture it happening, it might happen! I believed that we were going to get through it.

About eight inches of water had now accumulated in all living spaces as a result of the ingress of water through closed "watertight" hatches and doors. The men of the *Dewey* formed bucket brigades in the mess hall and after living compartment, and succeeded in controlling the level of that flooding.

The pounding and rolling of the ship grew worse. We were now going over consistently to 68 and 70 degrees. With each roll as I watched the inclinometer go farther and farther, I would dispatch a silent prayer, "Dear God, please make her come back!" On at least three occasions, the officer of the deck, other bridge watch personnel and I observed the inclinometer go over against the limit of its scale, which on the bridge was 73 degrees, and still the ship rolled. Engine room personnel later reported that they had witnessed their inclinometer swing against its stop at 75 degrees, while the ship rolled even farther. I marvelled at the fact that we had recovered each time it happened, and responded to each recovery with relief and thanksgiving.

Fragmentary reports reached me from our engineers. With each giant roll to starboard, the forced draft blower intakes, which fed air to the boiler furnaces and were located on the main deck, were submerged. From 500 to 1,000 gallons of water gushed into the firerooms on each such roll.

In the forward fireroom, Andrew Tolmie, a veteran chief watertender, was fighting the storm with great skill and courage. When excessive rolling made it impossible for the pumps to take suction on the sloshing water, he rigged hose suction lines. Being flexible, they could always be kept submerged. The pumping continued uninterrupted. Tolmie and his men grabbed the fittings and projections in the overhead. When they would have plunged across the fireroom with each giant roll, they pulled themselves up, raised their feet, and hung free of the deck. On some rolls they lost both their footing and their hold on the overhead, and fell into the starboard bulkhead, plunging shoulder deep into the sloshing water, often striking some pump or piece of machinery on the way. It was bruising, painful, and exhausting. At any moment it could be fatal.

During one of these rolls the starboard fireroom hatch sprung open on the weather deck. Water poured into the airlock. Tolmie somehow clawed his way over blistering hot steam lines, climbed up the airlock ladder, and struggled with the hatch wheel until it was secured. He could have drowned in that flooded space, and it's a wonder he didn't. It took a healthy measure of guts to stay below decks under those conditions. Tolmie and his men had them in abundance.

The other engine spaces were sweating it out through a similar ordeal and meeting it with similar courage. In the after fireroom Oliver Fowler, watertender first, was leading his men just as Tolmie was leading his. In the engine rooms the conditions were in some ways even more appalling. Temperatures of 160° made them almost untenable. Despite efforts to secure the weather-deck hatches, seawater was forcing its way through them into the ship.

In the after engine space, where a hatch was located directly over the main electrical switchboard, salt water repeatedly spewed down on the wiring. Flash-overs, short circuits, and fires erupted. Chief Electrician's Mate Charles William Ross, with his electrical gang, kept electrical power available for several hours, but the deluge of salt water proved overwhelming. Finally, at 1130 all electrical power was lost. Only the dim battle lanterns provided light below decks.

Now the presence of Bob Gibson manifested itself in a very positive way. When terror gripped one of the older engineers to the point where he froze and seemed unable to function, Bob broke the tension with a few light-hearted comments. He made his men realize that everyone had the right to be frightened as long as they continued to help one another and didn't panic. This was leadership at its best. In his sixth day as chief engineer, Bob Gibson earned a generous share of credit for the superior performance of the *Dewey*'s engineers. The man who froze managed to surmount his fear and later performed well. After the storm we learned that he was one of the two people on the *Dewey* who had previously experienced a typhoon. He therefore knew better than the rest of us what there was to fear!

In the after engine room with Ross was Dorwin Hill, chief machinist's mate. The repeated loss of lubricating-oil suction required the most vigilant and expert engineering practices. Chief Hill and his men applied them. By 1130 we were having to stop the port shaft so frequently that we just secured it for about two hours. Even though our maneuverability had been severely limited, the little bit of control that resulted from the intermittent use of engine power to keep the wind and sea abaft the port beam, made a positive and possibly a decisive difference. Had we lost engine power earlier, we would have been completely at the mercy of the sea just that much longer. Throughout the majority of the approximately twelve hours of the ordeal, engine power was kept available and used to good advantage. Engineers like Hobson, Keith, Walker, Mann, Longville, and many others stuck to their posts. They gave the ship the help she needed to successfully battle the fury of the storm. None of them could have escaped had we capsized.

Back in the dark shaft alleys, Garland Sewell, watertender third class, the "Oil King," was entirely alone, with no light except that of his electric torch. He remained at his station throughout the storm and attended the fuel oil manifolds, transferring oil between tanks as the situation required. He also would have been trapped if the ship had rolled over.

In the steering motor room the hatch succumbed to the pounding seas that swept across the weather deck. Seawater short-circuited the steering motor. The ship had to be steered by hand. This was a herculean task, requiring the combined efforts of at least six or eight men. The steering motor room crew was equal to it.

All of these conditions were made known to me by messenger. I later learned that Chief Ross made several trips from one engine space to another to make repairs and coordinate damage control work, each time crossing the sea-swept main deck, where death beckoned on every roll. His reports of conditions below were invaluable.

The barometer was still falling. At 1200 it was 28.10, a drop of .74 inch in the last hour.[9] The seas continued to rage, more than sixty-feet high, and the sustained wind velocity was more than 100 knots. On the bridge we were finding it difficult to remain on board. As the ship lurched to starboard, we had to grab a vertical stanchion, or some similar piece of the ship's structure, and hang on for dear life. Many times I found myself hanging by my hands, with feet completely clear of the deck, in such a position that if I released my hold, I would drop straight down, through the starboard pilot house window into the sea. Several times I looked down past my dangling feet, and saw the angry sea through the open window, directly below them. On one occasion I lost my footing and plunged headfirst across the pilot house, striking my face against a projecting angle iron, which jutted out from the pilot house bulkhead about three feet above the deck. It dazed me for a minute or two. When I came to, on my hands and knees, I heard someone saying, "Call the doctor, the captain's broken his nose." I assured him I hadn't (and I hadn't) and soon felt none the worse for wear.

We rolled so far that the torpedo director, on the starboard wing of the bridge, was submerged. We remained that way for at least a minute each time. At one point I saw Frank Bampton standing with feet apart on the starboard pelorous stand, bailing solid green water with his helmet. I called to him, "Hell, Frank, you're going to have to bail the whole damned Pacific Ocean." He responded, "I've got to do something."

I saw Dave Bate standing braced against the pilot house bulkhead, looking wet and miserable, as did everyone, and thought to myself that it would have been better for him if we had found it too rough to transfer him to the *Dewey* just in time for a typhoon. He could just as easily still have been riding that big fat oiler. He must have read my mind, for when he saw me looking at him a moment later, he lurched over to my vicinity and said, "After all, Cap'n, we can't live forever!" I said, "No, but we can sure as hell try!"

In a recent letter, Dave Bate recalled; "At the beginning of the storm on the 18th, I was on the port wing of the bridge, trying to be of help, but mostly staying out of the way of you and Frank, who were very busy indeed. Anyone on that wing of the bridge had to keep low, because the sting of the rain and spray was painful. The wind seemed strong enough to tear off our rain gear. So I recall spending a lot of time in a sitting posture, leaning against the outer bulkhead. On one or two occasions I went into the pilot house. Once Captain Mercer called me in. He and I chatted about the chances of coming out of the storm alive. I recall that he was most pessimistic. . . ."[10]

We had no chaplain on the *Dewey*, but one of our leading quartermasters, Lawrence P. Johnson, quartermaster 2/c, acted as Protestant lay leader. "Preacher" was leading some of the bridge watch in saying aloud a continuous flow of prayers for the ship's safety. It seemed quite natural and proper. I was too preoccupied to join them, but I added a few silent pleadings of my own. I heard them saying the words to the "The Navy Hymn."

"Eternal Father, strong to save,
Whose arm doth bind the restless wave,
Who bidd'st the mighty ocean deep,
Its own appointed limits keep;
O hear us when we cry to Thee
For those in peril on the sea."

The *Dewey* couldn't stand much more. The rolls to starboard were coming more frequently now and we were remaining over, almost on our beam-ends, for longer periods—each a breathless, prayer-filled eternity. I still believed that we were going to make it.

Several times during those heavy rolls Preston Mercer and I found ourselves hanging by our hands, I from a vertical stanchion and he from the frame of his bridge chair, so that we were almost face to face. On one of those occasions he said to me, "If we go over and you end up in this sea, do you think you can make it?" The question brought instant flashbacks of Ginny and my son. I had too much to live for to lose it all now by drowning. I answered him, "Yes, I think I can." He confided that he doubted that he could, that he was not a strong swimmer. Then he continued, "I don't feel too badly about it, I've had a good life, and," with a smile, "my insurance is all paid up, but I feel sorry for all of these youngsters, many of them married and with families. Their lives have hardly begun and a lot of them wouldn't make it." I said, "Well, Commodore, I'm betting on the *Dewey*. I think she'll get us through." He closed the conversation by saying, "Skipper, I agree with you."

Searching for some emergency measure that might improve our stability, I decided to cut off the mast at bridge level. I reasoned that to do so would remove the heavy radar antenna from a great height, and thus lower the center of gravity. I told Preston Mercer of my intention. He said he thought it might help. I sent for Steve Yorden, our first class shipfitter, and his cutting torch. He soon arrived on the bridge, complete with his walrus mustache and his equipment, lighted the torch, and said, "Where do you want'er cut, Cap'n?" At that point my eye traveled once more up the mast to the radar antenna. This time my attention was caught by the starboard yard-arm, a 3-inch pipe across the mast near the top. Suspended from it were our signal halyards. As I looked I had a mental picture of the mast hinging at the bridge level, not breaking clean, the yardarm swinging down like the sharp end of a huge fire axe, punching through the ship's side right into the fireroom. The chance of thus holing and otherwise damaging the ship had not occurred to me until that moment. The risk was too great. I changed my mind, and abandoned the whole idea. It was still entirely up to the *Dewey* and such help as might come from Above! We had done all we could in our prestorm preparations.

In the wardroom, which is the battle-dressing station on a destroyer, the doctor was examining several patients who had been injured. The *Dewey* took another agonizing roll to starboard. Doctor and patient fell straight across the wardroom, from the port to the starboard transom. Neither one was injured by this abrupt shift of stations.

In the after crew's quarters, despite the chaos of flooding and a bucket brigade, two youngsters had wedged themselves in their bunks. Unimpressed by the seriousness of the situation, they amused themselves by keeping score of the number of tubes of toothpaste, toothbrushes, razors, and the like they saw drop out of the port angle-iron and fall straight across the ship to the corresponding starboard angle-iron. Near-misses didn't count!

Boatswain Miller came over to me and asked, "Captain, are we going to abandon ship?" I said, "Not if I can help it, Boats. I don't want to get into that water if we don't have to. So long as the *Dewey* doesn't abandon us, we're not going to abandon her." He seemed reassured.

We had left a few rounds of 5-inch ammunition in the ready service lockers near the guns. At about 1145 the wind ripped the metal tops off of three of them. Their projectiles and powder tanks spilled out and fell overboard when we next rolled to starboard. Most of our ready supply of depth charges, which were fastened to "T"-shaped arbors, held upright in six-inch-high cylinders welded to the main deck, were blown up out of the containers and spilled overboard. It was as though providence had decided to give us a hand and jettison the last possible increment of topside weight.

At about 1230 I climbed and scrambled out to the port wing of the bridge. Frank Bampton was walking up the portside bulkhead of the emergency cabin. On each giant roll to starboard he walked up to the top and sat on the director platfrom railing with his feet dangling over, ready to step off into the sea if we capsized. It occurred to me that he had chosen a good avenue of exit—one that might be least likely to entangle or trap him. Dave Bate described it in these words: "The sight that I will probably never forget was at the height of the storm, when from my sedentary position I observed Frank Bampton walking several steps up the side of the conning tower in absolute certainty that he was going off into the Pacific Ocean for a swim. He was completely surprised, when oh so slowly the ship began to right itself, and he was persuaded, (by its return to an upright position) to walk leisurely backwards, down the conning tower onto the bridge deck."[11]

Through the cloud of driven spray and spume I could see that one of the guy wires running up to the forward stack had some slack in it—enough so that the wind was causing it to snap taut every few minutes. It was going to break. I wondered just what effect it would have. I warned our signal gang to take cover from the wire's possible whiplash. There wasn't long to wait. As I watched and wondered the wire parted with a report like a small saluting cannon. It whipped across the port wing of the bridge, but fortunately injured no one. At once the forward stack collapsed and crashed across the deck on the starboard side, knocking overboard the whaleboat and one boat davit. The flattened stack reminded me of an old sock that had been thrown across the ship by some playful giant. Its top was under water, but since its juncture with the furnace uptake was essentially unbroken, and the fireroom was under pressure, the smoke and gases continued to issue forth from below the sea's surface. This incident broke the steam line to the ship's whistle and siren. It vented some 400 pounds of boiler-pressure steam with a roar that could be heard even above the gale. It seemed as though a steam line in the fireroom had carried away. My first thought was for the men down there who would be scalded to death in a matter of minutes. I concluded that our forward fireroom gang were all casualties. Not for a half hour or so, when Tolmie reported to me on the bridge, did I learn that the only serious damage was to one pair of underdrawers, scorched by the flashback that occurred when the stack first fell. He commented, "It didn't really matter, Cap'n, he'd probably have had to burn 'em anyway!" The forward fireroom was still operating, with control of flooding from the blower intakes well within the capacity of our steam fire and bilge pump. I breathed a sigh of relief and said a silent prayer of thanks. The deliverance of the fireroom gang from what I had thought was certain death seemed miraculous.

Apparent almost immediately when the stack fell was a new feeling of increased stability. The reduction of sail area, the added loss of the whaleboat (which had been scooping up hundreds of gallons of water every time we rolled to starboard) and the davit, and the lowering of the weight of the stack itself, all helped. We were not rolling quite so far and not remaining over on our side for quite so long. I reflected on how fortunate it was that we had neglected to secure the whaleboat properly. If it had been rigged in we probably wouldn't have lost it. It would have made a difference.

By 1300 the aneroid barometer went completely off the scale. The quartermaster recorded it at 27.30.[12] At about 1330 it went down "to the 'U' of 'U.S. Navy,'" probably less than 27 inches. Preston Mercer estimated it to be 26.30. The wind was at an estimated 125 knots. It could have been more.

By 1400 the pressure had begun to rise again and the barometer read 27.70. When Preacher made that report to me, I said, "Thank God! We're going to make it." He smiled, nodded, and silently shook my hand.

Dave Bate's comment on this phase of the storm notes: "When we thought the storm might be abating ever so slightly, you called me into the pilot house and asked me to go below and talk to the officers and men who were down there, to reassure them, and to come back and report to you. Up to that point I had been convinced we were going down, and that chances of survival were slim. I had been fairly stoical when the stack had blown over and the whistle was screaming, and all seemed lost. But when I started to go down that ladder I became terrified. However, I did go below, and talked to the officers and crew as you had requested."

It took a special brand of guts to leave the relative safety of the bridge, from which escape into the sea was assured, and descend into the dark compartments, which were tightly closed, and from which escape would have been difficult, if not impossible. However, I considered it essential that we do whatever we could to reassure the more than 200 officers and men who were shut in below decks, and with whom we otherwise had no communication. It looked to me as though they had another five hours of typhoon to endure as the rear half of the storm swept over us. I wanted them to know that we were through the worst of it, and that they hadn't been forgotten. (Paymaster "R. D." McMillan, who was one of those confined below deck, recently commented that he had never before seen grown men, convinced that they were going to die, kneeling openly in common prayer. It was a moving sight.) No matter how he felt, Bate descended into those dark compartments, presented a calm exterior, and delivered the kind of hope and encouragement that the situation demanded. It was a courageous and valuable service to the men of the *Dewey*.

As the barometer hit bottom, we experienced a noticeable drop in wind velocity. We were very close to and perhaps even within the eye of the storm. During the lull a messenger from the chief engineer managed to scramble up to the bridge. He reported that the engines were ready to go at any time the weather permitted, and the flooding in the engine spaces was under control. (They had used the main circulating pumps, which had a huge capacity, to pump the bilges.) I thanked him and said that we'd get word to the chief engineer when we wanted to move ahead, but for the moment we would continue to lie-to.

We should be about halfway through now, I thought, and should be out of it by about six o'clock this evening. By 1435 the wind had slackened to an estimated 80 knots.

During the remainder of the storm we repeated many of the same incredible experiences that had befallen us during the first half, but we were definitely riding just a little bit better. I felt confident that the ship would take us safely through it. She did. There were many tense moments, but our luck held.

At about 1800 we came out of the typhoon as you come out of a cloud formation in an aircraft. One minute we were in a thick soup of violent wind and spray, and the next we were out in the clear—not sunny and bright, but with greatly increased visibility. The seas were still mountainous and confused, and the wind was still close to hurricane force. We were able to make turns for three knots. I figured that it would be enough to move us slowly toward the rest of the fleet while we inspected our damage and got ourselves ship-shape.

Just astern of us and about two miles away the destroyer escort *Tabberer* emerged from the tempest. Using his signal light he flashed, "I have just lost my mast." I signaled back, "Cheer up, I have just lost my stack." Then he asked the course to Ulithi, and we gave him that information. He appeared to be heading considerably to the left of the course we had selected (220° T) to rejoin the fleet. I wondered why he didn't choose to remain in company, but concluded that the skipper had some good reason to proceed independently and thought no more of it. Events were soon to prove his selection of course to have been nothing short of providential.

As Preston Mercer left the bridge at about 2100, he said, "Well, Skipper, we've weathered an experience which will become famous in history. Everyone will want to hear about it. Tell them as well as you can what it was like, but don't expect anyone to believe you, for no one who has had no similar experience can conceive of anything like these past twelve hours." At that point I didn't really give a damn whether anyone would believe it or not!

We continued to steam independently on course 220° T at 3 knots. At about 2300 we noticed the loom of a searchlight sweeping back and forth over the horizon on our port beam. I was still on the bridge, and it occurred to me at once that the light was probably from the *Tabberer*, and that he might have found someone in the water. I turned the ship in that direction, and headed over to see what was happening. If any kind of rescue operations were under way, I knew that the *Dewey* could be of some assistance. We had heard snatches of TBS conversations by the *Tabberer* with some other ship, in which he had used the term "survivors." We did not hear mention of any other ship's name, but in the light of our own close call, I suspected that some destroyer had capsized. All efforts to raise the *Tabberer* on TBS and by flashing light in order to clarify the situation proved futile.

The turn to the left headed us more directly into the sea, and we began to pitch and pound heavily. As the *Dewey* rose up on the crest her bow would break clear of the water as far back as the bridge, then she would plunge down into the trough, slam her bottom against the surface with a terrible crashing noise, bury her nose in the sea, shudder, shake, and groan, and then painfully struggle up to do it all over again. It was a motion we had come to know only too well during the past two days! I called the commodore on the phone and explained to him what we were doing, so that he would understand the reason for the slamming. He responded that he thought we should turn back to our previous heading. Pointing out that we did not yet know the nature and extent of the structural damage suffered by the *Dewey* during the storm, he suggested that there was some risk that the pounding would aggravate whatever damage might have been incurred, and that in his opinion that risk was unacceptable. He concluded by recommending that I resume our previous course and proceed to the rendezvous point. I took his advice and turned back to 220° T. For the second time his mature judgment may have been a crucial factor in our survival.

As we resumed our previous heading I had a grave foreboding of the full consequences of the storm. The *Tabberer*'s use of the word "survivor" had convinced me that at least one ship had capsized and sunk. I wondered which ship it was, and if there would be more.

CHAPTER 8

The Tempest Takes Its Toll

Most of the other destroyers with Task Group 30.8 on the morning of 18 December, like the *Dewey* found themselves in a furious fight for survival. The storm engulfed them with explosive suddenness. Once in it, they were totally engaged, their every energy and every resource instantly called upon to remain afloat and stay alive.

With stability characteristics that we now know were deficient, the *Farraguts* (*Aylwin*, *Dewey*, *Hull*, and *Monaghan*) already had two strikes against them. They took the worst of it. But even the more stable 2,100-ton *Fletchers* had the fight of their lives. Of these, the well-ballasted *Hickox* rolled 70 degrees, and was very nearly lost. The *Spence*, with almost no ballast, didn't have a chance. For her, the necessary righting moment simply wasn't there.

Aboard the *Aylwin*, operating as the flagship of CTG 30.8, Bill Rogers had been making special preparations for the storm since the evening of the 17th. Beginning at 1200 that day (Sunday), his barometer reading went from 29.79 to 29.66 in just three hours.[1] The magnitude of the change was enough to signal the possibility of an approaching typhoon. He started at about 1700 to move his ready service ammunition and topside stores down into the ship. Efforts continued throughout the night to make the *Aylwin* as secure and as stable as possible.

On the morning of the 18th, repair parties were organized to make security inspections and set up special communications. Electricians were stationed at strategic points to handle electrical fires, should they occur. By 1100 the weather conditions were wild. The barometer read 28.58 inches.[2] The wind was from the north at an estimated 100 knots. When Task Force 38 changed course from 180° to 220° T and increased speed to 12 knots, the *Aylwin* swung rapidly around to 260° T.[3] She was in the trough of the sea. Full left rudder failed to bring her back. She had been rolling heavily before, but now she went all the way over to 70°, and stayed there for what seemed like an eternity. Bill stopped the engines. When the ship partially righted herself, he attempted to turn back to the south. He couldn't do it. When he tried to go ahead, the rolling became more severe. Finally, by putting the rudder into the wind and backing, he succeeded in twisting back to the south, but at that point he lost steering control. Again he stopped the engines. The ship's head swung back until she was in the trough. She rolled to 70 degrees, hung there for at least fifteen seconds, and then righted herself to sixty degrees.

Four times during the next twenty minutes the *Aylwin* heeled over to 70 degrees. The whaleboat was torn loose, ripping away both davits. At 1120 steering control was regained. Bill struggled to keep the wind about 30 degrees abaft the port beam, using his engines to provide steerageway. Despite his efforts, the elements consistently took control. They would swing the ship into the trough, and she would heel over again, almost to the limit. Each time she fought her way back.

At 1330 the ventilation blowers failed. Engine room temperature quickly rose to 180 degrees. The spaces had to be abandoned. The engines were stopped. All hatches were closed. For the next six hours, the officers and men of the *Aylwin* hung on desperately. The ship was tossed, and shoved, and beaten. It was brutal treatment. The savage thrust of the gale and the mountainous waves forced her over, but each time she refused to yield that extra degree that would have meant defeat. Each time, she succeeded in righting herself, at least part way. The fear of capsizing invaded the consciousness of every man. There were moments when it was almost heart-stopping.

At 1930 a leak was reported in the engine room. Fire and bilge, submersible, and main circulator pumps were put into operation. The water rose to at least a foot over the floor plates before it was brought under control. The addition of free-surface liquid further reduced the ship's stability. At 1950 material condition "Affirm" was set throughout the ship. All hands donned lifejackets. It looked as though the battle was lost. Repair parties shored up the engine room bulkheads to better withstand the flooding. It seemed that no ship could continue to take such punishment, yet the *Aylwin* refused to quit. The officers and men were just as stubborn. All of them hoped, and some of them prayed, for their deliverance.

Finally, at about 2000, there was a marked change. The storm had spent its fury. The wind subsided. Visibility improved. The seas began to diminish. The *Aylwin* had survived! For Bill Rogers and his men, it was like a last minute reprieve from a death sentence.

In reporting the details of his ship's ordeal, Bill noted that the experiences of the typhoon provided hard evidence of the fact that *Farragut*-class destroyers were not sufficiently stable. Speaking of his own ship, his concluding words were, "That she did not capsize was miraculous."[4] That seemed to say it all.

The *Hull* was assigned to Task Unit 30.8.3, the northernmost of the three oiler units.[5] After rendezvous with Task Force 38 on the 17th, she had been directed to deliver 120 bags of U.S. mail, which she was carrying for some thirty ships of the force. It proved to be an especially difficult task in those rough seas. In late afternoon, after having made delivery to the battleship *South Dakota*, and with eighty bags remaining aboard still to be delivered, the *Hull* resumed her station in the screen. Further delivery was deferred until after the return of better weather.

During the night the skipper ordered his first lieutenant and executive officer to inspect the ship for security, to improve the below-deck stowage wherever possible, and to remove all loose gear from the topside. Those orders were carried out.

After daybreak on the morning of the 18th, the *Hull* conformed to the movements of her formation. According to Roy Lester, the machinist's mate who was stationed at the throttle, speeds of 15 to 22 knots were used during the 8 to 12 watch.[6] Although the engine turns used were equivalent to those speeds, the ship's actual speed in the sea state then existing was probably considerably less. Jim Marks indicated that he doubted if the *Hull* ever achieved a speed through the water in excess of 10 knots during the morning.[7]

Like her squadron mates, the *Hull* found the weather conditions severe. The seas were mountainous, the winds consistently 80 to 90 knots, with gusts to 115, and the visibility was reduced to zero because of spindrift and torrential rain.[8]

The combination of wind-driven rain and spray created a multitude of recurring electrical failures for the *Hull*. Radio, radar, and steering motor casualties were generating critical operational problems. At about 1042 the surface search radar went out of commission. The skipper reported this development to his screen commander (Commander Destroyer Division 110, in the *Laws*), and asked that he be kept advised of courses to be steered to maintain position in the formation, and to avoid danger. Commander Edsall (CDD 110) responded at about 1050 that according to his radar presentation, the *Hull* was pretty well on station, and that he would keep Marks informed as necessary.

Some of the other ships of this unit now were experiencing great difficulty. At about 0950, the *Cape Esperance* had reported that she was unable to keep up with the formation. Captain R. W. Bockius, her commanding officer, announced on the voice radio that he had given up the attempt.[9]

Each new change of course required the ships of the screen to reorient to the same relative bearings from the guide. It was an ill-advised requirement. It meant that the escorts had to increase speed above that of the formation in order to regain station. They already were having difficulty keeping up with the formation on the base course. Had the OTC directed "Turn" instead of "Corpen" movements,[10] it would have alleviated the problem. The execution of "Turn" signals would have allowed the individual ships to turn directly to the new course, rather than requiring that the entire formation wheel around the corner, like a marching column, to the new heading.

Intent on maintaining station, Jim Marks complied with the signaled course changes until it appeared that his ship was almost "in extremis." Then he began maneuvering in the best manner to avoid damage from the sea. Earlier, when the storm first engulfed them, he had been encouraged by a report from the executive officer that two security inspections of the ship that morning had confirmed that she was well secured for heavy weather. He was also well aware that with 125,000 gallons of fuel aboard, the *Hull* was above the minimum level that would have required ballasting with seawater. The guidelines for ballasting were prescribed by the Bureau of Ships, through the type commander (Commander Destroyers, Pacific Fleet). It was logical to conclude that as long as the ship maintained a fuel or combined fuel and seawater ballast reserve greater than the prescribed minimum, its stability would not be in jeopardy. For the *Farragut*-class destroyers we now know that such a conclusion was invalid, but on 18 December 1944, the men on the ships didn't know it. The ship's company of the *Hull* probably felt, as did many of us on the *Dewey*, that no ship of the United States Navy could capsize as long as she remained in compliance with ballasting instructions applicable to her class.

At about 1100, Edsall called and told Marks that if it would help him to keep station, he could close the main body. This would have enabled him to reduce speed, and it was a helpful suggestion. There was no acknowledgment for the message. Jim's voice radio had failed.

Conditions aboard the *Hull* had been bad all morning, but now they were worsening by the minute. By 1130 she was rolling to limits never before experienced by anyone on board. As the wind velocity rose into the 100-knot range, she suffered storm damage similar to that which had befallen the *Dewey*. First her motor whaleboat was smashed at the bow. Then with savage pounding from the sea, the boat was torn away from first one and then the other of its davits, and dumped into the water, a jumbled mass of wreckage. Depth charges were ripped loose from the K-guns and tossed overboard. Fortunately, the charges had been set at "Safe," otherwise they would have exploded and caused severe damage.

Again like the *Dewey*, the *Hull*'s stacks were under a terrific strain from the gale. The gusts near the eye of a typhoon can be in excess of 200 knots. The wind's force increases proportionately as the square of its velocity. Doubling the velocity produces four times as much force. A 110-knot wind would have generated about 78 pounds of pressure per square foot of exposed sail area.[11] If we assign a conservative 600 square feet as the sail area of one stack, this amounts to 23 tons of sustained pressure. The gusts would have generated correspondingly greater pressure. Sensing the magnitude of this force, Jim Marks thought that the wind's thrust might rip off one or both of the stacks. For a few brief moments he considered that if he could cut one loose, it might lower the center of gravity, reduce the wind pressure, and lessen the rolling. This option was soon dismissed. He correctly concluded that no man could have existed on the exposed topside long enough to do the job. It was still possible that the wind could blow down one or both stacks, but that decision rested entirely in the hands of Fate.

So fierce was the blast of the typhoon that its roar drowned out almost every other sound. It was next to impossible for the skipper to make himself heard, or to hear what was said to him. Marks tried every possible combination of rudder and engines. He attempted to run away from the wind and sea, and to bring them as far on the port quarter as possible. Like a groggy prizefighter who has been hammered until helpless, the ship could not respond. She was hanging on the ropes, barely able to fight back.

Jim began to wonder if the ship's bridge structure was going to disintegrate. The wind's force seemed strong enough to tear it apart. As he watched, he saw the metal covers of ready-service ammunition boxes ripped away, despite their heavy screw-down hasps. They were blown overboard, like leaves on a blustery November day in Minnesota.

The *Hull* was pushed over bodily by every giant gust. She was yawing violently. Shortly before noon, steering control was lost from the bridge. The well-trained crew quickly regained control in the steering motor room. The chief engineer, Lieutenant (j.g.) Sharp, reported that the forward fireroom blowers had stopped. It was no wonder. Seawater was flooding into the blower air intakes. The after fireroom watch now took control of the steaming boilers, again attesting to the training and discipline of the crew. All bells (signals) to the engine room continued to be answered with the engine power requested.

Exceptionally high-velocity gusts of long duration now caused the ship to lurch and heel violently, often more than 60 degrees to starboard. The junior officer of the deck was catapulted through the air to the starboard side of the pilot house. The executive officer took his place beside the helmsman. He saw to it that orders to the helm were properly interpreted and promptly executed.

Shortly after twelve o'clock the ship rolled to 70 degrees. As the gale momentarily subsided, she righted herself. Jim Marks felt that the prolonged gust he had just witnessed was "the worst punishment any storm could offer."[12] Then came the knockout punch. The wind's force exploded with incredible fury. The overpowering thrust of this savage blast pounded and shoved the *Hull* with merciless force. She slowly heeled over on her starboard side. This time she exceeded her limit. There was no way she could right herself. Still the gale blew. It held her down in the water until the life went out of her, and her struggles ceased. Now the seas came flooding into the pilot house, and through every open ventilation duct into the ship.

She remained on her beam ends, at an angle of 85 or 90 degrees, as the water poured into her hull and superstructure. Finally, she began to capsize. A valiant destroyer had lost her fight with the sailor's oldest enemy, the sea itself!

Jim Marks remained on the port wing of the bridge until the water surged up to him. He observed his crew scrambling to the uppermost part of the ship as she lay on her side. As he watched, he noted that every man was wearing a lifejacket. He recalled that he had seen to it, just three months ago, that every jacket was equipped with a whistle and a waterproof survival light. At least they had a chance of being seen, or making themselves heard. He stepped off into the sea as the ship capsized. He felt the suction as she went down. A few moments later he also felt the concussion of the boilers exploding. Neither event caused him any ill effects. Once in the water, he could see only a few feet. The storm compressed the visible world around him into a tiny sphere, with himself at the center. He was surrounded by violence, tossed and tumbled, and held under water repeatedly to the limit of his endurance. It was all accompanied by the deafening roar of the gale. Worst of all was the overwhelming sickness of heart that now must have blotted out every other emotion as he thought of his lost ship and his shipmates, many of whom were certain to lose their lives.

Of the 245 men and 18 officers aboard the *Hull*, probably as many as a hundred were trapped below decks, unable to escape. Those who were able to get clear and endure the elements until rescued owed their lives to the foresight of their skipper, who had ordered all gun-watch personnel to leave their stations and don lifejackets about a half-hour before the ship rolled over.

As the *Hull* sank beneath the waves, there were about a hundred and sixty officers and men in the water. A few managed to cling to three life rafts that bobbed to the surface. The remainder had only lifejackets to help them stay afloat. All were at the mercy of the raging sea. Now for each it became an almost hopeless battle for his own life. The mountainous waves made it impossible to remain on the surface. They were tumbled head-over-heels by the breaking crests, gasping and struggling to get their heads clear for a breath of air. As the day wore on without rescue, and darkness finally came, the chances for their survival steadily diminished. It was amazing that any of them lived through it.

On the morning of the 18th, the *Monaghan* was busy screening Task Unit 30.8.2, the southernmost of the oiler units. Like the *Dewey*, *Aylwin*, and *Hull*, she found the seas mountainous and the steering difficult.

At 0800 the *Monaghan*'s "Oil King" (Joseph C. McCrane, water-tender second class, from Clementon, New Jersey) made his routine soundings of the fuel tanks. He reported to the captain that the ship had about 130,000 gallons, or 76 percent fuel on board.[13] As had been the case with the *Hull*, this was above the established minimum below which ballasting would have been required. A certain sense of security was suggested by that fact.

The *Monaghan*'s difficulties first became apparent to us on the *Dewey* at 0927 when we heard her report to CTG 30.8 that she was unable to steer the base course (180° T), and was on a heading of 330° T. This aimed her toward the *Dewey*'s task unit (TU 30.8.4). Captain Acuff advised Bruce Garrett to try using more speed.[14] In the light of hindsight, it was not good advice.

At 0936 Garrett called Acuff and reported, "I am unable to come to the base course. Have tried full speed, but it will not work."[15] The next transmission we heard was the *Monaghan*'s report that she was out of control. Hoping to provide some reassurance, I called Bruce on TBS to tell him that the *Dewey* was in similar circumstances, and that we had given up trying to maintain station, or even to remain with the formation. As noted in the preceding chapter, we had tentatively identified the *Monaghan* on our radarscope, and determined that she was then only about 3,000 yards away from us.

By about 1045 the *Monaghan*'s rolling had become violent. She was reacting very much like the *Dewey* and the *Hull*, and her officers and crew were growing more and more apprehensive that she might capsize. Her generators and steering motor failed. Soon there were no communications between the bridge and the steering motor room. From about 1115 on, she had no lights and no power. Dead in the water, she was completely at the mercy of wind and sea.

Bruce Garrett, with a total of one week of command experience, was reacting like a veteran. He became gravely concerned about his ship's stability, and at about 1100 directed that fuel oil tanks #10 and #11 be ballasted. With 76 percent fuel aboard, nothing but a keen awareness of the danger of capsizing would have dictated such an action. The report of the senior survivor (McCrane, the "Oil King") states that he immediately went to the shaft alley, opened up the valves to #10 and #11 fuel oil tanks, and connected them to the firemain. He then notified the engine room to start the fire and bilge pump in order to pump seawater into the designated fuel tanks. Since his line of communications was through the steering motor telephone, he was never certain that the pumps were started as requested.[16] It probably made little difference.

Testimony at the court of inquiry indicated that there were reports from the engine room and firerooms, about five or ten minutes before the ship capsized, that the structure of the overhead in those spaces had begun to rip loose from the bulkheads.[17] While we cannot be certain now of precisely what those fragmentary reports meant, it appears possible that the basic hull structure of the *Monaghan* was beginning to crumble. If that was so, massive flooding of the engineering spaces would have occurred.

Since no officer survived her loss, we can only imagine what transpired on the bridge of the *Monaghan* that morning. Probably it was very similar to the situation on the bridge of the *Dewey*, except that at some point, during one of those giant rolls, the *Monaghan* failed to right herself. However, we do have a vivid account of the ship's loss from the report submitted by McCrane, which states: "Before the final roll there were forty or fifty of us in the after gun shelter. We stopped work and hung on. We began to get scared. All of us were praying like we never prayed before, some of us out loud, too. The man next to me kept repeating on each roll, 'Don't let us down now, Dear Lord. Bring it back, Oh God, bring it back.' We all felt the same way, and soon a few of the guys joined in. Then when we came back we'd shout, 'Thanks, Dear Lord.' The next thing we knew we were on our side.

"When it came, someone threw open the hatch, and we started to scramble out. Under the circumstances, most of us were pretty orderly and there was hardly any hysteria. The fellows started helping each other, particularly the shorter men who couldn't reach the hatch.

"I climbed out . . . and stood on the bulkhead. The waves were knocking me about, but I didn't want to shake loose, because I saw what happened to men who had jumped off. . . . They were pounded to a pulp against the side of the ship. But finally a big wave shook me loose, and I went scrambling along . . . until I was lucky enough to grab a depth charge rack. I walked along the torpedo tubes. Another wave hit me and I went into the air.

"The next thing I knew I was struggling in the water, trying to keep from being pounded against the ship. Water and oil were blowing against my face. I was choking and beating the water with my arms and legs like a puppy. I saw I wasn't getting anywhere, so I calmed down and got away gradually, but I was losing strength when suddenly someone hollered: 'Hey, Joe, grab that raft back of you.' It was a fellow named Guio [Joseph Guio, Jr., gunner's mate third class of Holliday's Cove, West Virginia] who later died on the raft. Thirteen of us got to it and hung on the sides like they did in that Noel Coward movie, *In Which We Serve*. I never saw the movie, but I remember those guys hanging on from a preview I saw."

This was at 1230. The *Monaghan* sank from view at about that time. McCrane's account continues: "We . . . started to help some of the badly injured on the raft. One of these was Ben Holland [ship's cook first class from McMinnville, Tennessee]. He was typical of the badly injured, with a big gash on the back of his head and on his foot. Guio, the guy who yelled to me about the raft was another. He had part of his foot torn off.

"Before we got the bottom of the raft down, it turned over four or five times . . . we had to fish around and help the wounded back on . . . we were getting pretty tired and weak. After we got the bottom down, we all climbed aboard—thirteen of us—that first night.

"I broke out the emergency rations—Spam, hard biscuits, and stuff like that—and the water. I limited them to a biscuit and a cup of water two or three times a day. As soon as we opened the Spam, the sharks started nosing around. We all ate a little, drank our mite of water, and tried to get some rest.

"That first night we just missed being saved. We saw the lights of a ship and started hollering and yelling, waving our arms. But she passed by without seeing us. About this time I put my arms and legs around Guio because he was naked and suffering from the cold. Just then he said, 'Joe, can you see anything?' I thought he meant the ship and told him I could. 'I can't see a thing,' he answered.

"A few minutes later he closed his eyes—and we got ready for our first burial at sea. Doil Carpenter [seaman first class from Torrance, California] said a prayer, and we put Guio, the guy who probably saved my life by yelling about the raft, over the side."[18]

It was a pitifully small band of men from the *Monaghan* who clung desperately to their raft and prayed for rescue, as the 18th of December, 1944, came to an end.

Efforts by the *Spence* to fuel on the 17th continued throughout the daylight hours. At 1730 she tried to fuel from an oiler by the astern method. After about fifteen minutes, the lines parted. A final attempt was made before darkness set in, but it too was futile. The night of the 17th brought a welcome respite to the officers and crew, who by that time were almost exhausted. They must have found the situation discouraging. Certainly Jim Andrea, after a full day of the most difficult shiphandling, several narrow escapes from collision, and an alarmingly low fuel state, must have felt a heavy burden of command responsibility.

In his narrative report of the loss of the *Spence*, the senior survivor, Lieutenant (junior grade) A. S. Krauchunas, tells the story from the vantage point of the ship's supply officer: "In the morning (18 December 1944), the weather had become worse and no attempt was made to fuel. During breakfast in the wardroom, the officers conversed with the captain over the problems that had been encountered, or would present themselves during the day. The chief engineer, Lieutenant (junior grade) L. D. Sundin, USNR, said that the plant was operating on one boiler and that we had enough fuel for another twenty-four hours at our speed, 8 knots. At this time I understand they had started to take on ballast, how much I do not have any idea."[19]

The testimony of three other survivors, two of whom were engineers, establishes the time at which ballasting commenced as between 1000 and 1040. According to Chief Watertender George W. Johnson, about 16,000 gallons of seawater ballast (or less than 10 percent of capacity) had been taken aboard prior to capsizing. Some free-surface liquid therefore was introduced into the ship just before she capsized.

The ship was in damage control condition "BAKER," the normal wartime cruising condition, which left open those watertight doors necessary to permit a normal flow of traffic. At about 1050, the ingress of seawater into the engine room caused the main switchboard to flash-over, and all electrical power and lights were lost. The emergency diesel generator failed to cut in (although it had been tested successfully just ten minutes earlier). The electric bilge pumps, which were in use to control flooding, stopped. The ship was proceeding at a speed of 11½ knots. The captain had the conn, and was attempting to steer the formation course and maintain his assigned station in the screen. Until about 1115, the ship had been rolling heavily to port as much as 43 degrees. At that time the roll increased. Now the *Spence* went to 47 degrees. She hung at that angle for several minutes without righting herself, then at about 1123 the roll to port continued. Relentlessly, she slowly rolled all the way over on her side. She remained there for about seven minutes; then she capsized, broke in half, and went down.

Krauchunas described it: "At about 1000 I understood that we were maintaining our course and station properly. I went down to my stateroom. . . . Shortly all the lights went out, . . . it was about 1050. . . . I then left my stateroom, feeling very uneasy, and went into the captain's cabin on the main deck. Arriving there, I found the doctor, Lieutenant (j.g.) G. C. Gaffney, MC, USN, sitting in the chair feeling very low. . . .

"At about this time the ship developed a port list . . . we were changing course at the time; as a result . . . our rudder was locked at hard right. At approximately 1110 we took a hard list to port and stayed there momentarily and then came back. Our next roll to port capsized the ship. Immediately I jumped from the bunk in the captain's cabin into the passageway leading to the main deck. Arriving there the entrance was covered with oil and water gushing through, and I immediately rushed to the radio shack passageway, which was not underwater at this time. I went through, and immediately the water closed in behind me, covering the entrance completely. I had no lifejacket because no thought of the ship capsizing came to my mind. . . .

"Upon sliding into the water, I swam towards a floater net, which was adrift at least twenty yards away. I picked up a lifejacket in the water and put it on. I reached the floater net, which contained approximately twenty to twenty-five men, and the net floated back to the ship, which by this time was completely capsized. The men struggled to push the net away from the ship and it was several minutes before we were washed away from the hull. Soon the

Spence was shut off from our view by the gusts of wind and rain. The net was turned over completely and men were shaken off, including myself. I was pulled beneath the surface for a great length of time . . . I finally broke the surface and saw the floater net twenty yards away. I reached it and found that several men had not returned. The storm was so severe that one could not face directly into the wind. After what seemed several hours . . . an uninflated yellow rubber raft came floating by. Two or three of the men inflated it and jumped in. . . . The yellow raft was immediately blown out of sight and we were left alone again.

"Our floater net contained all the necessary equipment . . . [it] consisted of two 5-gallon kegs of water, two food kits [contents unknown], a medical kit, . . . flares, flashlights, die markers, etc. During the storm the medical kit and the two food kits became detached from the net and floated away. The storm died down after darkness fell on the evening of 18 December, and there were only nine men left. [Krauchunas names only eight.] . . . Lieutenant (j.g.) A. S. Krauchunas, Lieutenant (j.g.) John Whalen, E. F. Traceski, QM2/c, Albert Rosley, TM3/c, C. F. Wohl, WT3/c, M. D. Sehnert, S1/c, C. L. Ground, S2/c, and Heater [initial unknown], S1/c.

"During the night of 18 December, we opened the kit containing flares and made a thorough check of the contents. It was decided not to use any . . . until an opportunity arose. This was a bad decision, because when the opportunity arose we found that the kit had broken off the raft and was gone, leaving us with two cans of die marker, which I put in my trouser pockets. The night passed without any deviation from the normal."[20]

Krauchunas's definition of "the normal" appears to have been somewhat unique. In any case, it is clear that the suddenness of the *Spence*'s capsizing caught him with his guard down. Probably the majority of his shipmates were also caught by surprise. The thought that they might roll over was simply inconceivable. To many of them, the trauma of capsizing must have been overwhelming.

The stability characteristics of the *Hickox* closely paralleled those of the *Spence*. Technically they were sister ships. The commanding officer of the *Hickox*, Commander J. H. Wesson, had ballasted when his fuel reserve fell below the 70 percent mark several days earlier. On the 17th, after it became apparent that fueling was not going to be possible, he took on more ballast. On the morning of the 18th, since he had been directed to be ready to fuel, he partially deballasted, but as soon as it became clear that fueling would have to be deferred, he again added ballast. When he completed the process at

1010, he had 246 tons of seawater and 76 tons of mixed diesel and fuel oil in his tanks.[21] Thus, while the *Hickox* had only 14 percent of her fuel load aboard, her tanks were filled to about 60 percent of capacity. About 76 percent of the liquid was seawater. By the time she encountered the full fury of the storm, she was in a much more stable posture than the *Spence*. Even so, she encountered severe problems, and very nearly capsized.

In an earlier chapter it was noted that the *Hickox* had joined Preston Mercer's task unit (TU 30.8.4) and had been stationed in the screen. At 1030 on the 18th, Wesson turned left to avoid collision with an unidentified ship, observed by radar to be on a steady bearing. The *Hickox* at once found herself in the trough of the sea, unable to extricate herself. Yawing and excessive rolling, already creating problems, immediately worsened.

Wesson tried for about an hour to turn the ship to the formation course, without success. He then decided to abandon all station-keeping efforts and ride out the storm at a speed of two or three knots. The steering motor room started taking water. At 1130 steering control was lost from the bridge. A shift was made to hand steering. The accumulation of water in the steering motor room now threatened to drown the men who were operating the hand cranks. They were almost submerged on each heavy roll.

Efforts to steer the ship had to be abandoned. Wesson concentrated on the control of flooding. It was necessary to open the watertight door in the after crew's living compartment in order to provide access for bailing out the steering motor room. About two feet of water immediately flooded from the latter into the compartment. In the meantime, the ship was rolling almost to her limit, sometimes as much as 70 degrees, most of the time returning only part way to an upright position.

All power aft was lost at 1130. A bucket brigade was the only alternative. The men worked in almost complete darkness. There was no ventilation. Several suffered severe fatigue and heat exhaustion. In the engine rooms the temperature and humidity rose until it was impossible to remain in those spaces. The strenuous efforts of all hands in the after part of the ship controlled the water level. An electric power line was rigged to the power supply of gun #5. It enabled them to make use of an electric submersible pump in the steering motor room. By 1745 the compartment was clear of water and hand steering was put back in operation.

As the storm finally abated, another attempt was made to turn out of the trough. At 1746, with the ship headed on 260° T, the *Hickox* was able to turn to course 135° T. Speed was gradually increased, and course was set for the new fueling rendezvous, now scheduled for the morning of the 19th.[22] The *Hickox* had won her battle, but it had been a mighty close call!

Most of the other destroyers experienced serious difficulties on the 18th. Many were severely battered. This was especially true of those in company with Task Group 30.8. In every case the trouble began with heavy rolling or pitching, or both. This was followed by: loss of steering control; an unavoidable twisting into the trough of the sea, which put the ship "in irons"; a period of alarmingly excessive rolls to the lee side, often to as much as 70 degrees; the loss of lights and power; the critical flooding of engine spaces, firerooms, and living compartments; the failure of radars, radios, and ship control equipment; and structural damage to the hull, whaleboats, stacks, masts, and antennas.

The crews of the destroyers with the logistic support group, including especially those of the *Hull*, *Monaghan*, and *Spence*, had fought the elements with all of the energy and skill they possessed. In every instance, heroic measures were required. In every instance they were forthcoming. For the lost ships, even those were not enough!

CHAPTER 9

The Small Carriers Prove Their Mettle

Please note

I was in charge of the fore fighting I on the flight Deck

Some of the first indications of the severity of the storm came from avoiding actions initiated and reported by the smaller flattops (both CVLs and CVEs). Their skippers were all four-stripers, with commensurate maturity and experience. When they began to encounter serious problems, they promptly detached themselves from the formation and sought more favorable conditions. Although they too were concerned about stability, and were aware of inherent structural weaknesses in their ships, their most urgent troubles arose from the failure of aircraft moorings. Steel pad eyes, welded to the decks for securing the planes, were torn off during periods of heavy rolling. The planes broke loose. They slithered and crashed across flight and hangar decks, colliding with other planes and with the ship's structure, rupturing gasoline tanks, and creating the immediate and grave risk of massive conflagrations. Fires did erupt aboard the CVLs *Monterey* and *San Jacinto*, and CVEs *Altamaha* and *Cape Esperance*. The crews of those ships, with courage and resourcefulness, fought the fires, and in every case brought them under control.

The *Monterey* was operating as a unit of Task Group 38.1 on the morning of the 18th. Captain "Slim" Ingersoll had determined the day before that a "storm of considerable intensity" was brewing.[1] Since then a continuing effort had been made to secure the ship and her aircraft for heavy weather. Palisades had been rigged on the flight deck, double security watches were stationed, and roving patrols were established on the flight and hangar decks.[2]

At 0813, when the attempt to fuel was determined to be infeasible and course was shifted from 060° T, to 180° T, the wind and sea were on the starboard quarter. Immediately the ship began to roll heavily. Captain Ingersoll ordered flight quarters sounded, and put all air department personnel to work checking aircraft cables and lashings, adding to and reinforcing them wherever practicable. The heavy rolling and hurricane-force winds made it extremely difficult to work on the flight deck.

The USS *Langley* rolls heavily during the typhoon. Behind her, the *New Jersey* plows ahead on an even keel, providing a marked contrast in stability.

The rolls became more severe. By 0838 they had reached 34 degrees. Four fighter planes on the flight deck broke loose and tobogganed across the deck. They plunged overboard on the port side, tearing off the landing signal officer's safety nets and platform on the way. Another fighter plane went overboard from the flight deck at 0906.

At 0908 Ingersoll received a report that a plane was adrift on the hangar deck. In about two minutes he felt an explosion. Immediately a bad fire erupted. The crew was called to general quarters. The task group commander was informed that the *Monterey* had a serious fire and would alter course to the right to reduce her rolling. She was brought around to a new heading of 240° T, 60 degrees to the right of the base course. Her speed was gradually reduced, and she rapidly fell behind the formation. The units of TG 30.8 now began to overtake her.

The cause of the fire was the runaway plane, which had torn loose from its moorings, crashed into another plane on the port side, punctured the gas tanks on both aircraft, and exploded. The fire quickly engulfed the hangar, and grew in intensity as it was fed by fuel from other ruptured gas tanks. One plane after another was involved. The fire was especially intense in the central section, where it enveloped the conflagration station, the trap door of which was blown open by a secondary explosion. This made it impossible to operate the sprinkling system controls located in that station, which had been designed to provide a protected control point for just such a contingency. Loose wreckage slid across the hangar and ruptured ventilation supply ducts on the port side. Within two minutes all of the engineering spaces, except the after engine room, were filled with smoke from the broken ducts. Those spaces had to be abandoned. Skeleton crews, using rescue breathing equipment, were quickly brought back into the forward fireroom and engine room. Now the hangar deck sprinkling system was operated from remote controls located in the machinery spaces. Water from the sprinkler nozzles quickly accumulated on the hangar deck and cascaded down the ruptured ventilation ducts into the engine and fire rooms. This flooding added a new dimension of risk to a rapidly worsening situation.

The accumulation of heavy smoke and flooding caused the skipper to stop his engines. He wanted to conserve steam for the major damage-control problems that now confronted him. At 0924 the *Monterey* was dead in the water, with all efforts focused on fighting the fire. Another explosion occurred on the port side in the vicinity of frame 75 on the second and third decks. The resulting fire flashed down through the ruptured ventilation ducts. The laundry space also was soon ablaze.

The heat from the fire on the hangar deck endangered the ready-service magazines on both sides of the flight deck. Where sprinklers could be manned and operated these spaces were quickly flooded. The explosions had ruptured the firemains to the 40-mm and 20-mm magazines. The gun crews, assisted by the air-group pilots, picked up the ammunition in those spaces, cradled it in their arms, struggled to the side of the ship, and threw it overboard.

Topside, the typhoon raged against the crippled carrier. Two more aircraft broke loose from the flight deck and plunged over the port side. They carried with them the radio transmitting antennas and 20-mm guns that were in their way.

The ingress of scalding water from the hangar deck via the ruptured ventilation ducts made it necessary to secure the fires in #2 fireroom. The ship was hove to on a heading of 255° T. The wind was increasing in intensity and the seas were mountainous.

At 0950, just after the task group commander had ordered the *New Orleans, Twining,* and *McCord* to stand by the *Monterey,* she was overtaken by the logistic support units. Now she was in the melee with the rest of us. It was at this point that the *Dewey* almost collided with her. Her well-trained and fearless crew gradually gained control over the hangar deck fire. They played ten fog nozzle·

equipped hoses directly into the heart of it. The entire sprinkling system was also at work. By 1025 the fires were extinguished. Meanwhile, the storm worsened, with sustained winds of 70 knots and gusts to 90. Although the *Monterey* was ready to go ahead again on all boilers, the skipper was deeply concerned over the mass of hot wreckage that now was loose in the hangar. It could not be secured until it cooled and the ship's rolling lessened. He realized that any maneuvering that would exaggerate the pitching and rolling would further aggravate the movement of the rubble. It then might cause more explosions and new fires. Since the ship had ridden well while hove-to, he decided to keep her dead in the water and ride it out. For the next four hours the crew hung on and fought to control the damage. By 1550 the wind had slackened to 55 knots. At 1625 the wreckage was secured. The sea and wind had diminished enough to warrant going ahead with the engines. The ship proceeded on a course of 130° T at 15 knots to rejoin Task Group 38.1.

The *Monterey* had suffered severe damage, but her captain had kept a cool head and exercised sound judgment. Just as importantly, her officers and crew had performed in magnificent fashion, matching each crisis with courage and skill. The ordeal took the lives of three men, critically injured ten more, and less seriously injured an additional thirty. It was a heavy price to pay, but the actions that were purchased with those casualties served to prevent a high toll, which would have been inevitable without them.

Another light attack carrier, the *San Jacinto*, warned by the bad weather on the 17th, had made very thorough preparations for the storm. The ship's gasoline system had been drained to reduce the hazards of fire, and additional security patrols were in constant attendance on the flight and hangar decks to check aircraft moorings. Roving patrols were established throughout the ship to handle any emergency. Additional lifelines were rigged, and the ship's damage-control organization was alerted and standing by to handle any situation. All aircraft had been degassed, debombed, and secured for heavy weather.[3]

By 0900 on the 18th, the ship was rolling to 35 degrees. At 0930, a plane in the forward part of the hangar deck broke loose. It was quickly secured. To prevent a recurrence, all aircraft mooring lines were tightened and doubled.

By 1030 the roll had increased to 38–40 degrees. A considerable amount of water had entered the hangar through the flimsy side doors. At 1035 the ship took a heavy roll to starboard, dipping the gun sponsons under water. The sea invaded the ship through every

opening. It pounded its way in through the hangar side doors and
roller curtains. It even came down the stacks, in sufficient quantity
to damage one boiler.[4]

An extremely heavy roll at 1035 caused one plane to break loose.
Within thirty seconds, and before the hangar deck patrols could
fight their way across the slippery deck to secure it, it had crashed
into another, and torn it loose from its moorings. The ship continued to roll violently up to 38 degrees. The runaway aircraft
crashed into others moored on the hangar deck. All of them soon
were torn loose. Now the crew was confronted with trying to secure
a huge, twisted, mass of wreckage, which slid wildly across the deck
each time the ship rolled. One of the loose planes struck the electric
activating device for the hangar sprinkling system, and the deluge
of water from that source added to the free-surface effect already
present.

While the hangar deck crew was engaged in the hazardous business of trying to lasso, capture, and secure the constantly moving
pile of wrecked aircraft, they also had to deal with three fires started
by broken electrical wiring. The accumulation of gasoline fumes

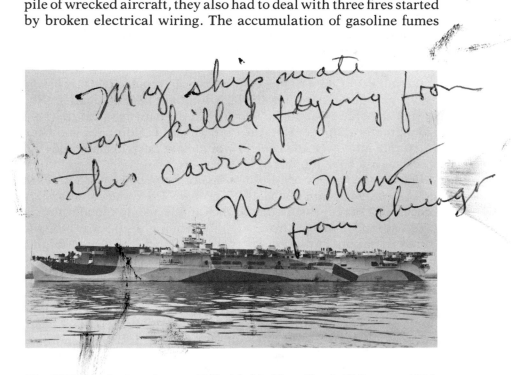

The USS *San Jacinto* departs Philadelphia Navy Yard, 17 January 1944.
Eleven months later she was fighting for her life in a typhoon, half a
world away from her point of departure.

was so intense that the smallest fire created the risk of disaster. The heroic actions required to contain these fires were exemplified by those of Commander G. E. Schecter. When a blaze broke out on the bulkhead in the middle of a hangar, and could not be reached because of the moving wreckage, he climbed up the bulkhead and along the overhead, with a fire extinguisher in one hand, and succeeded in putting out the fire before any serious damage had been done. With the most precarious handhold, he had traveled across the bulkhead like a human fly, some thirty feet above a shifting mass of wreckage. One slip would have cost him his life.[5]

Desperate measures were needed. The wrecked aircraft had to be secured, but it was suicidal to venture onto the hangar deck on foot. At any moment, the salvage crew could have been crushed by the mass of twisted airplanes. The sailors of the *San Jacinto* lowered themselves on lines from the overhead into the middle of the sliding, crashing mass of debris. Thus fastened, they were able to swing clear of the deck each time the ship rolled. When it righted itself, they were able to work on the level deck for a few minutes at a time. It was extremely dangerous. It took them about four hours to do it, but they finally managed to secure all of the loose wreckage. The danger of rupturing the boiler uptakes, or of punching a hole in the ship's side, had been averted.

Commander Cooper, the executive officer, reported: "Only heroic and superhuman efforts in the face of almost certain death on the part of the officers and men working in the hangar saved this ship from greater damage. Had they failed, and the uptakes had been fractured, all power and control would have been lost and the ship might easily have foundered."[6]

Finally, the chaotic conditions that confronted his men were best described by Captain Michael H. Kernodle, USN, the commanding officer, whose report stated: "To the uninitiated, the loud sound of crashing and tearing airplanes, the banging and tearing of the flimsy metal of ventilation ducts, the avalanche of heavy weights being thrown violently from side to side, the presence of much oily water on the deck, plus a large volume of steam escaping from the ruptured atmospheric exhausts within the enclosed hangar deck space, created a wholly frightening situation. However, regardless of these terrifying surroundings, men on the hangar deck were lowered from the overhead and skidded on deck in pendulum fashion on the ends of lines into this violently moving pile of rubble, and succeeded in securing it and holding the damage to a minimum, when to do so appeared to them to be almost certain death or serious injury."[7]

Kernodle added that he was proud of the courage and actions of his men during the storm. He had every reason to be. Thirty of the *San Jacinto*'s officers and men had been injured. There were no fatalities, and none of the injuries were categorized as serious.

Other CVLs reported similar experiences. By 0900 on the 18th, Captain G. H. DeBaun, USN, skipper of the *Cowpens* (with TG 38.1) found it necessary "to separate from the task group and follow such courses and speeds as could insure the complete safety, integrity and seaworthiness of the USS *Cowpens*."[8] Shortly thereafter, one of his fighter aircraft on the flight deck broke its moorings and caught fire. Quick action by damage-control personnel and deft shiphandling by DeBaun enabled them to jettison the burning plane over the side. Lieutenant Commander Robert Hoyt Price, USN, the acting air officer, was lost overboard at the scene of the fire. He was not recovered.[9]

The anemometer registered in excess of 100 knots, with one of its cups missing. The gale carried away the air search radar antenna from the foremast, and flung it into the sea about fifty yards off the port beam of the ship. It also carried away one radio whip antenna and severely bent the other. Mountainous seas smashed in two hangar deck roller curtains, flooded and rendered inoperative the TBS radio generator, tore loose gun sponsons, dished in gun shields and smokestacks, ripped loose one motor whaleboat beyond repair, bent the port paravane walkway, demolished sixty-five feet of life railing from the catwalks, entered the fireroom blower vents, and often poured down the stacks. The combination of wind and sea caused the loss overboard from the flight deck of seven aircraft, three jeeps, two tractors, and one Kerry crane; cracked the hangar deck bulkhead in two places; created a leak in the hull about nine inches below the waterline; and caused the loss of 550 feet of fire hose, 5 life rafts, and 13 floater nets.[10]

In the bomb magazine, bombs broke loose and went skidding about the deck. Only the heroic and tireless efforts of the officers and men of the aviation ordnance division made it possible to secure them. It took three miles of manila line to do the job![11]

The smaller escort carriers (CVEs), in company with the oilers, had an even rougher time of it. Captain R. W. Bockius, commanding officer of the *Cape Esperance*, estimated that his ship came within ten to fifteen miles of the eye. He reported a barometer reading of 28.69, wind of 80 to 90 knots with gusts to 115; seas mountainous and very confused; and visibility, with spindrift and rain, zero.[12]

The *Cape Esperance*, forewarned by local indicators, also had begun securing for heavy weather on the 17th. By the morning of the 18th, the aircraft on the flight deck had all been secured with a combination of manila line and ½-inch wire cable; 200 tons of fuel oil had been shifted from the starboard wing tanks to the port side; personnel were directed to remain on the port side of the ship unless their duties required them to move about; the forward elevator was placed in the down position to lower the center of gravity; and material condition "Affirm" was set throughout the ship.[13]

Bockius had dropped out of the formation at 0950, and was maneuvering to reduce the punishing effects of the sea. Rolling consistently to 36, often to 39 degrees, the *Cape Esperance* began to lose aircraft from the flight deck. First one and then another broke loose, crashed into adjacent planes, tore them loose, skidded across the deck and went overboard. One of these perched on top of the forward starboard stack and burst into flames, which quickly rose to the level of the bridge. The captain ordered all hands to leave the area of the fire except those necessary to conn the ship.[14]

Despite efforts to bring the *Cape Esperance* to a more comfortable heading, she continued to pound and roll excessively. When she plunged her bow into the trough, both propellors came clear out of the water. The *Miami* and the *Thorn* were directed to stand by her to render assistance.[15]

When it seemed that there were no alternative actions left, and the storm was gradually but certainly overwhelming the ship, Fate intervened. First the wind-swept spume extinguished the fire. A huge wave then tossed the airplane from the stack into the air and over the side. The mountainous seas, the wind, and the excessive rolls, all rose to a new level of violence. First one and then another of the aircraft on the flight deck were swept overboard. As the numbers lost mounted, the deck load lightened, the center of gravity was lowered, and the rolling gradually lessened. By the time thirty-two planes had been lost from the flight deck, the ship rode more easily. Now she found herself able to survive the mauling. Had she not lost the majority of her flight deck load (only seven were left), there is every indication that the ship would have foundered.[16]

Three war correspondents were aboard the *Cape Esperance*. They later indicated to the captain that they had not expected to see Christmas again, and noted that the storm was worse than battle, "because they could heave nothing at anybody, but just had to wait and take it."[17] They were not alone in those opinions.

Another CVE, the *Altamaha*, under the command of Captain A. C. Olney, USN, was operating with the southernmost oiler units. Her most serious troubles began when the following seas broke over the fantail and gushed through the hangar-deck curtains, flooding the after elevator well. Extremely heavy rolls caused a 6-ton aircraft crane to tear its deck fittings completely out of the hangar deck. Carrying a finger lift with it, the runaways quickly demolished three planes and two jeeps. The shifting mass of rubble was in danger of crashing through the ship's side. The hangar-deck crew had their work cut out for them. They confronted the challenge with typical courage and ingenuity.

At 1009, just after changing course to 090° T, and with the wind from 330° T at 80 knots, the planes on the flight deck began to carry away. The first fell into the forward elevator well, which had been opened to permit the escape of gasoline fumes from the hangar deck. This jammed the forward elevator in the lowered position.

The USS *Altamaha* steams peacefully through calm seas.

Soon a second aircraft crashed down the well on top of the first. Amazingly, no fire resulted from these mishaps.[18]

By 1130, with the wind in excess of 100 knots, the planes on the flight deck were crashing into the island, stacks, and walkways, and finally, whenever the roll exceeded 31 degrees, they were sliding off the deck into the sea. As they fell, they carried away life rafts, nets, and radio antennas. They inflicted major damage to the 20-mm and 40-mm gun batteries, all along the starboard side.[19]

The following seas, plus a broken firemain, soon flooded the after elevator well to a depth of four feet. Submersible pumps were repeatedly clogged with loose debris. The captain had to resort to a bucket brigade to control this flooding. The hazards confronting the men engaged in bail-out operations were enough to frighten even the most seasoned veterans, but they turned to, with determination and good humor. Anyone who fell became an immediate and prime candidate for drowning. It took them about five hours, all the while dodging the wreckage and struggling to keep their footing, to get it under control.[20]

Attesting to the velocity of the wind, Captain Olney reported that he "frequently saw the wings and tail surfaces of planes ripped

The typhoon's fury spent, a bucket brigade works to bail out the *Altamaha*'s hangar.

The USS *Altamaha* flight deck on the morning of 19 December 1944.

bodily from their fittings and blown over the side."[21] He also noted that at one point, when the ship was headed directly into the wind, the propellors of four planes parked on the bow, with new engines, began "windmilling" at about 200 rpm. A few seconds later, "these planes were torn from their moorings and flung like chips over the side."[22]

Finally, Olney concluded: "The retention of the full deck load (of aircraft) might well have resulted in the loss of the ship."[23] Once again, Fate had intervened with the positive force necessary for survival. Incredibly, casualties to personnel were remarkably few and relatively minor. Six men were treated for lacerations in the sick bay. The *Altamaha* had indeed been lucky.

While the escorts and small carriers, which were closest to the eye of the storm, were severely buffeted and in many cases escaped capsizing by the narrowest of margins, the bulk of Task Force 38 escaped serious structural damage. The battleships hardly knew they were in a typhoon. Their huge underwater hulls and comparatively small superstructures gave them a great advantage over the other types. The fact that the fleet commander and his staff were embarked in the *New Jersey* could well have been a factor in their failure to appreciate that the fleet was being overtaken by a typhoon.

The large attack carriers (CVs) were simply lucky to have been far enough south of the track to miss the full fury of the storm. There is good reason to believe that they would have suffered heavy damage, possibly with disastrous consequences, had they come within five or ten miles of the eye. They probably would have lost the majority of their aircraft, in which case the fleet would have been robbed of its principal offensive weapon. As to possible damage to the carriers themselves, the combination of mountainous waves and wind ve-

Wrecked aircraft clutter the *Altamaha*'s elevator after the typhoon.

The forward flight deck of the *Altamaha* as it appeared on 19 December 1944.

locities generating more than 78 pounds per square foot of pressure against a sail area of at least 27,000 square feet is awesome to contemplate.

One cruiser, the *Miami*, was close to the storm's center. She sustained major structural damage to her main deck and shell plating in the vicinity of the bow. Another cruiser, the *Baltimore*, suffered minor damage from the storm.

The oilers, with their inherent stability—the result of very low centers of gravity, heavy displacement, and relatively small super-structures—weathered the typhoon well. Although they were very close to the storm's center, six of them reported only minor damage.

Finally, the little fleet tugs, also with low centers of gravity and good basic stability characteristics, came through the ordeal with little or no serious damage, although the *Jicarilla* had an engine problem and had to be towed to Ulithi.

The Third Fleet's encounter with this devastating typhoon had tragic consequences, but few realized then, or understand now, how close Halsey's forces came to truly catastrophic losses of ships, aircraft, and human lives.

PART III

The Aftermath

The reason
the U.S.S. Altamaha
survived the storm
we took on a whole
lot concrete (slabs)
in
San Diego on our
shake down cruise
from Tacoma, Wash

CHAPTER 10

The Casualties Are Counted

It was very early on Tuesday morning, the 19th of December. Aboard the *Dewey*, at about 0100, we again saw a light over the horizon on the port side. We turned in that direction to investigate, but the pounding and slamming were still excessive. Once more we reluctantly abandoned the effort to assist in what we strongly suspected were rescue operations. The deck log of the *Dewey* for that date shows the following entry during the midwatch: "0100 Continued to see searchlight on port beam, but could get no response to signals. Started toward light, but extremely heavy pounding in very high seas caused the Captain to change course back to 220 degrees true."[1]

We continued to maintain steerageway until after daybreak, when the seas became smoother and we were able to make a superficial inspection of the hull. No critical hull damage was discovered. A message was dispatched to the fleet, task force, and task group commanders, apprising them of our position, course, speed, and the extent of damage then apparent.

The ship was a jumble of loose wreckage. Standing on the open bridge, and looking down and aft, it was, in the words of one of my Royal Navy friends, "a bit of a mess." The forward stack was draped over the starboard side, lying almost completely flat across the boat deck, and hanging down over the edge of the main deck, with the open top about three or four feet below the surface of the sea. A tangle of lines, guy wires, stanchions and debris cluttered the entire topside. The signal bridge watch-standers stood almost mesmerized by the sight, looking down and shaking their heads in awe, but laughing and joking with the sailors of the deck force who were beginning the job of cleanup and repair. I noted Steve Yorden's tan face turned up, facing in our direction, his white teeth showing, and his walrus mustache framing his smile. I couldn't help but contrast the circumstances of today with those of the day before, when Yorden had stood next to me, ready to cut the mast.

The ship's doctor, Lieutenant (j.g.) A. R. Baier, reported to me that he had examined all of those who had been hurt, and that aside from a few possible rib fractures and a lacerated scalp, the men of the *Dewey* had escaped serious injury. I had expected at least a few broken limbs. I remarked to him that it was great news, and then observed that the Good Lord had certainly been looking out for us. "Preacher" Johnson was standing on the bridge close enough to overhear this exchange, and when the doctor departed, he ambled over and stood next to me. "What do you think brought us through, Cap'n?" he asked.[2] I had been giving that question a lot of thought. I had recalled the dedication of our engineers, who had remained at their stations under conditions that were close to unendurable. I had also remembered the calm performance of the bridge watch, the thorough preparations for heavy weather by the deck force, and the staying power of the ship herself. These thoughts flashed through my mind again, and I responded, "A great crew saved us; that and some kind of miracle, I guess. Why, Preacher? What do you think?" "Oh, there's no doubt in my mind, Cap'n," he said. "There's your miracle, sir." With that he pointed up to the port yardarm. To my astonishment I saw that it was bent upward! There was no logical explanation for it. Even if we had rolled to 90 degrees, it couldn't have touched the water. Preacher explained that God's great hand had reached down, taken hold of the port yardarm, and pulled the ship back up, just as she was about to capsize. I said, "I see what you mean, and so far as I'm concerned that's probably the best explanation we'll ever get."

While the crew of the *Dewey*, like those of more than a hundred other ships, were busy clearing away debris and making temporary repairs, the fleet commander was trying to determine the location of his scattered force, and assess the seriousness of the damage wrought by the storm. He soon learned that the *Monterey*, *Cowpens*, *San Jacinto*, *Miami*, *Aylwin*, *Hickox*, and *Dewey* all had suffered major damage, and that "more or less minor damage" had been incurred by some nineteen other ships. Aircraft losses were determined to be substantial, but not crucial.

At 1355 on the 19th, Admiral Halsey addressed the following message to the fleet tug *Mascoma*, information to all task force and task unit commanders, and to Commander Destroyer Squadron One: "Do you have any information present position, condition, or last known position of *Spence* (DD 512), *Monaghan* (DD 354), or *Waterman* (DE 740)?"[3]

We felt certain, since they were still unaccounted for, that one or more of those ships had capsized. Preston Mercer responded to

Admiral Halsey's message with one that indicated that since the *Monaghan* was last heard from at 0945 the previous morning, at which time she was attempting to turn out of the trough to southward, and since the *Dewey* rolled more than 72 degrees to starboard on the same heading while heavily ballasted to port, he feared the

The "80-Degree Rollers" certificate was conceived and drawn a few days after the *Dewey*'s return to Ulithi for repairs of storm damage. It is the work of a young seaman named Sam D. Pierce, then a yeoman striker assigned to the ship's office of the *Dewey*. The drawing was reproduced by the USS *Prairie*, in sufficient numbers to deliver a copy to every officer and man then serving in the *Dewey*. Pierce painstakingly inscribed each individual's name in the space provided, using the same italic script as had been used in the certificate. They became prized possessions, often dog-eared from the ravages of time and rough handling, but valued mementos even so.

Sam Pierce is now the art director of a large photoengraving and litho plant in Atlanta. He graciously consented to the use of the certificate in this book. I am especially indebted to him, not only for his generous authorization to use his work, but for the graphic and dramatic manner in which he portrayed the miracle of the *Dewey*'s survival.

Monaghan may have capsized.[4] Recalling the critical level to which her fuel had fallen, we suspected that the *Spence* may have suffered the same fate. It was a chilling thought. We silently prayed that the missing ships would be found, no doubt battered, but still afloat.

Meanwhile, Admiral Halsey directed the *Dewey* to proceed immediately to Ulithi for repairs of storm damage.[5] We altered course and speed accordingly. As we steamed by ourselves for Ulithi, the Third Fleet gradually assembled, formed up in good order, and conducted fueling operations. The thirsty destroyers of Task Force 38 now filled their empty tanks. Even those that had been down to less than 15 percent of capacity on the 18th had managed to conserve their remaining supply and stretch it out for that extra day.

As we headed for the expert repair facilities of a destroyer tender at Ulithi, we did not know that the fleet commander had received a message from the *Tabberer*, sent just before one o'clock on the morning of the 19th, that reported: "Now engaged in picking up survivors of *Hull* (DD 350) in approximate latitude 13°32' N, longitude 128°11' E. *Benham* (DD 796) also in vicinity. *Hull* capsized with little warning at about 1030. Only two life rafts launched and neither yet sighted by us. Have ten enlisted survivors and will remain in area searching until after daylight or until otherwise directed. Amplifying report of own damage follows. Foremast of *Tabberer* (DE 418) carried away in wind of gale intensity 1830. All other damage minor. Able to make any speed up to 24 knots permitted by sea. All radars and radios out except emergency equipment."[6]

This message had not been addressed to the *Dewey*, but several hours later, as we scanned the many dispatches received and were able to decipher the call signs, our curiosity was aroused by this message from the ship we had encountered briefly the night before. We decoded and read it with heavy hearts. I was especially saddened and frustrated to learn that our suspicions about the searchlight we'd seen the night before had been correct, and that the lost ship was one of our own squadron mates. We hoped and prayed that many more survivors of the *Hull* would be rescued. Jim Marks was very much in my thoughts. Now our concerns about the *Monaghan*, *Spence*, and *Waterman* were even greater, and the magnitude of the loss of life that might be expected was staggering. Our hopes fell as we read the *Mascoma*'s negative response to Halsey's query about the missing destroyers.[7]

While the individual ships of the Third Fleet were slowly pulling themselves together and setting about the business of cleanup and repair, Admiral Halsey and his staff were going through the heavy load of radio message traffic regarding storm damage. By 0900 they had assembled a comprehensive picture of what they then knew. At 0922 local (– 9) time, the Commander Third Fleet sent the following operational priority, top secret dispatch to the Commander in Chief, Pacific Fleet:

"Typhoon center passed thirty miles north of fleet guide midday 18th. Tracked by surface search radar. Gusts to 93 knots. Fleet took beating. *Tabberer* (DE 418) reports *Hull* (DD 350) capsized with little warning at 1030. Only ten enlisted survivors at time of report. Several other stragglers still unreported. *Mataco* towing disabled *Jicarilla* to Ulithi. *Monterey, Cowpens, San Jacinto* being sent to Ulithi for survey of damage and repairs. Estimate now *Monterey* will be sent Pearl [Harbor] result of serious hangar deck fire which broke out during heavy rolling. *Dyson, Laws, Benham, Hickox, Aylwin, Tabberer* with assorted derangements will escort cripples. Fueling now proceeding in calm weather latitude 12°00′ N, longitude 129°00′ E. Strike intentions and movements of cripples in separate dispatches."[8]

Now Admiral Nimitz and his staff had their first indication that the Third Fleet's encounter with the typhoon had taken a heavy toll. Meanwhile, Admiral Halsey had directed an intensive air and surface search for survivors in the area through which the fleet had just passed.

At 2257, Commander Third Fleet notified Commander in Chief, Pacific. "*Tabberer* loaded additional survivors of *Hull* vicinity 14°57′N, 127°58′E. Rescued five officers including commanding officer and thirty-six men. Continuing search until relieved on station by CVE. . . ."[9]

On the night of the 19th I wrote to Ginny. Under the rules of wartime censorship I could not discuss the storm or even indicate we had been in it. Nevertheless, I counted on her to read between the lines, and said, "This ship and her crew (and the Commodore) have certainly won my admiration and respect. I don't know when I've served with a finer group. . . . Despite the fact that there was no opportunity to write, I don't know of any time when I've been closer to you in my thoughts than during these last two days." By the time this letter reached her she had already read newspaper reports of the loss of the *Hull* and *Monaghan*, and was worried about the status of the *Dewey*, which of course had not been mentioned by the media.

At 0443 on the 20th, Commander Third Fleet received from the *Rudyerd Bay* the first news of the loss of the *Spence*: "At 0030 in position 14°22'N, 128°09'E, *Swearer* (DE 186) picked up five survivors of *Spence* (DD 512). Statements indicate *Spence* capsized suddenly and believe few personnel survived."[10]

En route to Ulithi, at 1140 on the 20th, CTU 30.8.18, the commander of the escort carrier unit in the *Cape Esperance*, notified Commander Third Fleet: ". . . At 191100Z while in lat 12°55'30" North, Long 129°15'E heard *Waterman* (DE 740) calling CTG 30.8 and any ship on TBS. Unable to make any contact."[11]

One more straggler, the *Waterman*, had been accounted for. At least we knew she was afloat. Only the fate of the *Monaghan* now remained in doubt.

The *Dewey* arrived at Ulithi shortly after 1100 on the 20th, one of the first Third Fleet ships to reach the fleet anchorage following the storm. We were directed to moor alongside the *Prairie*, a veteran destroyer tender with excellent repair facilities and a hardworking, extremely well-trained crew. We had been serviced by the *Prairie* before and had established a fine relationship with the commanding, executive and repair officers. I was confident that we were in capable hands, and that if any tender could accomplish the repairs necessary, the *Prairie* could do it. As soon as we were secured alongside, the officers and men of the tender came aboard the *Dewey* to survey our damage. We outlined the repair actions we thought were required. They responded with comments on the feasibility of repair and a preliminary plan of action. One of the most important requirements was a thorough inspection of the hull and internal structure of the ship, to determine the extent of damage. This was undertaken immediately. So far as then could be determined, we had not suffered any significant hull or other structural damage except the loss of the stack. The tender repair officer assured us that they could build us a new one with no difficulty. A full assessment of the damage to electrical circuitry, 5-inch gun thyratron control equipment, the 5-inch gun director computer, and the anchor windlass, was going to take at least a week.

On the way back to Ulithi I had given considerable thought to the matter of stability, and the extent to which the *Dewey* had rolled. It seemed likely that the responsibilities of the Bureau of Ships would be reviewed in the course of any investigation. I anticipated that BuShips representatives might take a defensive stance concerning the adequacy of our stability, and that they might dispute any claim that we had rolled to the maximum limit established by the design of the ship. As a matter of fact, none of us knew the exact limit to which we had rolled. It appeared to me that the best response to such questions was to avoid any arbitrary statement as to the

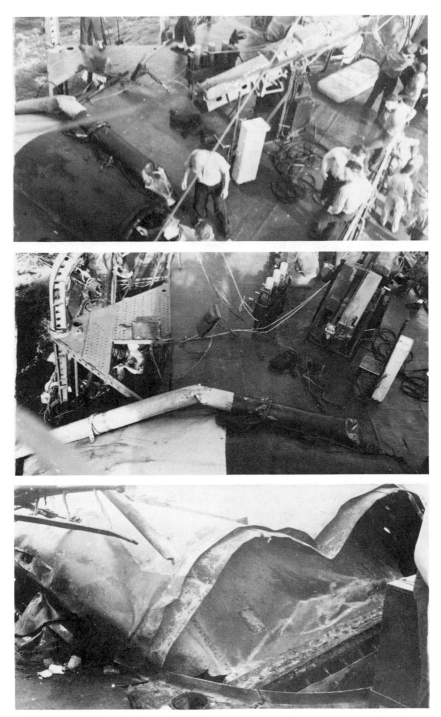

The USS *Dewey*—Typhoon damage.

precise number of degrees. The *Dewey*'s sailors were a bit unhappy with their skipper because he wouldn't confirm their claims that we had rolled 80 degrees. Nevertheless, I found it a much less vulnerable position to respond to the question asked by everyone, "How many degrees did you roll?" with, "I don't know the precise number, but we rolled to the limit of the inclinometer with the starboard wing of the bridge in the water." Then I added, "When I hung by my hands from a vertical stanchion in the pilot house, I looked directly down past my feet, through the bridge window, into the sea. Had I let go, I would have dropped straight down into the water." The usual reaction to this response was silence.

Meanwhile, Admiral Halsey had taken the Third Fleet back in the direction of his launch-point, to resume air strikes against targets on Luzon. Again he encountered the bad weather created by "our" typhoon, the tail end of which he had overtaken. At 0135 on the 21st, he sent General MacArthur a message, which read: "Regret unable strike on 21st due to impossible sea conditions. Am retiring eastward."[12]

Soon the other cripples arrived at Ulithi. Bill Rogers came in with the *Aylwin*. She also moored alongside the *Prairie*. We exchanged stories about the typhoon, and neither of us would have preferred to have been in the other's shoes. We were both convinced that the *Hull* and *Monaghan* had capsized because of their inherently poor stability. The loss of the latter had not yet been confirmed, but there remained little doubt that she too had gone down.

On 21 December, Admiral Nimitz sent a message to Admiral Halsey, indicating that he was flying out to Ulithi from Pearl Harbor, accompanied by Vice Admiral Murray and Rear Admiral Sherman, to arrive on the 24th and break his flag in the *New Jersey*.[13] There could have been little doubt in Admiral Halsey's mind that this visit would focus attention on the typhoon experience.

Also on the 21st, Commander Third Fleet directed the Commander of Service Squadron Ten at Ulithi (CTG 30.9) to: "Convene investigations to investigate causes foundering *Hull* and *Spence*. Hold all survivors for interrogation and until investigations are completed or until otherwise directed."[14] At the same time, Halsey sent Nimitz this message: "My 202235 initiates investigation into causes foundering *Hull* and *Spence* as preliminary measures. Request if practicable that CinCPac initiate ultimate desired administrative measures employing personnel not attached to Task Force 38. Please advise."[15]

While none of these messages concerning the investigation were addressed to us, Preston Mercer's personal intelligence network got word to him, and he conveyed the news to Bill and to me. The complex task of analyzing what had happened had begun.

Admiral Halsey sent Admiral Nimitz a summary of the Third Fleet's status late on the 21st: "Preliminary reports indicate *Hull* (DD 350) rolled over and sank in approximate position 14°55′N, 127°55′E, on 18 December. Five officers including commanding officer and thirty-six men rescued by *Tabberer* (DE 418) also thirteen men rescued by *Robert F. Keller* (DE 419). *Spence* (DD 512) rolled over and sank in approximate position 14°42′N, 127°48′E on 18 December. Total *Spence* survivors 24 including 1 supply officer, rescued by *Tabberer* (DE 418), *Swearer* (DE 186), *Gatling* (DD 671). *Monaghan* (DD 354) also apparently lost as 6 survivors rescued so far no details yet. . . ."[16] This message also was addressed to Admiral King, Commander in Chief, United States Fleet.

On the 22nd, Jim Marks arrived in Ulithi aboard the *Tabberer*. He immediately came aboard the *Dewey* to make a personal report to Preston Mercer. I was not present during that meeting, and Mercer never discussed it with me, nor did I expect or wish him to do so. Jim Marks did stop by my cabin and talk to me briefly about his harrowing experience in the water. I recall his telling me how he was battered by the huge waves until he finally accepted the fact that he was going to perish. However, he ingested so much salt water that it made him sick. In the process of retching, he involuntarily and even unconsciously, struggled to get his head above water for a breath of air. He felt that he would have drowned had he not gotten sick. Jim's face was a mass of salt-water sores, especially around his mouth. His eyes were blackened. He clearly showed the strain of his ordeal. I could not even begin to appreciate the sadness and despair that I knew he must feel, and I sympathized with him. Unfortunately, such things are difficult to verbalize, and I could find no way to express adequately what I felt. I was deeply thankful that he had survived.

Early on the morning of the 22nd, Admiral King sent a message to Admiral Nimitz, information to Admiral Halsey, which simply asked: "Has *Monaghan* been accounted for?"[17] Admiral Nimitz responded on the morning of the 23rd when he sent the following message to Admiral King: "Preliminary and incomplete report on storm damage to 3rd Fleet 18–19 December. *Hull* (DD 350) and *Spence* (DD 512) capsized. Survivors 41 and 24 respectively. *Monaghan* (DD 354) has not been heard from since receipt of an intercepted dispatch at 0945 on the 18th stating she was turning to a southerly course. ComDesRon One in *Dewey* (DD 349) reported that while on same course *Dewey* rolled more than 72 degrees to starboard though heavily ballasted to port. *Monaghan* believed lost. Board of investigation is being convened."[18]

It is of interest to note that Admiral King apparently did not have a report of the loss of the *Monaghan* until 23 December, five days after the event. Positive confirmation of the loss was received by King from Nimitz in a message which stated: "Six survivors recovered from *Monaghan* state she capsized and remained afloat about one half hour thereafter."[19]

The long nightmare of the Third Fleet's involvement in the typhoon of 18 December 1944 had ended at last. Now it would be the task of a court of inquiry to investigate the episode, determine how it happened, and fix responsibility as might be appropriate.

CHAPTER 11

Search, Recovery, and Heroism

On 18 December, the destroyer escort *Tabberer* was assigned to the antisubmarine group (TG 30.7), operating generally to the east about ten miles from the logistic support group (30.8). Like the majority of the escorts that morning, the *Tabberer* had great difficulty steering. Concerned that this lack of control might generate a collision situation, and with commendable initiative, the commanding officer (Lieutenant Commander Henry L. Plage) increased speed to 15 knots and headed east to get clear of the other ships in his unit. By 1115 he found himself in the trough of the sea, unable to turn out of it.[1]

The destroyer escorts were more stable than many of their cousins, the destroyers. They were designed with hulls almost as large, they were beamier, slower, and less powerful; their armaments were lighter, and their superstructures were smaller. As a consequence, their centers of gravity were generally lower, and their metacentric heights and righting arms correspondingly greater. Despite these positive stability characteristics, and with 75 percent of her capacity of fuel aboard, the seas were so rough that the *Tabberer* still rolled to 72 degrees. Unlike the destroyers, however, she recovered rapidly even from the worst rolls. The danger of her capsizing was considerably less than that which applied to the *Farraguts*.

During the afternoon there were storm-related casualties to her engines and electrical equipment, but at no time did she lose power. However, her mainmast was under terrific strain as it whipped from side to side. At about 1400, one of the mast's guy-wire insulators crumbled and allowed the wire to become slack. The mast was no longer securely braced, and it began to work loose. The amount of slack increased as the afternoon wore on, and at 1828 the mast buckled over completely. It had to be cut away. Shortly thereafter, the *Dewey* was sighted, and the exchange of signals described in chapter 7 took place.

The USS *Tabberer*—Heroine of the rescue effort. The plucky DE retrieved fifty-five of the ninety-eight officers and men who survived the loss of their ships.

At 2150, Chief Radioman Ralph E. Tucker, who was rigging an emergency antenna near the stack of the *Tabberer*, heard a cry. Squinting into the darkness, he saw a small light in the water on the starboard beam. He shouted, "Man overboard!" The signal watch turned on a 24-inch searchlight, aimed it in the direction of the small light, and quickly spotted a man in the water. Lieutenant Commander Plage assumed that the victim had fallen from the *Dewey*. He immediately brought the ship around, deftly maneuvered it into position, and recovered the man. The seas were still very rough, and this evolution was not easy. The ship was difficult to steer, and great care had to be exercised lest the victim be run down and injured, or caught under the hull and drowned. Plage demonstrated the skill of a veteran seaman, and performed the rescue without a hitch.

Immediately after being hauled out of the sea, the lucky sailor informed his rescuers that he was a survivor from the *Hull*, and that there should be some of his shipmates in the water close to where he'd been found. The skipper of the *Tabberer* at once initiated a careful search of the area. By flashing light, he also notified a nearby destroyer (thought at the time to be the *Dewey*) of the *Hull*'s reported loss.

The *Tabberer*'s account of this message exchange, and of the events immediately preceding and following it, differs from that recorded by the *Dewey*. In his report of the rescue, Plage wrote, "The storm eased rapidly and at 1940 this vessel gained visual communication with USS *Dewey* (DD 349) and both set course 153 degrees true, speed 8 knots, proceeding to Task Force 38 rendezvous, with *Dewey* standing radar guard for this ship and giving courses to steer and speed to make by visual signals. At 2130 we were steering course 155 degrees true, speed 11 knots." The *Dewey*'s deck log for the period commencing at 1800 reads: "Steaming as before; swinging left slowly from heading 270 degrees T to course 220 degrees T. 1830 Sighted ship starboard quarter, identified as *Tabberer* (DE), underway and in no need of assistance. 1900 Steady on course 220 degrees T."[2] This was the last entry before 2000, and no subsequent entry mentions the *Tabberer*. It thus appears that the *Dewey* and the *Tabberer* could not have been in company for long. There is a discrepancy of an hour and ten minutes in the time of the ships sighting each other. The *Dewey* was on a course of 220 degrees true at 1800 and for the next several hours, while the *Tabberer* was steering 155 degrees true from at least 1940 (and probably earlier) until 2150. I was on the bridge at the time of the encounter. It is my recollection that the *Tabberer* asked the *Dewey* for the course to Ulithi, that we signaled it to her, and that she appeared to diverge from us from then on. It was close to dusk, and as the daylight faded, she was soon out of sight in the darkness. We wondered at the time why she did not remain in company. In any case, the ships were darkened, and once out of sight, any particular one easily could have been confused with others showing on the radar screen.

The next entry in the *Dewey*'s log notes that at 2000 she was steaming as before (on course 220° T) and that at 2300, "Sighted searchlight on the horizon bearing 120° T and attempted to close. 2320 Unable to safely maintain course; came to 225° T, proceeding toward fueling rendezvous."[3] We thought at the time that the light we saw must be from the *Tabberer*. The facts support that conclusion.

There does not appear to be any way now, thirty-six years later, to resolve discrepancies in the record. One possible explanation is that the bridge personnel on the *Tabberer* may have confused some other destroyer with the *Dewey*. During the storm, on the afternoon of the

18th, the *Tabberer* had determined that the *Hickox* and *Benham* were within a mile or two of her position. The record confirms that the *Benham* remained in company with the *Hickox* throughout the storm, that ComDesDiv 104, in the *Hickox*, was informed of the *Hull*'s loss by the *Tabberer* when the latter rescued the first survivor, and that he (CDD 104) directed the *Benham* to "assist in search for survivors of *Hull* as practicable."[4] The *Benham* apparently rejoined the *Tabberer* (although out of sight from the *Dewey*) and searched the area with negative results until midnight, at which time she departed for the next morning's rendezvous. It thus appears that it was either the *Hickox* or the *Benham* that was notified of the recovery of the first *Hull* survivor, and not the *Dewey*, as the *Tabberer*'s report indicates.

Shortly after the first rescue, the *Tabberer*'s crew crowded up to the weather decks and lined the rail, straining their eyes to locate more survivors. They heard a whistle. Soon the searchlight located a new victim in the water. Plage maneuvered his ship and picked up another man. By this time the skipper had devised a rescue technique that he repeated many times during the next forty-eight hours. Aware that he would have very little control of the ship at low speed in rough seas, he determined that he could make a safer approach to each man if he steamed to a point about fifty feet upwind of and broadside to the victim and then allowed the ship to drift down to the pickup point. Considering the winds that were blowing, the time it took to drift down was probably less than it would have taken to maneuver alongside under power.

From 2215 through the remainder of the night, Plage and his men, already tired from battling the typhoon, kept at it. They wanted desperately to rescue as many men as they could. Their dedicated efforts produced outstanding results. Not only did they rescue the lion's share of those who were recovered, they wrote an epic tale of selfless service and heroism while they were doing it.

Lifejacket lights, whistles, and yells helped them find the men in the water. To enhance their search efforts, Plage stopped his ship every ten minutes, turned on his running lights, and swept the surface with the white shafts of his searchlights. They would have served as a beacon to attract any Japanese submarine that might be lurking in the area. Plage must have thought of that possibility many times during the next two days. He accepted the risk, and carried on with his rescue efforts.

The deep troughs of the sea were like black trenches. The searchlights could not penetrate them. The skipper realized that there could be men in those dark and cavernous valleys who could see the

Tabberer, but who could not themselves be seen. He determined that he would do his utmost to find all of them. His zeal was contagious. Officers and crew reflected his enthusiasm. For the next two days they concentrated on nothing else but rescue.

During the first night they had picked up eleven men by midnight. For a while they seemed to find one, or occasionally two or three together, every twenty minutes or so. As they listened for cries and whistles, they became conscious of the background noise on their own ship. Plage had his electricians turn off all ventilation blowers in the vicinity of the bridge. It seemed to help.

By 0810 on the 19th, the *Tabberer* had picked up nineteen survivors from the *Hull*. Number nineteen was Jim Marks. According to Plage, "he was pretty far gone, very weak, he couldn't help himself at all. We just had to drag him aboard. . . ."[5] The *Tabberer* went on with her search. Again at 0830 she recovered two, at 0852 two more, another at 0854, and one each at 0908, 0920, 0930, and 0950.

Most of the single survivors seemed to be between 1,000 to 1,500 yards apart. Based on that observation, the *Tabberer* began an expanding box search, designed to cover 1,500 yards on each side of the ship's track. They couldn't see a man's head beyond that range in the sea conditions then prevailing. It was still choppy and windy. They dropped a green dye marker at each turning to serve as a visual reference point.

At 1310 the *Tabberer* was directed by Commander Third Fleet to join other storm-damaged ships at a rendezvous, ninety miles south of her present position, at sunset. At 1400, Plage reluctantly started for the designated meeting point. At 1406 he sighted and picked up victim number twenty-nine, then resumed his course to the rendezvous. At 1515 he picked up seven more survivors. This group included Lieutenant (j.g.) George H. Sharp, chief engineer of the *Hull*, who had lashed his group of seven together early that morning to make them more visible and facilitate their rescue. When they had sighted the *Tabberer* early that morning, several had wanted to swim off in her direction by themselves. Lieutenant Sharp had been observing the *Tabberer*, and he correctly deduced from her course changes that she was conducting a systematic search. He was confident that she would eventually reach them. He prevailed on the men to remain together. They owed their lives to him for his intelligent leadership. After their recovery Plage resumed the course to the rendezvous.

Each individual rescue produced its own problems. Typical was the case of Boatswain's Mate First Class Louis A. Purvis, from Chatham, New Jersey. A rugged individual and a strong swimmer,

Purvis was one of several *Tabberer* crewmen who involved themselves personally in the rescue operations. Wearing lifejackets with lines fastened to them, and tended by their shipmates on deck, these men entered the water and assisted the survivors during each rescue. On one such occasion, Purvis swam out to help a man who appeared to be unconscious. When he reached him he found that he was dead. As he turned and swam back to the ship, the slack in his line became snagged under the hull. As the ship rolled, the line grew taut and pulled Purvis under water. He managed to hold his breath, but almost as soon as he came back up and filled his lungs with air, another roll took him under again. Now he was pulled all the way under, and found himself banging against the ship's bottom almost down to the keel. Desperate to free himself, and unable to loosen the line, he slipped out of his kapok lifejacket. Meanwhile, his shipmates on deck were frantically searching for him, fearing that he had been trapped under the ship. As soon as he was free, he ducked under the keel and came up on the other side. Without a jacket now, and almost exhausted from the ducking, he needed help. His buddies heard his shouts, rushed to the other side of the ship, got a line to him, and hauled him back aboard, somewhat the worse for wear. Two hours later, Purvis was back in the water again, assisting more survivors.

Another rescuer who spent most of the night of the 18th and practically all day on the 19th in the water helping the victims was Lieutenant Howard J. Korth, from Bay City, Michigan. Korth was the *Tabberer*'s gunnery officer. A class of '42 graduate of Notre Dame, where he played guard on the football team, Korth was a powerful youngster and, like Purvis, a strong swimmer. Both of them were caught under the rolling ship more than once, but they kept at it and helped many of the rescued who were too weak to help themselves. Both were recommended for Navy-Marine Corps Medals for heroism.

Once the survivors were brought to the ship's side by Korth and Purvis, their shipmates, clinging with one hand to cargo nets that had been draped over the side, reached down, grabbed the victims under the arms, and literally lifted them on board. The job called for men with great physical strength and courage. The *Tabberer* had them.

Early in the afternoon of the 19th, as the ship approached a lone survivor, those on board could see an 8-foot shark swimming close to him. Immediately, *Tabberer* riflemen began firing Tommy guns and 30-caliber Springfields to at least scare it away. The survivor was nearly exhausted and unable to swim. At this point, the executive officer, Lieutenant Robert M. Surdam, who was on the main deck supervising the pick-up operations, saw that the man might be attacked before he could be brought aboard. Without a moment's hesitation, and with no lifejacket himself, Surdam dove into the water, swam to the victim, grabbed him by the back of his jacket, and towed him back toward the ship. Tiring fast from the exertion of pulling the victim back through heavy seas, Surdam had covered about half the distance, but he still had another thirty yards or so to go. Sizing up the situation, and reacting at once to it, Torpedoman First Class Robert L. Cotton, one of those helping on the cargo net, dove in and swam out to assist Surdam. With the shark circling about twenty feet away, the two of them towed the survivor to the ship's side and assisted him up the net.

At 1600 Plage rescued survivor number thirty-eight. He picked up numbers thirty-nine and forty at 1630. It was clear now that the *Tabberer* could not make the designated rendezvous point on time, but Plage dutifully changed course to head in that direction again. He then debated whether he should notify Commander Third Fleet that he had decided to remain in the area to search until the next morning. Before he came to any decision, a message was received from Admiral Halsey, directing that he continue the search until dawn. When the men of the *Tabberer* were informed of this development, they cheered. Although most of them had not slept for thirty-six hours, they did not want to abandon their comrades who might still be in the water, desperately hoping for rescue. Just at dusk those on the *Tabberer* heard a now-familiar cry. At 1830 they recovered their forty-first survivor from the *Hull*.

An all-night search produced negative results. At 0840 on the 20th, the *Rudyerd Bay* and her escorts relieved the *Tabberer* of her rescue duties, and relayed new instructions that she was to return to Ulithi. Plage came to course 110° T, and increased speed to 15 knots. At 1050 he sighted a life raft. He proceeded to close it, and found that it contained ten survivors from the *Spence*. He quickly recovered them and resumed the search. At 1106 he rescued *Spence* survivors eleven and twelve. Numbers thirteen and fourteen were picked up at 1115 and 1127. Plage notified the *Rudyerd Bay* of his latest find.

At 1225 the *Rudyerd Bay* and her escorts again arrived on the scene and again relieved the *Tabberer*. This time, she finally proceeded to Ulithi, carrying fifty-five very fortunate officers and men, who probably would not have been alive had it not been for the heroic little destroyer escort. Lieutenant Commander Plage and his men had distinguished themselves with a magnificent performance. Both the commanding and executive officers were reservists, as were most of the officers and about 90 percent of the crew. Four years earlier, Plage had been an insurance investigator in Florida and Surdam an industrial analyst in a commercial bank in Albany, New York. Speaking to this point at a press conference in February 1945, Surdam commented that the *Tabberer*'s performance with a crew of reservists was, "a great indication of what the Navy can do in the way of training."[6] True enough, but it was also an indication of the high caliber of the young men of the United States of America at that time in our history.

Other search-and-rescue operations on a massive scale were conducted throughout the four days following the typhoon.

Beginning at 1848 on the 18th, Admiral Halsey directed Task Force 38 to conduct a thorough search of the area through which the fleet had passed. Although the *San Juan, Cabot, Hancock,* and *Iowa* all reported hearing whistles, or briefly sighted lights in the water, the ensuing destroyer searches for survivors that first night were in every case negative. At 0700 on the 19th, Third Fleet carrier aircraft and surface ships launched intensive searches for survivors of the *Hull.* The destroyers *Blue* and *Moore* were specifically directed to search in the vicinity of the position reported by the *Tabberer.* Their search was futile. On the morning of 20 December, the *Rudyerd Bay* reported that one of her escorts, the *Swearer,* had rescued survivors of the *Spence* at 0030.

Chapter 8 described the loss of the *Spence* and included the narrative provided by Lieutenant (j.g.) Krauchunas, the senior survivor. On the night of the 18th he was one of nine men on a life raft, hoping and praying that they would be rescued. Except for the extreme discomfort of their situation, the night passed without incident. His narrative continued: "The morning of the 19th December, 1944, was a very clean bright day. During the morning we sighted two planes, but could not attract their attention, and during this attempt to attract them, we used one of the die markers. . . . Ensign George W. Poer, USNR, floated away from our raft on the evening of 19 December. The condition of Lieutenant (j.g.) John Whalen and Hester, S1/c, was growing worse, due to exhaustion and consumption of salt water. Lieutenant (j.g.) John Whalen slipped from the floater net into the water at approximately 0300, 20 December 1944. Hester, S1/c, slipped from the raft a few moments later. These two men had been held on the life raft by the other men for the last eight or nine hours. During our stay in the water, I took personal supervision over the water kegs, and gave each man a drink every 2½ to 3 hours, including the men that slipped off the raft. Upon our rescue we still had a full keg left. We were picked up by the USS *Swearer*

(DE 186) at latitude 14°27'N and longitude 128°07'E at 0400, 20 December 1944."[7]

Third Fleet carrier aircraft conducted an intensive air search for survivors that morning. Results were negative. At 2028 on the 20th, the destroyers *Cogswell* and *Knapp* were reported to have rescued four additional *Hull* survivors. At 2342, Commander Third Fleet directed Task Force 38 to conduct an intensive surface search, covering the widest possible front, en route to the next morning's rendezvous.[8] At 0130 on the 21st, Admiral Halsey canceled strike operations against targets on Luzon because of increasingly bad weather. All efforts now were concentrated on a continuing search for survivors by surface ships and aircraft.

Shortly after daylight on the 21st, the *Monaghan's* survivors were rescued by the destroyer *Brown*. In chapter 8 the narrative report of Joseph Charles McCrane told of the *Monaghan's* loss, and described how thirteen survivors clung to a life raft. By the next morning only twelve were left. His story continued: "The next day we were all confident we would be picked up. Planes passed over us, but it was still pretty rough and our little raft must have been hard to see. A TBF went right over us. That night another fellow died after he had gone berserk and started to drink salt water. We tried to stop him, too. Another fellow started swimming around the raft and we lost him as well as Holland, who died of his injuries."[9]

The next day and night passed in about the same way. One man went over the side of the raft and was lost, and two more swam to another unoccupied raft. They were never seen again. Meanwhile McCrane had applied first aid to the remaining men, bandaging their cuts and applying sulfa powder and ointment.

On the morning of the third day, McCrane said he felt things were beginning to look grim. He was trying to keep up his hopes as well as those of the other survivors.

"Pretty soon we saw some fighter planes come over," he continued, "and we knew we were either near land or one of our carriers. They later turned out to be carrier planes. These two planes banked over us and dropped some of those water markers. Twenty minutes later we saw the most wonderful sight in the world, a tin can [destroyer] steaming at full speed right at us.

"A few minutes later she was alongside with everyone shouting advice. Someone threw us a line and soon we were safe. She turned out to be the USS *Brown*, a 2,100-tonner. They told us when we got aboard that a shark was right on our tails the whole time we were being rescued. Well, he's welcome to the rest of the spam, anyway."[10]

The war diary of the *Brown* for 21 December, despite its brevity, conveys some of the grim tragedy of the rescue effort: "0905 *Brown* left formation to investigate life raft. 0911 Life raft empty; no identifying markings. *Brown* proceeded to rejoin. 0930 *Brown* proceeding to investigate second life raft. 0935 Recovered life raft, empty. 1033 Sighted life raft with survivors, two miles to port. 1046 *Brown* recovered twelve men and one officer, survivors of USS *Hull*, all in fair condition. 1120 Life raft with survivors reported by CAP [Combat Air Patrol]. *Brown* proceeding to investigate. 1130 Sighted life raft two miles to the south. 1140 Recovered six men, survivors of USS *Monaghan*; several sharks about. 1141 Proceeding to investigate floater net reported by CAP. 1156 Floater net close aboard, contains one body partly eaten by sharks. 1159 Body slipped from net and sank when recovery attempted. *Brown* proceeding to rejoin TG 38.1. 1320 Sighted life raft, proceeding to investigate. 1328 Recovered empty life raft. No identifying marks. 1610 rejoined formation."

The final rescue had been made. The *Tabberer* had picked up fifty-five men, forty-one from the *Hull* and fourteen from the *Spence*. The *Robert F. Keller* picked up thirteen and the *Cogswell* found one, from the *Hull*. Finally, the *Brown* rescued six from the *Monaghan*, the only survivors from that ship, and thirteen from the *Hull*.

The intensive search continued through the 22nd of December. Ninety-eight officers and men were recovered. Seven hundred and ninety had been lost. For those who may wonder if the search effort was adequate in the light of the number of men known to be missing and the circumstances then obtaining, there was a war to be fought, and that had to be the top priority. The ships of the Third Fleet needed to anchor in a safe harbor and repair the extensive damage wrought by the storm. They could not remain too long in the same area without running the risk of detection by Japanese submarines or aircraft, with consequent additional and more serious damage likely to be inflicted. With these considerations in mind, the fleet commander decided to terminate the search, return to Ulithi, and get ready for the next phase of the campaign. It was a sound decision.

CHAPTER 12

Assessment of Damage, Repairs, and Investigation

There were two essential tasks to be accomplished during the Third Fleet's stay in Ulithi. The first was to complete an assessment of damage and accomplish the necessary repairs. The second was to conduct a formal investigation of all circumstances relevant to the fleet's involvement in the typhoon. Both had to be undertaken on a priority basis. Time was extremely limited. The next combat operation called for the departure of Task Force 38 no later than 30 December. In order to provide the necessary logistic support, the ships of TG 30.8 had to be ready at the same time.

Admiral Halsey quickly sized up the full extent of the fleet's damage and informed Admiral Nimitz. In addition to the loss of the three destroyers, major structural damage had been incurred by three light carriers, two escort carriers, three destroyers, and one cruiser. "More or less minor" damage had been inflicted on nineteen other ships. Aircraft losses amounted to 146 planes lost or damaged beyond economical repair. Ninety-four of these were from the escort carriers and thirty-three from the light carriers. The remainder were from the cruisers and battleships.

The damage that probably was of greatest concern to the Third Fleet staff was the reduction in radar capacity. Storm-related casualties involving radar equipment were suffered by many of the major combatant ships not previously mentioned, as well as by those reported to have been damaged. This imposed a critical reduction in the fleet's air search, aircraft detection, and aircraft tracking capabilities. In the environment of the Western Pacific at that time, with Japanese kamikaze attacks a constant threat, any significant cutback in air search radar performance amounted to a loss in air defense capacity. This was unacceptable. The Commander Third Fleet quickly concluded that immediate and drastic corrective action was required. Accordingly, early on the 21st Admiral Halsey fired off an operational priority message to Admiral Nimitz, reporting the fact that, "Storm damage has further aggravated critical radar material situation in fleet."[1] He listed the carriers *Cowpens, Cabot, Lexington, Ticonderoga, Essex,* and *Langley,* the battleship *Iowa,* and "many others" as needing immediate repair or replacement of radar equipment. He also requested that civilian contract engineers be flown by first available government air transportation to Ulithi, and that replacement parts be delivered as soon as possible. The message closed with the comment, "Necessity for completing essential radar work prior departure Task Force 38 from Ulithi next operation justifies maximum transportation effort."[2] No doubt he got what he asked for, since there was no delay apparent in the conduct of scheduled operations. This should not be taken as an indication, however, that repairs had been completed by the time of the next sortie. In all probability, when the Third Fleet put to sea on 30 December, they took with them many of the civilian contract engineers who had been flown out to Ulithi to assist with the storm-damaged radars.

The material inspections conducted after arrival in Ulithi disclosed other storm damage not previously apparent. Damage to the shaft of the battleship *Iowa* was typical. While en route to Ulithi after the typhoon, she had experienced excessive vibration in one of her propellor shafts. Suspecting that some serious derangement had occurred, an inspection by divers after arrival in Ulithi disclosed damage to the shaft. Replacement of the tail shaft was indicated. Accordingly, on 26 December Admiral Nimitz ordered the *Iowa* detached from the Third Fleet, to proceed to Pearl Harbor for drydocking and repair.[3] Other structural and machinery damage did not become evident on some ships for several weeks, as we discovered for ourselves on the *Dewey.*

As a result of the fleet's typhoon damage, the repair facilities at Ulithi were taxed to their capacity. Repair personnel on the tenders and repair ships, as well as the crews of the damaged ships themselves, worked around the clock to make the fleet combat-ready. It all added up to a hard-working Christmas period, but those of us who were aboard the *Dewey* considered ourselves lucky just to be alive. No doubt that same feeling prevailed aboard many of those other Third Fleet ships that spent the Christmas of 1944 safely at anchor in Ulithi Atoll.

With regard to the second task, that of investigation, Admiral Nimitz arrived in Ulithi and broke his flag in the *New Jersey* on the 24th of December. There is little doubt that he had given considerable thought to the administrative action to be taken to investigate the circumstances of the Third Fleet's encounter with the typhoon. Navy regulations required such an investigation whenever any naval vessel was lost or damaged, but aside from that fact, good administrative practice dictated that the circumstances be examined in depth, to establish responsibility, determine if any offenses had been committed, and fix blame wherever indicated.

It is apparent that the composition of the court of inquiry had been determined prior to Admiral Nimitz's departure from Pearl Harbor on the 21st, since he brought Vice Admiral Murray with him and arranged to pick up Vice Admiral Hoover en route when he stopped overnight at Guam. One can assume that some eyeball-to-eyeball discussion of the storm took place on Christmas Eve between Admiral Nimitz and Admiral Halsey. It is also possible that on Christmas Day Admiral Nimitz took time to talk privately with the members of the court, or at least with Vice Admiral Hoover, for the purpose of outlining broad policy guidelines.

On 25 December 1944, Admiral Nimitz formally appointed Vice Admiral John Howard Hoover as president of a court of inquiry, to convene on board the USS *Cascade* at 10 A.M. on Friday, 26 December, to inquire "into all the circumstances connected with the loss of the USS *Hull* (DD 350), USS *Monaghan* (DD 354), and the USS *Spence* (DD 512), and damage sustained by the USS *Monterey* (CVL 26), and the USS *Cowpens* (CVL 28), and other damage sustained by ships of the Third Fleet as a result of adverse weather on or about 18 December 1944."[4]

The precept directed the court to investigate the causes of loss and damage, injuries to and loss of personnel, and the responsibility for them. It also directed the court to include in its findings a full statement of facts, its opinion as to whether any offenses had been committed or serious blame incurred, and in case it determined that offenses had been committed or serious blame incurred, to specifically recommend what further proceedings should be taken.[5]

The court was authorized to administer oaths to witnesses in the taking of testimony, and its attention was specifically invited to sections 725 and 734 of *Naval Courts and Boards*. These two sections dealt with the established procedure for a court of inquiry. The first (section 725) was applicable in the case of the loss of a ship. It stipulated that the commanding officer's report containing the narrative of the disaster should be read in court in the presence of the commanding officer and the surviving officers and crew. The commanding officer was then to be asked if the narrative just read was a true statement of the loss of the ship, and whether he had any complaint to make against any of the surviving officers and crew. The court was then required to ask the surviving officers and crew if they had any objections to the narrative just read, or if they had anything to lay to the charge of any officer or man with regard to the ship's loss. Section 734 dealt with the definitions of the terms "Defendant" and "Interested Party," and the rights accorded to them in the process of the inquiry. A defendant was defined as: "A person whose conduct is the subject of investigation." Section 734 went on to indicate that a defendant would be notified of the gist of evidence that implicated him, and accorded the rights of an accused before a court-martial—namely, the right to be present, to have counsel, to challenge members, to introduce and cross-examine witnesses, to introduce new matter pertinent to the inquiry, to testify or declare in his own behalf at his own request, and to make a statement and argument. An interested party was defined as: "Any person, not a complainant or defendant, who has an interest in the subject matter of the inquiry." Section 734 also stated that any person designated by the court as an interested party was to be allowed to be present during the inquiry, to examine witnesses, and introduce new matter pertinent to the inquiry in the same manner as a defendant.[6]

In addition to Vice Admiral Hoover, Vice Admiral George D. Murray and Rear Admiral Glenn B. Davis were appointed as members of the court of inquiry, and Captain Herbert K. Gates was appointed judge advocate.[7]

Vice Admiral Hoover was serving as Commander, Forward Area, Central Pacific, at the time of his appointment as president of the court of inquiry. Then fifty-seven years of age, he had completed submarine training in 1924 and after completion of flight training in 1929, was designated a naval aviator. In 1941 he commanded the aircraft carrier *Lexington*. After the attack on Pearl Harbor he had served as Commander, Caribbean Sea Frontier, and then as Commander, Aircraft Central Pacific. Already the recipient of two Distinguished Service Medals, Admiral Hoover's service assignments covered an exceptionally wide range of naval experience. However, his experience as a combat commander at sea during World War II was limited.

Vice Admiral Murray had been designated a naval aviator in 1915. At the time of Pearl Harbor, he was the commanding officer of the carrier *Enterprise*. In that capacity he had participated in many of the early carrier task force raids and in the Battle of Midway. He was a carrier task force commander during the Battle of Santa Cruz on October 25, 1942, when his flagship, the *Hornet*, was so severely damaged that she had to be sunk by our own forces. After a stint as commander of the Naval Air Training Center at Pensacola he was assigned as Commander Air Force, Pacific Fleet, and had been there four months when Admiral Nimitz took him to Ulithi to become a member of the court of inquiry. He was then fifty-five years old.

The court's junior member was Rear Admiral Glenn B. Davis. A gunnery expert, he was transferred in July of 1942 from duty as assistant chief of the Bureau of Ordnance to command the battleship *Washington*. In that capacity he was awarded the Navy Cross for his part in the night action of November 14–15, 1942, near Savo Island. In April 1943 he assumed command of Battleship Division Eight, and was in the thick of the action in the Pacific from then until his assignment as a member of the court of inquiry, at which time he was fifty-two years old.

Captain Gates was a specialist in mechanical engineering, with a master's degree in marine engineering. He had served in the repair ship *Denebola* and the destroyer tender *Prairie*. In May 1944 he became the commanding officer of the tender *Cascade*, and was still so serving when he was assigned as judge advocate of the court of inquiry. He was then forty-three. His background in marine engineering and ship repair was undoubtedly helpful to the members of the court as they strove to gain an appreciation of how the ships of the Third Fleet reacted to storm conditions and storm damage.

The court of inquiry met at 0940 on 26 December, aboard the *Cascade*. The first order of business was to decide to sit with closed doors. Casual observers and the curious were thus excluded. The decision was made to have fleet command witnesses testify first. Apparently, the reason underlying this decision was the realization that the wartime commitments of the Third Fleet would soon take all of its principal commanders to sea again. The business of the court would be subject to inordinate delay if their testimony had not been concluded prior to the fleet's departure on the 30th. The court would have to cover a lot of ground in just four days![8]

The court called Lieutenant Commander James A. Marks, U.S. Navy, commanding officer, USS *Hull* (DD 350), and informed him that in view of the loss of his ship he was a defendant. (This was for the record. He already had been advised informally as to his status.) Jim Marks introduced Captain Ira H. Nunn, U.S. Navy, as his counsel. Captain Nunn had a service-wide reputation as a legal specialist and was very well qualified to represent the defendant.[9]

The court next called Captain Preston V. Mercer, U.S. Navy, Commander Destroyer Squadron One, and informed him (again for the record) that in view of the loss of the *Hull* and *Monaghan*, both attached to his squadron, he was an interested party. He was advised that he would be allowed to be present during the entire course of the inquiry, to examine witnesses, and to introduce new matter pertinent to the inquiry in the same manner as a defendant.[10]

The way was now clear to begin a parade of fifty-four witnesses, whose testimony would occupy the court's attention over a period of eight days. The record does not give any indication of a deliberate strategy for the conduct of the inquiry, and the sequence in which witnesses were called appears to have been dependent more on their availability than on any logical plan.

In the meantime, I was very much preoccupied with the business of inspecting and arranging for the repair of the *Dewey*'s damage. Captain Mercer had advised me, however, that he felt certain I would be called as a witness before the court of inquiry. To that end he suggested that I refresh my recollections by reviewing the official ship's log and my own written narrative report. I appreciated his advice, and prepared myself for the time when I would be called to testify. I also gave some thought to the whole typhoon experience. Many questions came to mind, not only about the events of 18 December and the day before, but about the matter of stability. I recalled our very serious concerns about some obvious deficiency in the *Dewey*'s handling characteristics before we left Puget Sound Naval Shipyard in September. Now I wondered whether the Bureau of Ships would be found negligent for its failure to initiate some positive corrective action to improve *Farragut*-class destroyer stability. Preston Mercer had informed them of his concerns about the *Dewey* by telephone on 26 September, and they had received a dispatch report of the *Aylwin*'s inclining test conducted on 24 September showing a significant reduction in her metacentric height. The only logical conclusion that made sense to me was that there must be some gross deficiency in the inherent stability of the whole class. After all, two *Farragut*s had capsized, despite being fueled to 75 percent of capacity, while two others, similarly fueled, had come so perilously close to capsizing that their survival was nothing short of miraculous.

Other questions occurred to me. I could not understand how it could have happened that the Task Force 38 destroyers had been allowed to deplete their fuel supplies to such a low level. I also wondered about the failure of the fleet commander to take effective action to avoid the storm. The bulk of the young officers on the *Dewey* had determined from local weather indicators on the 17th that the fleet was being threatened by a typhoon to the southeast of us. I knew from conversations with Bill Rogers that the officers of the *Aylwin* had come to the same conclusion. None of us were geniuses. Why hadn't the Third Fleet staff been just as aware of the threat as we were? Why had the fleet and task force commanders taken the time and incurred the additional risk involved in attempting to fuel on the morning of the 18th, when it was obvious to us that fueling would be impossible?

During those next few days, I formed some opinions about the typhoon experience. I was certain that both the Bureau of Ships and the high command of the Third Fleet had been at fault, and that between them they would share the blame for the fleet's losses and damage. By the same token, I felt sure that both Preston Mercer and Jim Marks would be found blameless.

With regard to the *Dewey*'s experience, I was confident that Preston Mercer's testimony would cover the matter of the shipyard postrepair trial and the BuShips response to his request that the ship be given an inclining test. I had no concern about adverse criticism concerning the way in which the *Dewey* had been handled, and I looked forward to appearing as a witness before the court of inquiry with considerable interest.

CHAPTER 13

Command Aspects

The captain of a ship of the United States Navy, regardless of his rank or the size of his command, is held totally responsible for her safety and administration and for the welfare of her officers and crew. Except in those combat situations where destruction of the enemy is the first priority, the safety of the ship is paramount. Anything that happens while at sea falls within the cognizance of the commanding officer. If the ship performs well, he is given credit for it. If she performs poorly, he is held accountable. Ship losses, collisions, groundings, boiler or gun explosions, and major fires—especially if they involve the loss of life or major damage to the ship—are notorious "captain-breakers," although there have been some notable exceptions. The skippers involved in a few of these tragedies have emerged from the inevitable investigations with commendations for the exemplary manner in which they handled the emergency. This has been especially true in those cases where ships were lost in combat. It is a tough command philosophy, not without some injustices, but on balance it has been straightforward and fair. It demands self-reliance and competence. It does not tolerate passing the buck. Most importantly, it has been a major factor contributing to the traditional dependability and high-quality performance of the United States Navy.

When engaged in antisubmarine escort duties, the commanding officers of destroyers and other escort vessels—in addition to being responsible for the safety of their own ships—are also obligated to provide protection for the heavy ships of their respective formations. This unique additional responsibility is a natural inhibitor. It restricts the freedom of action normally available to the captain of any other type of ship. During World War II, the destroyer's ability to provide antisubmarine protection was dependent upon the placement of its sonar detection equipment between the submarine and the ship being protected. Position in the screen was therefore vital to the execution of the mission. The need for accurate station-keeping could not be lightly disregarded. Even when unusually severe sea conditions developed, a destroyer skipper normally would not have felt that he could say, "To hell with the formation, I'm going to look out for my own ship," and then proceed independently on a course of his choice. To do so would have left a hole in the screen, and jeopardized the ship or ships he was escorting. On the other hand, the skipper of a battleship, or a carrier, or an oiler, with no special responsibility for the safety of any ship but his own, normally would have been expected to abandon his station and take whatever independent action was necessary for his ship's safety. This difference in command responsibility was a crucial consideration as the destroyer skippers of the Third Fleet made their decisions on the 18th of December, 1944.

The manner in which several typical commanding officers handled their ships and exercised command during the typhoon has been covered in previous chapters. Those higher command responsibilities that governed major tactical decisions—such as the launching of air strikes, whether or not to fuel the escorts, the selection of rendezvous points, courses and speeds to be used, fleet or task force dispositions, task group formations, and the conduct of air operations—all reposed at the senior levels. They were under the cognizance of the fleet, task force, and task group commanders. It was to answer questions about these higher command responsibilities that the court of inquiry called the senior commanders of the Third Fleet and their principal staff officers to testify. Since there was no particular order to the sequence of their appearance before the court, they are discussed here generally in a high-to-low progression of seniority. The testimony of Admiral Halsey, because of its importance, is excepted from that sequence, and has been reserved until last.

The first witness on December 26th (the first day of the proceedings) was Rear Admiral Robert B. Carney, Admiral Halsey's chief of staff. The court obviously intended his testimony to set the stage for all that followed. He was asked to give a brief narrative of the fleet's movements, the reasons therefore, and such events as he considered pertinent that took place on December 17th and 18th. Admiral Carney responded with a very comprehensive statement. He first outlined the general strategic situation and described the Third Fleet's air strikes against Luzon on the 14th, 15th, and 16th. He noted that additional strikes were scheduled for the 19th, 20th, and 21st and pointed out that the plan called for a retirement from Luzon toward a fueling rendezvous for the morning of the 17th. He described how existing wind and sea conditions made that fueling difficult and presented some of the considerations that governed

Admiral Halsey's decisions. The following extracts and paraphrased comments from his testimony summarize his narrative: "The wind was across the sea," and it was "impossible" to find a satisfactory course for fueling. The Commander Third Fleet concluded at about midday on the 17th that, "there was a tropical disturbance to the eastward of the fleet position." It was estimated that "the tropical disturbance was moving in a northwesterly direction and that it would recurve to the northeast." This estimate was based on a study of the current weather map, and it "conformed to the history of December typhoons." The estimated position of the tropical disturbance was passed by message to the task force and task group commanders early in the afternoon of the 17th. During that same afternoon, the seaplane tender *Chandeleur* reported a "tropical disturbance generally to the eastward" of the fleet. The weather deteriorated during the night, but "we were unable from available data to accurately determine the existence of a typhoon system nor to accurately estimate the storm's character or movement." Not until mid forenoon of the 18th did we have "accurate information that a genuine typhoon did in fact exist, where it was, and what it was doing." Although the fleet commander could not at that time accurately plot the location of all fleet units, he estimated late in the forenoon of the 18th that the bulk of the fleet would be south of the storm's track, but that "there was a possibility of some stragglers being farther to the north." Admiral Carney then noted that the storm center passed the *New Jersey* about thirty miles to the north; that it was seen and tracked by radar, and that it was of small size and considerable intensity. He pointed out that two considerations were governing the fleet commander. The first was the need to extricate the fleet from the storm, and the second was the commitment to resume offensive operations. With regard to the missing ships, Admiral Carney explained that "Air searches and searches by surface vessels were initiated to the extent possible, with the concurrent necessity for getting back to the Luzon area for the resumption of the offensive operations."[1]

Asked if it was normal for destroyers to have only 15 percent fuel on board, Carney's answer was "No. The operations were extensive by the necessity for high speed run-ins initially on the night of the 13th and by three consecutive days of carrier strikes. The obligation of Task Force 38 was a heavy one and those operations did not permit interim fueling or topping off." The defendant then cross-examined the witness. Among the questions asked by Marks were the date and time when Commander Third Fleet was first advised of dangerous weather, and whether or not local observations proved helpful in determining the path of the storm. Responding to the first of these, Admiral Carney said, "The first information from an outside source, that is, a source other than the fleet units in company, came from the *Chandeleur* about half-past two in the afternoon of the 17th." To the second question he replied, "As I previously stated, it was not until the forenoon of the 18th that we were able to determine the position, course, and speed of the storm."[2]

After Admiral Carney withdrew, the court determined that the record of its proceedings would be classified Secret. Its next witness was Captain Ralph E. Wilson, assistant chief of staff for operations, staff, Third Fleet. In the course of his discussion he explained that during all of the 16th, the fleet staff had the weather situation under observation. It appeared to them that the fleet would pass through a relatively weak front, and that considerably to the southeast there was a tropical disturbance of medium intensity. He then commented on the fueling operations that were attempted on the 17th. He noted that after two hours the weather became so bad that the operations were suspended, and a directive was sent to the fleet to proceed to a fueling rendezvous the next morning, well to the westward. Wilson explained that the fleet commander changed the rendezvous point twice, so that in all, a total of three were set, one at 17° N, 128° E, one at 14° N, 127°30' E, and one at 15°30' N, 127°40' E. All were selected on the basis of the best weather information available at the time, and each was intended to be clear of the storm's path, yet not in dangerous proximity to land-based enemy air forces. When Jim Marks cross-examined Wilson, he asked him the basis for the decision to change course to 060° at approximately 0700 on the 18th, by which time it must have been apparent that weather conditions made fueling next to impossible. Wilson replied, "The 060° course . . . was set by the officer in tactical command, and I assume he chose a course into the wind while attempting to fuel the low destroyers alongside the carriers."[3]

As indicated earlier, the officer in tactical command was Commander Task Force 38, Vice Admiral John S. McCain. The court asked him only ten questions. His answers have been incorporated into the following paraphrased summary: He did not appreciate the speed with which the storm was overtaking his force. He thought that a movement of 100 to 200 miles would be sufficient to avoid it. Uppermost in his mind was the commitment to strike Luzon. The location selected by Commander Third Fleet for the fueling rendezvous on the 18th appeared to him to be satisfactory at the time it was chosen. He was not consulted regarding the changes in rendezvous points. Storm considerations did not begin to dictate the disposition and movement of Task Force 38 until the morning of the 18th. Asked if he had any opinion regarding statements by other commanders that there were clear indications that the storm was drawing closer and increasing in violence on the 17th, he replied in the negative. When questioned regarding inadequacies in the weather reporting system, he avoided a direct response. He confirmed that Commander Third Fleet ordered the course change to the southward on the morning of the 18th after attempting to fuel, and that he (Commander Task Force 38) had ordered the destroyers to attempt to fuel from the heavy ships on that same morning. The court posed no question regarding the decision to change course to 060° T for fueling at about 0700 on the 18th, nor of the length of time that course was held. Admiral McCain made no mention of either of these points.[4]

Vice Admiral McCain's chief of staff was Rear Admiral Wilder D. Baker. He testified that: CTF 38 did not have timely warning that a severe storm was approaching on the 17th; CTF 38's weather information was obtained from plane reports and weather notices; on the 17th, CTF 38 estimated the storm to be bearing roughly 135° T from the task force, heading on a northerly or northwesterly track; he (Baker) thought the southernmost of the three rendezvous points was best; the task group and task force commanders were asked only once by Commander Third Fleet for their estimates of the weather, early in the morning of the 18th, and there was no other exchange or thought on the subject.[5]

The judge advocate also called Commander James H. Hean. He was Task Force 38's tactical officer and navigator. He provided the court with a detailed analysis of the movements of Task Force 38 from the termination of fueling operations on the 17th, to the evening of the 18th. In the course of his testimony, he indicated that: CTF 38 advised Commander Third Fleet, at 0430 on the 18th, that there was little possibility of fueling from the oilers; at 0500 Commander Third Fleet canceled the morning rendezvous, "and ordered all units to take 180° T"; at 0555 CTF 38 gave Commander Third Fleet his estimate of the location of the storm's center as 12°30' N; 131°00' E, and estimated it to be moving northwest at a speed of 12 to 15 knots. Thus the OTC, at 0555 on the 18th, provided the fleet commander with an estimate of the storm's location and track that placed its center about 200 miles to the southeast. It indicated that the Third Fleet could expect to collide with the outer periphery of the disturbance in a matter of a few hours. Commander Hean also noted a change of course to 150° T at 0616, which headed the fleet almost directly at the approaching storm. He stated that that course was changed at 0710 to 060° T, and speed set at 10 knots for fueling. Commander Third Fleet's message to cease fueling was received by CTF 38 at 0802, and course was changed to 180° T at 0806.[6]

The task group commander of Task Group 38.1 was Rear Admiral Montgomery, embarked in the carrier *Yorktown*. On 26 December he was injured while getting into a boat and had to be hospitalized on the USS *Solace*. He therefore was not available to testify before the court of inquiry, and Captain John B. Moss, his chief of staff, was called as a witness instead. When asked whether he had at all times had a clear picture of the nature and movement of the storm, Moss replied that CTG 38.1 had all of the information disseminated by the Fleet Weather Central (at Pearl Harbor), as well as the opinion of the aerologist of the *Yorktown*, and that both sources of information had given accurate estimates of the storm's location. (This appears to be inconsistent with testimony by Third Fleet staff representatives.) He also indicated that no specific orders were issued to prepare for the storm.[7]

Task Group 38.2 was under the command of Rear Admiral Gerald F. Bogan, embarked in the carrier *Lexington*. (The carrier *Hancock*, flagship of Vice Admiral McCain, was also a unit of TG 38.2.) Admiral Bogan testified that during fueling operations on the 17th, the *Lexington*'s aerologist reported to him that a cyclonic storm was forming to the northeast. Bogan further indicated that at about 1500 on the 17th, the Pearl Harbor weather summary was received showing a "severe cyclonic storm" only about 160 miles away, in approximately the same location as that estimated by the *Lexington*'s aerologist. After receipt of the Pearl Harbor weather summary, Bogan reviewed the rendezvous point selected by Commander Third Fleet for the next morning and advised Commander Task Force 38 (information to the fleet commander) that improved conditions would be found farther to the south.[8]

Rear Admiral Frederick C. Sherman, in the carrier *Essex*, was the Commander of Task Group 38.3. When called as a witness, he said that he had not received timely warning of the storm's approach, but that on the 17th his staff aerologist reported a typhoon 500 miles to the northeast. In the light of the wind's direction, its increasing intensity, and the falling barometer, Sherman estimated the storm to be not to the northeast, but "to the southeast and much closer than 500 miles." He also stated that although he was "not particularly happy over the last rendezvous," he did not convey that reaction to any higher authority.[9]

The court called Captain Jasper T. Acuff, Commander Task Group 30.8, as a witness. As previously noted, Acuff was embarked in the *Aylwin*. He outlined the disposition of the oiler units, the task unit assignments of the *Hull*, *Spence*, and *Monaghan*, and the directives received from higher authority until 1127 on the 18th, at which time the *Aylwin* lost all power. (CTF 38, on learning that Acuff's flagship was in trouble, had directed the individual task unit commanders of TG 30.8 to take charge of their units and to follow the movements of CTF 38.) Acuff testified that he and the commanding officer of the *Nehenta Bay* discussed the location of the rendezvous point selected for the morning of the 18th while en route to it the night before. The two agreed that it did not look good, but Acuff, like Mercer, concluded that Commander Third Fleet "had better information than we had when he ordered the change in rendezvous." Accordingly, no question regarding the choice of rendezvous point was transmitted to the fleet commander.[10]

Preston Mercer, already designated as an "interested party," had reason to be personally concerned over the court's proceedings and its recommendations. He had been the OTC of the center oiler unit (TU 30.8.4). The *Spence* had been officially assigned to that unit on the 17th. At the time of her loss, the *Monaghan*, although not assigned to TU 30.8.4, had been in close physical proximity to Mercer's flagship, (the *Dewey*). Further, he was the squadron commander of the *Hull* and *Monaghan*, and in that role had heavy responsibilities for the state of training and the material condition of both ships. It was obvious that the court might raise questions, not only about his actions during the storm, but also about his performance of duty for several months prior to the 18th of December. It must have occurred to him that he might be asked whether there had been any indication of problems concerning the stability characteristics of *Farragut*-class destroyers prior to the storm. However, if any of these points worried him he gave no outward indication of it. I had the impression that he went off to participate in the court's proceedings with a perfectly clear conscience, confident that his actions before and during the storm would stand up under the closest scrutiny.

During the course of his testimony, Mercer stated that: when asked by Captain Acuff for his recommendation on the afternoon of the 17th, he had advised that fueling operations cease and that the task group move to the southwest; he obtained estimates from the three destroyers lowest in fuel that they could steam for another 24 to 48 hours at 15 knots; it was "recommended" that the three destroyers (*Spence*, *Hickox*, and *Maddox*) should ballast to 50 percent; he didn't like the change in rendezvous for the morning of the 18th, but since he had "no detailed aerological information" and had confidence in the judgment of his seniors, he did not protest. He covered the experience of the *Dewey* in considerable detail, generally consistent with the narrative set forth in chapter 7. With regard to the stability of the ships of Destroyer Squadron One, he noted that during the recent Navy Yard overhaul, he had vigorously resisted the addition of topside weight and was successful in obtaining new and lighter 20-mm gun mounts to replace those previously installed, with an attendant reduction in topside weight of about 3,250 pounds per ship. He also stated that during the Navy Yard period, the *Aylwin* had been inclined, and that her new metacentric height was determined by the shipyard to be 1.54 feet, a significant reduction from the 1.92 feet computed for the *Monaghan* when she was inclined in 1942. (It was standard practice to incline just one ship to determine the characteristics of her entire class. These statistics, therefore, were considered applicable to all *Farragut*-class destroyers at the time of the tests.) Mercer also noted that during its recent passage from Pearl Harbor to Ulithi, the second division of the squadron had rolled excessively (about 45 degrees in only moderate weather) and had found it necessary to slow and strike ammunition and other topside weights below. He noted that all commanding officers, and most of the officers and men who had been in the ships any length of time, were very much aware of their lack of stability and that it was a matter of constant concern. He made no mention of the *Dewey*'s postrepair trials, or of our mutual concern over her stability at that time, or of his call to BuShips requesting an inclining test prior to the ship's deployment. He stated that he had inspected the *Monaghan* on 25 November, and the *Hull* on 5 December, and had found their watertight integrity to be "up to a proper standard." He indicated his belief that "it was only due to the most extraordinary weather conditions and their lack of stability that the *Hull* and *Monaghan* were lost."[11]

Captain Mercer was specifically questioned concerning the commanding officers of his ships. The following verbatim extracts from his testimony are relevant:

Q. "Will you please compare the experience, capabilities as observed by you, of the commanding officers of the *Hull* and *Monaghan*, with the remaining commanding officers of your squadron?"

A. "The commanding officer of the *Monaghan* was in the squadron for such a very short time that I had practically no opportunity to make a sound estimate. He handled his ship well in formation, kept her on station in the screen, but that was the limit of my opportunity to observe him.

"The commanding officer of the *Hull* has been separated from his squadron a great deal. Likewise, when she was with us for a very short time, his ship was handled well, and I have no criticism whatever of his ability. The commanding officers of the *Dewey* and *Aylwin*, whose experiences are more pertinent than the other ships of the squadron, each had considerable advantage over the commanding officers of the *Monaghan* and *Hull*. The commanding officer of the *Dewey* previously commanded a four-stack destroyer for nearly a year. The commanding officer of the *Aylwin* was in the *O'Brien* when she sank, and had a very thorough course in damage control. The commanding officer of the *Hull* had served in the North Atlantic and experienced very heavy weather, and perhaps did not appreciate that the *Hull* was not as stable as previous destroyers in which he was embarked. I believe that the commanding officers of the *Monaghan* and *Hull* have at least average ability and judgment compared with their contemporaries."

Q. "How does the service experience of the commanding officers of your squadron compare with that of the commanding officers of other squadrons?"

A. "The commanding officers of the ships of my squadron are the most junior in destroyers, being of the Naval Academy Class of 1938. The commanding officer of the *Spence* was in the Class of 1937, and now there are a few commanding officers of the Class of 1938 in other destroyers."[12]

Preston Mercer also responded to a question from the judge advocate as to which destroyer squadron in the fleet was in his opinion the least stable, by stating that there was no question in his mind that it was Destroyer Squadron One. This concluded his testimony.[13]

When the survivors of the three lost ships were called to testify, narrative accounts of their loss, prepared in each case by the senior survivor, were read to them. With the exception of a few minor technical details, they stated that they had no objections to these narrative reports, and that they had nothing to lay to the charge of any officer or man with regard to the loss of their ships. The commanding officer of the *Hull* was asked if he had any complaint to make against any of the surviving officers and crew on the occasion of the loss of the ship. Jim Marks said that he did not. The record of proceedings notes that when it came time to hear the narrative of the loss of the *Hull*, the members of the court, the judge advocate, the parties to the inquiry and their counsel, and the surviving members of the crew of the *Hull*, all assembled in the pilot house of the *Cascade*. It is assumed that this was done to provide a setting similar to that which confronted Jim Marks in the pilot house of the *Hull*. It must have been a dramatic point in the proceedings.

Jim Marks read the narrative that formed the basis for the account contained in chapter 8. In the course of his testimony he made it clear that he was aware from the first time he went to sea in the *Hull* that her stability was very poor compared to his previous ship. He also stated that if he had been released to operate independently the morning of the 18th, he would have turned south immediately, and thus might have cleared the storm safely. He did not specifically mention his responsibility to remain in his screening station, but it should have been obvious to the court that he did not feel free to leave the formation.[14]

In the morning of 28 December, I received a message from the *Cascade*, directing me to report aboard at 1400 that day, to appear as a witness before the court of inquiry. I made the trip by whaleboat (our coxswain knew the way by that time, he'd been delivering Preston Mercer to the *Cascade* for three days) and arrived about a half-hour early. Bill Rogers was already there. We were seated in a large passageway outside the wardroom. Captain John Crawford, skipper of the cruiser *Miami*, and Commander Joe Wesson, skipper of the *Hickox*, were also waiting to testify. We learned that Commander Jim Farrin, the assistant maintenance officer on the staff of Commander Service Squadron Ten, was in with the court and had been there since 1300. We also learned that Admiral Halsey had appeared as a witness before the court that morning. The scuttlebutt was that Admiral Halsey had made the comment before going in to appear that he didn't know who should be court-martialed, himself or the Bureau of Ships, but that someone should be! It sounded like the sort of thing Admiral Halsey might have said, but the origin of the story was somewhat vague, and I took it with a grain of salt.

Commander Farrin completed his testimony at about 1415. Captain Crawford, Commander Wesson, and Bill Rogers were then called in that order. Each took about fifteen minutes to testify. I was called at about 1500. When I entered the wardroom I saw before me about a dozen people, all dressed in freshly laundered khaki uniforms and seated at a long table, half of them with their backs toward me. I was escorted by the marine orderly to a seat on the near side. The members of the court were to my left, and I noted that there were two vice admirals and one rear admiral, and that each of the former wore the gold wings of a naval aviator. I didn't focus on any of the faces, but saw Preston Mercer and Jim Marks sitting next to the members of the court. Everyone looked very serious, but Mercer smiled when I glanced at him. I took note of the green felt cover on the table and thought, "This is 'the long green table'!" (Being court-martialed in the Navy had long been referred to as "sitting at the end of a long green table.") A Marine colonel (later identified as Colonel Brooks) sat across from me. Four chief yeomen were seated to my right, all of them recording testimony as it was given. I was impressed by the somberness of the prevailing mood and also by the polite and almost friendly manner in which questions were posed. I found myself wondering whether Admiral Halsey's testimony had surprised them. Captain Gates swore me in, informed me of the subject matter of the inquiry, asked my name and present station, and then asked me to explain the cause of the *Dewey*'s electrical difficulties and what influence they may have had on the flooding of the engine room. Admiral Hoover asked me how far my ship had rolled. I responded as briefly as possible to these queries, summarizing the electrical damage, and indicating that I had personally witnessed the inclinometer rest against its stop at 73 degrees. By 1510 I was finished and had been excused. I felt that the court had asked perfunctory questions and that they contributed little of significance to the inquiry. Nevertheless, I assumed that Preston Mercer had covered the *Dewey*'s experience in considerable detail and reasoned that it probably would have been redundant to ask me to go through the same narrative. I never learned what any other witness said until I read the record of proceedings for the first time in October 1978.

Admiral Halsey's testimony provides a comprehensive summary of the Third Fleet's experience, and is quoted verbatim from the record:

Q. "Admiral, did you consider that you had timely warning or did you know that a severe storm was approaching around the 16th and 17th of December?"

A. "I did not have timely warning. I'll put it another way. I had no warning."

Q. "There has been testimony from other commanders that the local conditions indicated the approach of the storm. Was that evident to you?"

A. "The local conditions commencing on the 17th were very bad. So bad that I ordered the destroyers that were alongside the tankers and heavy ships to clear. A disturbance was indicated,

but whether it was a severe storm or merely a local disturbance, there was no way of determining. We still thought it
was a storm that had curved away to the northward and
eastward, and we determined to get away from it."

Q. "When fueling had to be stopped on the 17th of December due
to increasing bad weather, what were your considerations?"

A. "The general picture was sour. I had numerous destroyers
that were very short of fuel that had to get fuel on board. We
endeavored to fuel by the astern method. This did not work for
many reasons, the main one being lack of rigging on tankers
for fueling astern. I was under obligation to make a strike on
Luzon, but of course a strike could not be made until the fleet
was fueled. I was also obligated to avoid by that time what I
considered a storm the magnitude of which I did not know. On
several previous occasions we had had a fairly good track of
typhoons and were able to keep on the outer fringe. . . . I got
but one report, as I remember, of a possible disturbance, and
that came from the *Chandeleur* and it was obtained by one of
her planes. The report was some 12 to 14 hours late in arriving, due to being a mere routine report and did not agree with
the aerologist's position, of what he termed at that time a
tropical disturbance. Up to the forenoon of 18 December,
when an unsuccessful attempt had been made to fuel, I was
still under the impression that the tropical disturbance would
curve to the northward and the eastward and its severity was
not indicated."

Q. "At what time did the storm considerations begin to govern
the disposition and movement of the fleet, if at all?"

A. "On the forenoon of the 18th, it was very definitely apparent
that we were very close to a violent disturbance of some kind,
which I believed was a typhoon. We were completely cornered
and in the dangerous semicircle. The consideration then was
the fastest way to get out of the dangerous semicircle and get
to a position where our destroyers could be fueled."

Q. "During the night of the 17th a number of rendezvous were
selected. Do you know the circumstances under which those
changes were made?"

A. "To my recollection we took a generally westerly course up to
midnight. We had decided that we would go to the southward
and westward for a fueling rendezvous. We later changed that
to the northward and westward so that we would be in a better
position to strike Luzon on time. That thought of striking
Luzon was uppermost in our heads right up to the last minute."

Q. "What seemed to be wrong with the weather service in this case?"

A. "It was nonexistent. That's the only way I can express it. After the horse was out of the stable we established a system so that such a thing couldn't happen again. Heretofore we had always received reports. This time there was one report of a disturbance that came in. As I recollect, the only report that was brought to my attention was a report from the *Chandeleur*. These reports are brought back by planes to the base and analyzed at the base and sent out on the normal circuits, usually 12 to 24 hours late. It is the first time in the four months that I've been operating in this area that I haven't had reports to enable us to track a storm. The Third Fleet was the first to report the storm."

Q. "Admiral, is it your belief now, in the light of subsequent events, that this cyclonic disturbance developed independent of the former weather reports of a disturbance?"

A. "No, I believe that the two disturbances are identical."

Q. "You have stated that you felt the storm was curving to the northeast. Do you know the basis on which this idea was formed?"

A. "I am no weather expert. There was a front to the northward of the tropical disturbance, extending as I recall it, in a northeast and southwest direction. There was also a high-pressure area coming down from the China coast and moving to the southward. My aerologist expected the disturbance to impinge on this front and be deflected to the northward and eastward. Because of the position of the high-pressure area moving to the southward, he expected this pressure area to aid and accelerate this deflection. Tropical disturbances generating in the equatorial belt, due to the motion of air over the earth's surface and the consequent motion of air, tend to curve to the northward and eastward. This disturbance, as we had it plotted, was north of the equatorial belt. There have been numerous storms during the four months I have been operating in this area, and without exception they have followed this general rule. In addition, my aerologist informed me that in a study of past typhoons during the month of December, three out of four curved to the northward and eastward. Lacking definite knowledge of the movement of the storm I was governed by the above considerations."

Q. "Had you any idea there were any vessels in your force that were very low in stability [and] that were low on fuel?"

A. "Having spent a great many years in destroyers and having been in some very severe weather in ships ranging from 160 tons to 1,200 tons, I knew there had been grave doubts as to their stability from time to time, particularly when in a light condition. I believe that some time before we got into the worst of this storm we sent out a general signal advising everybody to ballast down.[15] I had been on a 1,200-ton destroyer when they first put the 5-inch guns on the outboard side of the galley deckhouse and had them roll considerably, but never had one turn over. In this connection, of the three destroyers that were lost, two of them, the *Hull* and *Monaghan*, I have been told without checking, had about 75 percent of their fuel on board. The *Spence* was very low on fuel."

Q. "What caused you to discontinue fueling on the morning of the 17th?"

A. "The USS *Spence* came along the starboard side of the *New Jersey* for fuel. The exact time she was alongside I am not sure of. However, she had a hose line on board and that was broken once or twice. She was riding away up ahead and she'd drop well astern and charge ahead and drop astern. Of course, during this time she was pitching and rolling heavily. The estimates from the *New Jersey* are less than 1,000 gallons of fuel were transferred. Some one-and-a-half hours after the *Spence* came along the starboard side of the *New Jersey*, the USS *Hunt* came along the port side. Before discontinuing fueling, the *Hunt* had received 23,000 gallons of fuel. She also carried away the hose line. I gave the order to discontinue fueling because of what I considered a very grave danger of damage to the *Spence* in her endeavor to fuel."

Q. "Comparing the conditions of the 17th fueling with those of the early morning of the 18th, what is your estimate of the weather conditions?"

A. "On the morning of the 17th I was under the impression that we were on the fringes of a disturbance. On the morning of the 18th there was no doubt in my mind that we were approaching a storm of major proportions and that it was almost too late to do anything."[16]

Both Captain Mercer and Jim Marks declined the opportunity to further question Admiral Halsey. He was informed that he could make any additional statement that he wished concerning anything related to the subject matter of the inquiry, which in his opinion should be made a matter of record. He replied that he had nothing further to add. He was duly warned not to discuss the proceedings of the court. Admiral Halsey informed the court that he "had an interest" in the subject matter of the inquiry, in that he was the fleet commander. In other words, he designated himself as an interested party. He regretted that he would be unable to be present during the inquiry and therefore waived his right to be present. He requested that he be allowed to be represented by counsel. This request was granted, and he withdrew.[17]

CHAPTER 14

Weather Forecasting

One of the most important aspects of the investigation was that which concerned the fleet commander's weather forecasting service. This chapter will deal with that function as it was presented to the court. Relevant facts that were not made known during the investigation, but which have come to light in researching this book, will be dealt with later in the critique (chapter 17).

Immediately after they heard the testimony of Rear Admiral Carney and Captain Wilson, the court of inquiry called Commander George F. Kosco, the Third Fleet's aerological officer, as a witness. Apparently they wanted a first-hand account from Admiral Halsey's weather man as to precisely what had gone wrong. It was obvious that something had.

Commander Kosco graduated from the Naval Academy in 1930. After his commissioning he served six years at sea, followed by three years at MIT, where he was awarded a master of science degree in aerology. He then served two years in carriers, followed by two years ashore in aerological assignments. During his tour ashore he had spent three months in the West Indies doing special hurricane research, flying into and around hurricanes in order to determine their characteristics. At the time of the typhoon he had been the Third Fleet's aerological officer for about one month. He was considered to be the most experienced aerologist in the Third Fleet.[1]

Kosco's testimony made it clear that he relied heavily on radio weather reports for his basic forecast data. He explained that the first indication of the storm's existence came on the morning of the 16th, when reports from Guam and Ulithi showed force 4 winds (from 11 to 16 knots) from the east southeast and the west, respectively. He reported to Admiral Halsey that he suspected a tropical storm was forming somewhere between Ulithi and Guam, but that it was a weak disturbance. He also indicated that he expected it to collide with a frontal system and change course to the northeast. This prediction was based in part on the history of previous typhoons. Usually there was only one in December, and, said Kosco, for the past fifty years 75 percent of those storms had passed off to the northeast. The remainder had moved west into the Philippines.[2]

On the night of the 16th, Kosco noted that Pearl Harbor's weather report showed a weak tropical storm, and that it was located between Ulithi and Guam, confirming his own analysis. Again he reported to Admiral Halsey, and this time also to the chief of staff, that he didn't think the disturbance would cause any trouble for the Third Fleet.[3]

Kosco said that on the 17th he reviewed earlier aircraft weather reports received from Kwajalein, Pearl Harbor, and Saipan. They seemed to show a definite cyclonic pattern of wind circulation, and he estimated the storm to be at 15° north and 136° or 137° east. (This would have placed it about 380 miles east of the flagship.) When the fleet encountered bad weather on the 17th, he assumed it was from the frontal system he had predicted the day before. He further noted that on the 17th the barometer, "went up for regular periods as it should from about four in the morning until ten, and then fell normally," and that the wind was backing from northeast to north. He concluded that they were "not going to be caught inside of it."

Kosco recounted the events that had occurred at about noon on the 17th, when he and others of the fleet staff were having lunch aboard the *New Jersey*, and the *Spence* was observed to be experiencing great difficulty remaining alongside. When Admiral Halsey got up from the table and commented that they had better terminate fueling operations, Kosco ran up to his office to see if he could determine what was happening to the weather. He concluded that they had to contend with a tropical storm, not a typhoon. He reviewed his weather maps again, and reported to the fleet commander that the disturbance was located at about 15° north and 138° east. (This would have placed it sixty miles farther away than his first estimate.) The fleet commander reported this position by radio at 1414, local time, to the Commander in Chief, Pacific, and to all task force and task group commanders of the Third Fleet.[5] A few hours later, Kosco realized that he had made an error in his estimate of the storm's location. He revised it on his own weather charts by moving the position of the storm center westward to about 15° north and 135° east, but the correction was not broadcast to CinCPac, or to the Third Fleet task force and task group commanders. The record does not disclose when, or if, Admiral Halsey was informed that the position he had sent out to the fleet was in error. The corrected position, as plotted on Kosco's weather map, was about 320 miles from the flagship's position, roughly 130 miles closer than the first estimate. The storm's actual location at 1800 on the 17th, as determined by post-typhoon analysis, was about 160 miles east southeast of the flagship.[6]

As the afternoon wore on, the weather continued to deteriorate. The fleet staff concluded that the disturbance was somewhere to the east southeast. Now they began to consider the avoiding action that would be required. Noting that the *Chandeleur*'s report, received at about 1500, placed the center at 13° north, 132° east, (about 180 miles east southeast of the *New Jersey*), Kosco recommended that they go southwest. He told the court that he feared that if they headed directly south they would collide with the storm center reported by the *Chandeleur*.[7]

Kosco said that with the wind from the north, backing to the northwest, it appeared that the flagship was in the safe semicircle. During the rest of the afternoon of the 17th, the fleet staff monitored radio weather broadcasts and tried to figure out what to do. They realized that they were evaluating the storm on the basis of very meager reports. It was also clear to them that they somehow had to avoid it. At the same time, they became concerned that they might get too close to Japanese air bases in the Philippines. They decided to establish a rendezvous point for the next morning that would put them in a better position from which to launch offensive strikes and at the same time reduce the threat of attack by shore-based enemy aircraft. The final morning rendezvous was established at 2220, with security from air attack one of the primary considerations. The need to move the fleet to the southwest to avoid the storm apparently had become a secondary factor.[8]

At about 2230 on the night of the 17th (only ten minutes after the final morning rendezvous point had been transmitted to the fleet) Kosco met in the flag mess with Rear Admiral Carney and Captain Wilson. They examined the weather maps and discussed the situation. They concluded that they had done all that could be done for the time being. Kosco departed and went to bed. At about 0230 on the 18th he awoke with the vague feeling that "something was wrong." He went up to his office to check the most recent radio weather reports. There didn't seem to be anything significant. He thought that the barometer "was going up and down as normal," and the wind was constantly shifting to the westward. He concluded that these were signs of the passage of a tropical storm.[9]

It was Kosco's turn to take the staff watch from four to eight that morning. At about 0330 he proceeded to flag plot to relieve the watch. The staff watch officer told him that Admiral Halsey was up. Kosco decided that he'd better go inform him of the status of the weather. He told the admiral that the storm was increasing in intensity, and that their present northwesterly course would head them right into it! (They had turned northwest to head for the morning rendezvous.) Admiral Halsey sent for Rear Admiral Carney and Captain Wilson. They sat in the wardroom and examined the weather map. Kosco pointed out his estimate of the storm's track as it related to the fleet's position. Halsey asked what he recommended. Kosco told him that he thought they should turn south immediately. Kosco then left to relieve the watch. Shortly thereafter the admiral called him on the telephone and asked him to get Vice Admiral McCain's estimate of the storm's position. Kosco called McCain and relayed the question to him. McCain's only response was to say that he wasn't going to be able to fuel. (The record does not indicate whether Halsey was ever told of McCain's concern that he wouldn't be able to fuel.) Having gotten no indication of where the task force commander thought the storm was, Kosco called Rear Admiral Bogan, and asked him the same question. Bogan said he thought the storm was at 17° north, 131° east. (About 220 miles northeast of the flagship.) Kosco's estimate at that time placed it at 15° north and 131° east. (About 200 miles east of the flagship.)[10]

Meanwhile, Commander Task Force 38 apparently heard the exchange with Bogan and realized that he had failed to answer Kosco's earlier question. He called back, and reported that he thought the storm was at 12½° north and 131° east. This would have put it about 240 miles southeast of the flagship. (As later reconstructed by the aerology section of the office of the chief of naval operations, the storm center at that time was about 90 miles east-southeast of the *New Jersey*.) Both McCain and Bogan said they estimated it was on a northwesterly track at about 12 knots. The actual track was later determined to have been 290° T, at a speed of about 15 knots.[11]

Kosco now informed the staff that he thought his estimate of the storm's location was the best of the three, because it was more consistent with local weather signs. He figured that if the storm was to the north of his estimate they were no longer in danger, but that if it was to the south of it, they were. However, after turning to the south it was apparent from the wind's continued shifting to the west that they were in the navigable semicircle. Kosco advised the staff to hold the southerly course.[12]

Continuing his testimony, Kosco stated that when the fleet tried to fuel and headed back on a course of 060°, he indicated (it is not clear to whom) that the northeasterly course was going to take them back into the path of the storm. He commented to the court: "But one hour couldn't have made much difference—ten miles—we might have missed it by two or three miles less, and we were making slow speed and the destroyers needed fuel."[13] Then he noted that by eight or nine o'clock it had become clear that they were not dealing with a tropical storm, but were becoming engulfed in a typhoon. He estimated that it was increasing speed from about 5 knots to 20 or 25 knots, and that it was proceeding on a westerly course. At 0915 the fleet commander sent a message to the fleet, giving the position of the flagship, as well as the correct location of the storm.[14] The message also reported that the storm was increasing in intensity, (by then it was painfully self-evident), and that it was moving to the northwest, but might possibly move westward into the Philippines. (It seems apparent that neither Kosco nor Admiral Halsey were convinced by 0915 that the storm was a typhoon, since their message made no mention of it. However, the erroneous position of the storm, which had been broadcast at 1414 the day before, had been corrected at last, nineteen hours later!)

Kosco went on to say that the barometer wasn't doing anything definite until about 1000, when it began to fall very rapidly. (The deck log of the New Jersey shows readings of 29.52 at 1000, and 29.23 at 1400.) He noted that the flagship changed course to the southeast and began to ride more comfortably. He mentioned the fact that they sent a typhoon warning at 1300 and commented, "Until that time we had thought we were dealing with a tropical storm." Again he reiterated, "It was not apparent that the typhoon was forming. On the afternoon of the 17th, planes from carriers and search planes flew over the area and reported bad weather, but found nothing to be greatly excited about."[15] (But two planes from the Chandeleur had made in-flight reports, indicating that at least they thought they had found something to be excited about.)

Now it was time for members of the court to ask questions. They did, but the points raised were generally not very sharp. They asked Kosco whether he considered his sources of weather information adequate. He said that normally they were, but the typhoon had not been normal, and that they were inadequate for dealing with such conditions. They asked if there was a system for coordinating the information obtained by those ships having aerologists aboard, and whether the system had been employed during the period covering the typhoon. Kosco replied that there was such a system, and that he assumed it had been employed. Asked if he received information from all other fleet units having aerological equipment or personnel aboard, he said he did not. The court also asked if the operation plan required that units so equipped or staffed provide him with weather information. He said that it did not, unless the situation was

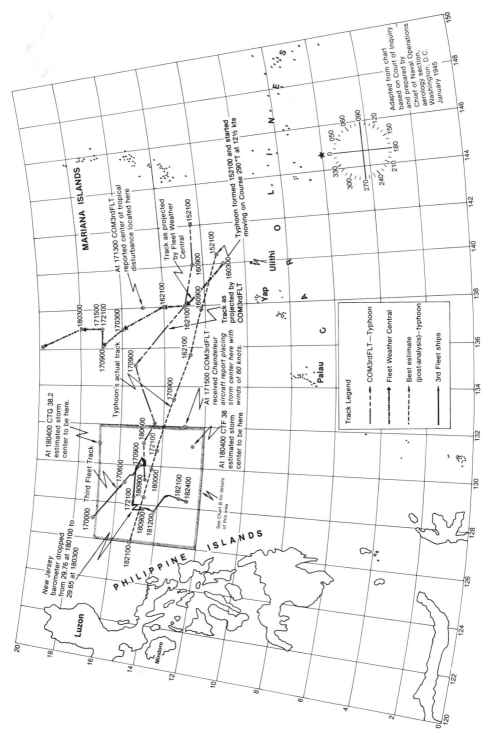

Chart A. Track of Typhoon 17–18 December 1944

Track Legend

COM3rdFLT—Typhoon	
Fleet Weather Central	
Best estimate (post-analysis)—typhoon	
3rd Fleet ships	

MARIANA ISLANDS

PHILIPPINE ISLANDS

Luzon

Mindoro

Palau

Yap

Ulithi

C   A   R   O   L   I   N   E   S

At 180400 CTG 38.2 estimated storm center to be here.

New Jersey barometer dropped from 29.76 at 180100 to 29.65 at 180300

Third Fleet Track

See Chart B for details of this area

At 180400 CTF 38 estimated storm center to be here

At 171500 COM3rdFLT received Chandeleur aircraft report placing storm center here with winds of 60 knots.

Track as projected by COM3rdFLT

Typhoon's actual track

At 171300 COM3rdFLT reported center of tropical disturbance located here

Track as projected by Fleet Weather Central

Typhoon formed 152100 and started moving on Course 290°T at 12½ kts

180300
171500
172100
170300
170900
170900
162100
162100
160900
160900
162100
170900
152100
152100
160300

170600
172100
170900
180600
172100
180000
180900
181200
182100
182400

Adapted from chart based on Court of Inquiry and prepared by Chief of Naval Operations aerology section, Washington, D.C. January 1945

000 010 020 030 040 050 060 070 080 090 100 110 120 130 140 150 160 170 180 190 200 210 220 230 240 250 260 270 280 290 300 310 320 330 340 350

deemed by the individual commanding officers and their task group commanders to warrant breaking radio silence. It is clear that the matter of breaking radio silence was not the governing factor. The commanding officers of those ships that were experiencing great difficulty in maintaining station had not hesitated to report by voice radio the actions they were taking. They did not report the specific weather conditions they were encountering because no one asked them to do so. It was generally assumed that those same weather conditions prevailed throughout the fleet. Their ships were a part of the fleet disposition, and they considered that they were in company with the fleet commander. There was no need to tell him about the weather, they reasoned; he was experiencing it, as they were.

Jim Marks now had the opportunity to question Kosco. He asked him to indicate the source of his weather reports, whether or not he received them according to plan, and if they were adequate. The court asked if Kosco could now plot the path of the storm. Kosco replied that he could track it accurately within 15 or 20 miles beginning with the morning of the 18th, but that previous to that time there was some doubt whether he could plot the track within 150 miles of its actual location. Finally, the court asked when Kosco first diagnosed the storm as a typhoon. Kosco replied that he made that diagnosis at about 0800 on the morning of the 18th, and that he had first sent that diagnosis to the other weather centrals at 1300 that day.[16] (No explanation was asked, nor was any offered, as to why, if the storm was identified as a typhoon at 0800, the fleet commander's message at 0915 made no mention of it.)

Preston Mercer did not question the witness. Kosco's testimony appeared to be at an end, and he withdrew. However, on the fourth day of the proceedings (December 29th), the court saw fit to recall him for further questioning. They had three specific queries: first they told him of Admiral Halsey's comment that he "had no warning" that a severe storm was approaching on the 16th and 17th of December. The court asked Kosco to account for that comment, in light of the fact that he was Admiral Halsey's aerological officer. Kosco replied that the admiral meant that he had received no warning of a severe storm, but that he did have a warning of a light, moderate storm in the area on both the 16th and 17th. Next, the court asked him to comment on Admiral Halsey's statement that the weather service "was nonexistent." Kosco explained that this storm had formed on top of the fleet, and that therefore there was no advance warning, as there had been in other storms that had formed some distance away. Finally, the court asked Kosco what weight he had given to Admiral Bogan's report at 1400 on the 17th

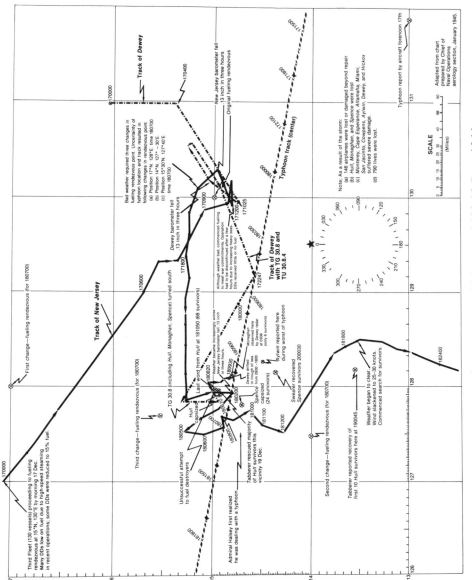

Chart B. Chronological summary of events, 0000 17 Dec. to 2400 18 Dec. 1944.

with regard to the storm's location and the recommendation that clear weather could be found to the south. Kosco answered that in the first place Bogan had not given the location of the storm in that message. He then added that the comment about heading south to find clear weather was very carefully considered; that it was rejected because of the *Chandeleur's* report of a storm center with 60 knot winds at 13° N and 132° E, which the Third Fleet staff judged they would encounter if they headed south. Kosco's testimony was finished. He was excused, and did not reappear before the court.[17]

Based on Kosco's account, and on information provided by weather charts and maps that he had submitted separately, the court of inquiry now had a comprehensive picture of the weather forecasting resources available to the Third Fleet. Of particular interest was the fleet weather broadcast, on which Kosco had placed so much reliance. It was sent four times daily from the Fleet Weather Central at Pearl Harbor, and was developed from data submitted by the outlying island stations in the Pacific. While this network provided a valuable service to the fleet, the location of its data-gathering points left large gaps in the vast ocean areas in which Pacific Fleet forces were operating. To fill those holes the Fleet Weather Central depended on supplementary weather observations by patrol aircraft, which were instructed to report weather conditions upon their return from the search flights that were their primary mission. When the patrol planes were able to provide data covering those ocean areas in which the fleet was operating, the Fleet Weather Central forecasts were of good quality. When such supplementary data was not forthcoming, the forecasts were spotty and unreliable for those areas that were unreported.[18]

On the fifth day of its proceedings (30 December 1944), the court called Commodore Dixwell Ketcham, the commander of Fleet Air Wing One, as a witness. They had been pondering the weather forecasting information obtained from Commander Kosco and others for the better part of five days. Now they wanted to know what orders had been in effect, at the time of the typhoon, governing the requirement for patrol aircraft to report weather conditions encountered during daily reconnaissance flights. Ketcham explained that every search mission beyond 75 miles was required to record hourly weather data, which was then submitted to the operations or weather office upon the plane's return to base. The base (usually a seaplane tender), then forwarded those observations by radio to Kwajalein, for retransmission with Priority precedence, to Fleet Weather Central Pearl Harbor and the weather stations at Manus and Saipan. The instructions also required that planes observing definite indications of a typhoon in their vicinity make an "in-flight" weather report using Operational Priority precedence, to the parent tender and to Commander Forward Area, Pearl Harbor, Manus, and Saipan. The parent tender then was required to forward that report to Commander Third Fleet if it was considered to be of sufficient importance. Ketcham indicated that there were no "special reports" (the "in-flight" variety) sent by his planes on the 15th or 16th of December. On the 17th, however, he said there had been two such reports by planes based at Kossol Passage (this was at Palau, in the Western Carolines, and was the location of the *Chandeleur*). The first report, from flight 9V440, sent at 170830 local time, gave winds of 57 to 65 knots from south, drizzle, visibility 500 to 1,000 yards, overcast, base of clouds 1,000 to 2,000 feet. The second report was from 21V440, sent at 171003 local time, and gave winds of 41 to 47 knots from northwest, visibility 500 to 1,000 yards, overcast, base of clouds 600 to 1,000 feet, with a thunderstorm. Ketcham did not relate the position of either reporting plane to the court, and no question was raised on that point. He went on to say that after receiving these two reports, the *Chandeleur*, at 171005 local time, sent to Commander Third Fleet (and others) a dispatch that reported a definite storm center with winds of 60 knots, at 13° N, 132° E. Commodore Ketcham also indicated that no orders were in effect at the time that would have prescribed special weather flights to search for storm centers. In other words, no flights were

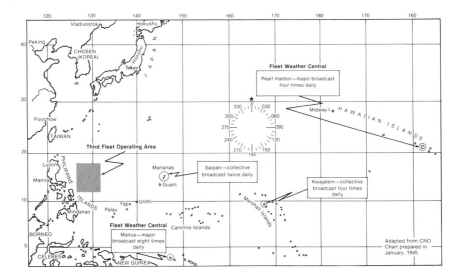

Weather Broadcasting Facilities, Pacific Ocean, December, 1944.

made to track and report on the movements of the storm center that had been located on the 17th.[19]

Still seeking answers to the complex weather problems that had confronted the fleet, and more importantly, the manner in which the fleet responded to them, the court now called as a witness Captain Wilbur M. Lockhart, the aerological officer on the staff of the Commander in Chief, Pacific. They asked him to provide a brief description of the weather in the Western Pacific from 15 to 18 December, as he had seen it from the vantage point of Pearl Harbor. Lockhart told of the confused weather picture in the Philippine Sea area that prevailed at Fleet Weather Central throughout the period in question. At 1200 Greenwich time on the 15th (Philippine Sea time is nine hours later), reports from Guam and Ulithi indicated "the possibility" of a "small disturbance" forming at 10° north, 141½° east (about 200 miles east of Yap). Fleet Weather Central's broadcast at 1800 Greenwich time on the 15th consolidated the Guam and Ulithi reports and passed them along to the fleet as a weak disturbance centered at 11° N and 140° E, (about 140 miles northeast of Yap) moving north-northwest at 12 to 15 knots. Twenty-four hours later, lacking any amplifying reports, Fleet Weather Central advanced the location of the disturbance on the basis of an educated guess. They placed it at 16° north, 137° east (about 240 miles north-northwest of Yap) moving north-northwest at 12 knots. Ocean area supplemental coverage on the 16th consisted of only one plane report from approximately 12½° N and 138½° E (about 180 miles north of Yap) that showed indications of a typhoon. However, the area within a radius of 600 miles to the northwest of that point was void of any reports. Fleet Weather Central personnel apparently were reluctant to accept the aircraft report without some additional verifying data. At 0000 Greenwich time on the 17th, the broadcast from Pearl Harbor indicated that the storm center had moved north-northwest, to 17° N, 137° E. (This was about 460 miles north-northwest of Yap, and 250 miles northeast of the storm's actual position.) About five hours later, the Third Fleet's storm report was received at Pearl Harbor. This was the message that placed the *New Jersey* at 14°59′ N, 130°08′ E, with a barometer reading of 29.71 and falling steadily, and forecast a tropical storm of increasing intensity at 15° N, 138° E, (about 330 miles north of Yap) moving north-northwest at 12 to 15 knots, with a predicted track recurving to the northeast. Fleet Weather Central personnel did not concur with the Third Fleet forecast, and considered sending a new report to correct it. However, they decided "it would rile the waters too much" to challenge the fleet commander's estimate, and they took no corrective action. It is not at all clear what estimated storm position they would have broadcast had they issued a correction, for their own projected track was grossly in error up to that point, with a movement much farther to the north than the storm's actual track. Not until 0600 Greenwich time on the 18th did Fleet Weather Central send a corrected estimate of the storm's position. It was, of course, too late. By that time the Third Fleet's battle with the typhoon was almost over.[20]

The court did not question Captain Lockhart concerning the aircraft report received by Fleet Weather Central on the 16th, which showed indications of a typhoon located north of Yap, nor was there any testimony as to what had been done to verify or further investigate that report. Lockhart noted that the Third Fleet's aerologists appeared to have overlooked the possibility that the storm might move to the west instead of the northwest; that "the actual weather was not read properly"; and that, "too much weight was given to a forecast from four or five thousand miles away" (referring to that from Fleet Weather Central). Lockhart also noted that the forecaster, "may have had more confidence in the Weather Central at Pearl Harbor than he had in himself." He concluded his testimony by responding to a final question by the court. Asked what would have happened if the fleet had headed to the southwest instead of the west after fueling on the 17th, he stated that, "If they had headed southwest at 10 knots or more they would have been in the safe semicircle and by hindsight would have been clear of the high winds as the storm center would have been at least 100 miles to the north of them."[21]

In chapter 13, the testimony provided by the task group commanders, as well as the commanding officers of several of the damaged ships, indicated that most of them were aware of the threat of a severe storm. All seemed to understand that weather conditions were steadily deteriorating from about midmorning of the 17th. Some suspected on the 17th that the local weather signs pointed to the approach of a typhoon. To be more specific: Captain John Moss told the court that Task Group 38.1 had ample information and warning concerning the storm; Rear Admiral Bogan, (CTG 38.2) testified that he had timely warning, and that he knew a severe cyclonic storm was approaching on the 17th; Rear Admiral Sherman, (CTG 38.3) stated that he was aware on the 17th that there was a typhoon to the southeast and that it was much closer than the 500 miles his aerologist had told him separated the storm from their position. As he drew near the end of his testimony, Sherman was asked if he had any observations that might assist the court. He replied, "Without meaning any particular criticism of our present-day acrologists, I'm inclined to think that they have been brought up to depend on a lot of readings they get from other stations. I think they are much weaker than the older officers in judging the weather by what they actually see. Whether anything can be done along these lines to either encourage or instruct them to watch weather that is then existing without waiting for reports from Pearl Harbor or other stations, I don't know. I think they should be taught to judge the weather by what they actually see."[22]

Among the individual ship commanding officers who testified, a few made very positive statements concerning their own analysis of the weather. Captain Ingersoll of the *Monterey* said, "We knew that a typhoon was somewhere around our area on the 17th, but the plot on the storm was certainly not very good. . . ."[23] Captain DeBaun of the *Cowpens* testified, "The weather followed the book description of a typhoon. We had swells, increasing winds, barometer dropped, all of that. A very good example of what is written up in Knight's *Seamanship*."[24] While DeBaun indicated that he was certain of the existence of the typhoon at 0800 on the 18th, it appears that he suspected its existence on the 17th, even though his aerologist repeatedly insisted that it was not a typhoon. Captain Kernodle, skipper of the *San Jacinto*, stated, "I received warnings continuously for 24 hours before I got into the storm, from my aerographer, from the action of the ship, and condition of the sea. I was fully aware of the storm and that it was going to be severe."[25]

Testimony by other commanding officers concerning the heavy-weather precautions that they took on the 17th strongly suggests that they too were aware of the approach of a typhoon the day before it struck. In most cases, they were not asked when they first became aware that they were going to have to battle a typhoon, but their preparatory actions provided eloquent testimony that they were readying their ships for more than the ordinary tropical storm.

The lack of supplementary weather observations by aircraft made it almost impossible for the Fleet Weather Central at Pearl Harbor to forecast the weather for the vicinity of the Philippine Sea with even a fair degree of accuracy. The weather broadcasts in some cases may have been worse than no broadcasts at all, because some aerologists in the fleet seemed to depend on them, and therefore gave too little attention to local weather indicators that would have been much more accurate.

To summarize, the three task force group commanders were at least aware that the threatening storm might be a typhoon. They were uncertain as to its location, but in no doubt as to its severity.

Several individual ship commanding officers were able to diagnose the approach of a typhoon on the 17th, using only the tools at hand. By contrast, the performance of the Third Fleet staff with regard to weather analysis was not very good. The court did not seek to highlight the comparison. Had they done so, the record of proceedings would have presented a picture that would have been even more damaging to the case of the fleet commander.

CHAPTER 15

Stability

Those characteristics of design that forecast how far the *Hull*,
Monaghan, and *Spence* could roll without capsizing were crucial to
any determination of why they were lost. It therefore seems remarkable that out of 167 pages of testimony that comprise the record of
proceedings of the court of inquiry, only seven were devoted to the
subject of destroyer stability. It seems even more remarkable when
one considers that the members of the court, by reason of their rank
and breadth of experience, probably were quite familiar with the
troubled history of naval ship design. It is of some relevance to
understand that history and to keep it in mind as the court's investigation is reviewed in a later chapter.

The design of ships, and the question as to which bureau of the
Navy Department had the primary responsibility for it, had been
the cause of controversy ever since the shift from sail to steam,
which began with the Civil War. The Bureau of Construction and
Repair shared the responsibility for ship design with the Bureau of
Engineering. Since the two bureaus frequently disagreed, several
Secretaries of the Navy tried to combine them, and thus eliminate
the cause of conflict. Starting in 1863, and again in 1886, 1899, and
1909, unsuccessful attempts were made to consolidate the two
bureaus. Failing to achieve their objective, the proponents of con-
solidation retreated and fell silent. For about twenty-five years an
uneasy truce prevailed. Little was heard on the subject until 1934,
when questions regarding the design of *Farragut*-class destroyers
resurrected the same old conflicts. Tension and animosity sim-
mered beneath the surface until 1940, when it was discovered that
the *Mahan*-class destroyers, which were next off the building ways
after the *Farragut*s, were top-heavy. The resulting interbureau battle was not resolved until the Secretary of the Navy, the Congress,
and the President of the United States all became actively involved.
The Bureau of Construction and Repair and the Bureau of Engineering finally were abolished. Congress established the Bureau of Ships
in their place on 20 June 1940. The matter of ship design was placed

entirely in the hands of the new bureau. Conflicts regarding the stability of destroyers were thus assumed to have been settled at last!

Since the responsibility for destroyer stability was at the core of the controversy, it would be logical to assume that the Chief of the Bureau of Ships and all of his principal subordinates, from the day the new bureau was established, were especially sensitive to questions regarding destroyer design. The need to delineate precisely who was responsible for monitoring the whole matter of destroyer stability (not only the initial design characteristics, but changes in those characteristics caused by shipyard alterations) should have been one of the first orders of business. Meanwhile, the fact that the *Farragut* class had marginal stability must have been common knowledge within the Bureau of Ships, and to some degree within the Pacific Fleet, beginning in 1942. (The *Farragut*s were discovered to be unacceptably top heavy and were given a "quick-fix" by removing one of their five-inch gun mounts at that time.) Now, only two years later, a court of inquiry was engaged in investigating the loss of three destroyers, two of which (the *Hull* and *Monaghan*) were *Farragut*s. Questions regarding the adequacy of destroyer design and the degree of responsibility of the Bureau of Ships for the loss of the three vessels must have occurred to the members of the court. Yet in the entire course of the investigation, no representative of the Bureau of Ships was called by the court to testify, and no questions were raised that sought to clarify the bureau's role as it pertained to the stability of the lost destroyers.

On Thursday morning 28 December 1944, Commander James M. Farrin, Jr., the assistant maintenance officer on the staff of Commander Service Squadron Ten (based at Ulithi) was called as an expert witness. (A brief explanation of the theory of ship stability is contained in Appendix 1.) The court was aware that the most commonly used indices of stability were the values of the metacentric height and the maximum righting arm. Farrin explained that of the two, the value of the maximum righting arm was the more dependable index. He testified that on the basis of data obtained from the *Monaghan*'s inclining test in 1942, the maximum righting arm in light condition (without fuel, water, stores, ammunition, men and their effects) was 0.6 foot, and the angle of inclination at which the value of the righting moment reached zero (the range of stability) was 52 degrees. Light service condition included fuel, one-half the capacity of water, one-third the capacity of stores, ammunition, and men and their effects. The 1942 inclining test data showed a maximum righting arm of 1.05 feet and a range of stability of 68 degrees

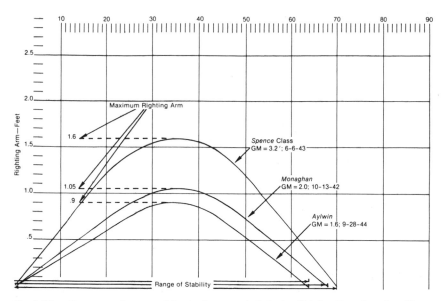

Stability Curves—*Spence, Monaghan* and *Aylwin*. (Light Service Condition Only)

with light service loading. Next, Farrin compared these values with those of the 2,100 ton *Fletcher* class, for which the corresponding figures were 1.2 feet (maximum righting arm) and a 65-degree range of stability in light condition, and 1.8 feet, 74 degrees, respectively, for light service condition. The metacentric heights for the *Fletcher*s were between 3.06 and 3.48 feet, roughly twice that of the *Farragut*s. Since the *Spence* was one of the *Fletcher* class, and for all practical purposes had no ballast on the morning of the typhoon, it appears that her range of stability (or maximum roll without capsizing) would have been closer to the 65 degrees of light load, than to the 74 degrees applicable to light service condition.[2] (See the Stability Curves—*Spence, Monaghan, Aylwin*.)

Commander Farrin explained: "For a ship subject to dynamic action in a seaway, the important consideration is the ability of the ship's stability to absorb the work done upon the ship by external forces of wind and sea. . . . From data given . . . on values of displacement, righting arm, and range, it may be seen that *Farragut*-class vessels have very much less ability to absorb dynamic forces than have the 2,100-ton and 2,200-ton destroyers. It may likewise be seen that the amount of energy which a ship in light condition may absorb is very much less than in fully loaded condition. . . . When damaged, or when free water has been admitted,

GM [metacentric height], righting arm, and range of stability are greatly reduced."[3]

The court asked Commander Farrin his opinion as to what might have caused the loss of the three destroyers. He replied: "In my opinion, the capsizing of these vessels was due to insufficient dynamic stability to absorb the combined effects of wind and sea. I would expect that, at least in the case of the *Spence*, stability should have been sufficient in the absence of free surface. . . . Failure to ballast in compensation for fuel used would also be a contributing factor. In the case of the *Hull* and *Monaghan*, with their dynamic stability appreciably less than the *Spence*, I consider it a possibility that the capsizing could have taken place without extensive free surface. Momentary synchronism of the encountered waves with the natural period of the ship would cause the amplitude of roll to build up quite rapidly."[4]

Farrin then was asked several questions about ballasting and the structural strength of destroyers in typhoon seas. He indicated that existing instructions for ballasting differed according to the class of vessel, but that generally speaking, *Farragut*-class destroyers would have been required to have a total of only 275 tons of fuel and water on board. Their total capacity of fuel oil was 607 tons. (Both the *Hull* and *Monaghan* were carrying in excess of 70 percent of their total fuel capacity, or about 450 tons, at the time of their loss.) Turning to the 2,100-ton *Fletcher*s, Farrin noted that their fuel capacity was 492 tons, and the ballasting instruction would have required the *Spence* to have about 200 tons of fuel and water ballast, or about 40 percent of capacity on board. As noted earlier, she had less than 15 percent when she encountered the storm. When it was pointed out that his estimates of *Farragut*-class stability characteristics were based on the *Monaghan*'s inclining test of 1942, he was asked what difference it would have made if he had based his computations instead on the *Aylwin*'s inclining test of September 1944. The value of the metacentric height for the latter was 1.54 feet, versus the 1.92 feet for the *Monaghan*'s earlier test. Farrin was unable to give a precise answer to this question, except to say that it indicated a condition of stability that was considerably less favorable. Finally, recalling the reports by other witnesses that the *Monaghan* had suffered structural failures, the court asked Farrin if he knew of any structural defects in the *Farragut*s, or if he thought that the *Monaghan* would have been expected to suffer structural failures under the conditions in which she found herself. To both of these he gave a negative reply, although he was hardly in a position to respond to the latter question, since he could not possibly have known what those conditions were. His testimony concluded, Farrin was excused and withdrew.[5]

On Sunday, December 31st, apparently feeling that they needed more detailed information regarding the stability of the *Spence*, the court called as a witness Lieutenant Commander John M. Court, also an assistant maintenance officer on the staff of Service Squadron Ten. It is apparent that he had been instructed to gather information about the *Spence* prior to his appearance. He stated that on the basis of his study he had concluded that the lack of fuel alone would not have caused the *Spence* to capsize. He then explained the effects of extensive free water in the bilges. (See Exhibit 16 from the Record of Proceedings that is shown below.) He had no specific estimate of the amount of free water actually present in the bilges of the *Spence*, but he noted that most of the other destroyers in the storm had reported at least a foot of water in their engine and fireroom bilges, and therefore assumed that the *Spence* may have had as much as one or two feet of it. He pointed out that one foot of water in her bilges would have given her a maximum righting arm of 1.35 feet, and that loss of positive righting arm (the point beyond which she would capsize) would have occurred at an angle of about 64 degrees. Two feet of water in the bilges would have decreased the maximum righting arm to 0.8 foot, and loss of positive righting arm

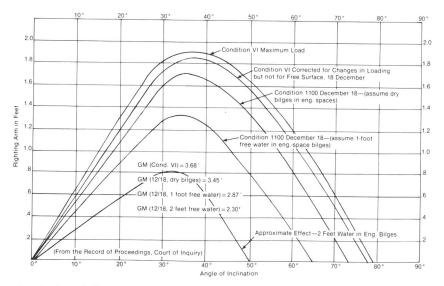

Statical Stability Curves—*Spence.*

then would have occurred at 50 degrees of inclination. Having presented this hypothesis to the court, he was asked what, in his opinion, had caused the capsizing of the *Spence*. He replied: "It was certainly contributed to by the condition of loading of fuel tanks. However, this factor alone could not explain the failure of the ship to right itself from an angle of 60 degrees. The effect of the wind, which I understand was estimated variously between 110 and 120 knots, is a factor that I have no accurate means of estimating. The fact that the ship was in the trough of the sea and subject to a form of rolling which builds up rather than counteracting further rolling, is also a factor which cannot be accurately computed. In other words, the natural tendency of the ship to roll in ever-increasing amplitude must be added to the effect of the wind as an incalculable. Both of these incalculable factors tend to reduce the effectiveness of the designed stability. It is my opinion that free water in the bilges contributed as much as did the lack of fuel to the failure of the ship to remain upright."[6] It was clear that no single factor could be cited as the principal cause of the loss of the *Spence*.

The investigation of the stability aspects of the loss of three destroyers had been completed. No other witnesses were called to testify on the subject. No one raised the question as to whether the *Aylwin*'s inclining test in September of '44 had been recognized by BuShips as evidence that her stability was only marginal, or if it was so recognized, why the ship and her unit commander were not so informed.

CHAPTER 16

The Court's Findings, Opinions, and Recommendations

On 3 January 1945, after hearing the testimony of fifty-four witnesses, the court of inquiry concluded its work and adjourned to await the action of Fleet Admiral Nimitz. In eighty-four separate findings, covering twelve typewritten pages, the court described the pertinent facts relating to the Third Fleet's encounter with the typhoon. Since they are generally consistent with the facts already related in earlier chapters, they will not be repeated here. The court also listed sixty-three separate "Opinions," covering seven typewritten pages.[1] Because they provided the basis for the court's recommendations, they are summarized in the following paragraphs.

It was the court's opinion that: The fleet movements directed by Admiral Halsey after the advent of bad weather on the 17th were logical, but he should have ordered special weather flights and weather reports from ships to cover the critical area from which no weather reports were being received. The large errors made in predicting the storm's location and projected path were the responsibility of the Third Fleet Commander. The report of a storm center received from the *Chandeleur* at 1424 local time on the 17th should have been given principal weight in determining how to maneuver the fleet. Admiral Halsey was at fault in not broadcasting danger warnings to all vessels early in the morning of the 18th. The aerological talent assisting Admiral Halsey was inadequate. Instructions should have been issued to commanding officers and unit commanders as to the relative importance of maintaining position in the formation versus maneuvering to minimize damage from the storm. Damage and losses were aggravated by efforts to maintain fleet courses, speeds, and formations during the storm. The southerly course ordered by Admiral Halsey at about 0530 local time on the 18th was a sound decision. The courses steered by the fleet from about 0700 local time on the 18th (for more than an hour) brought the fleet closer to the storm and contributed to the disaster; the course of 060° that morning was an error in judgment on the part of

Vice Admiral McCain, who directed it, and Admiral Halsey, who permitted it. Insufficient weather data was available to Admiral Halsey to fix accurately the position of the storm on 16 and 17 December. The recommendation given to Admiral Halsey by his aerologist on the 17th, to head west until the situation clarified itself, was sound advice, as was also the recommendation given at 0430 local time on the 18th, to head south. Too much reliance was placed on the weather analysis broadcast by Fleet Weather Central, Pearl Harbor. Search planes have a primary mission to search for enemy forces, and therefore are not the best vehicle for obtaining weather reports.

With regard to damage and losses suffered by the *Monterey*, *Cowpens*, *San Jacinto*, *Cape Esperance*, *Altamaha*, *Nehenta Bay*, and *Kwajalein*, the court was of the opinion that: the ships were handled by their commanding officers in an acceptable manner during the typhoon; damage was directly attributable to the storm; no blame attached to any officer or man serving in any of those ships on 18 December 1944 for loss of life, damage to ships, loss of aircraft or damage thereto. In the case of the commanding officers of the *Cape Esperance* and *Altamaha*, the court addressed itself to the question of independent action expected of commanding officers, and Opinion number forty (40), applicable especially to the two commanding officers mentioned, expressed these general policy guidelines: Weather conditions at sea may become so severe as to require independent action by a junior without reference to his senior. Such a situation confronted the commanding officers of the *Cape Esperance* and *Altamaha* on the morning of the 18th, when they chose to ride out the typhoon on courses that led to excessively deep rolling of their ships, causing the loss of aircraft that were torn loose from their moorings. Under the circumstances, tha actions taken by the commanding officers were justified, and they should not be held responsible for loss of the aircraft.

With regard to aircraft losses in general, the court expressed the opinion that no blame attached to any commanding officer, officer, or man serving in the vessels of the Third Fleet in which these losses occurred.

The court's opinions continued, that: the damages sustained by the *Dewey*, *Aylwin*, *Hickox*, and *Miami* (and the less extensive damage suffered by nineteen other ships) were a direct result of the typhoon, and no blame for those damages attached to any officer or man serving in those ships; the losses of the *Hull* and *Monaghan* were the result of insufficient dynamic stability. Elaborating on this opinion, the court explained that it had taken into account the fact that the *Dewey* and *Aylwin*, of the same class, had weathered the storm. It noted that although they had ballasted to the high side, both ships still came close to capsizing, and while it was possible that such ballasting made the difference between survival or loss, there was no reason to conclude that if the *Hull* and *Monaghan* had ballasted in the same manner, they would have remained afloat. The court pointed out that mountainous seas and winds up to 120 knots prevailed in some areas, and that within comparatively short distances, wind and sea conditions were markedly different. Continuing, the court stated: "It is considered entirely possible that momentary synchronism of the seas with the period of the ship could cause the amplitude of roll to build up quite rapidly. Add to this the very appreciable effect of a wind of 100 knots or higher on the large areas of upperworks of the destroyers and there is no safety margin left for ships of this stability. The quantity of free surface water that may have been present in the *Hull* and *Monaghan* is not known, but there can be little doubt that under the existing weather some amount of free water was present in the ships. While any such free surface would contribute to the instability, it is believed that the sea and wind then existing, together with the fact that both ships had lost steering and were rolling heavily in the trough of the sea, could have combined their effects so as to cause capsizing."[2]

In the case of the *Spence*, it was the court's opinion that her loss was due to the combined effect of:

(a) Synchronism of the waves with the ship's natural period of roll.

(b) The pressure of typhoon winds on the ship's structure.

(c) The ship's low fuel state.

(d) Lack of ballast.

(e) Free surface effect of water that entered the ship through numerous openings, since condition "Affirm" was not set. In the court's opinion, this was as much a factor in the capsizing as the lack of fuel or ballast.[3]

With regard to the stability of *Farragut*-class destroyers, which the court noted was markedly less than that of other destroyers, it was the court's opinion that tactical commanders should give greater consideration to their poor stability whenever storm conditions are encountered. The court also noted that: all of the lost ships were maneuvering and attempting to maintain station right up to a short time prior to capsizing; the commanding officers of the *Hull*, *Monaghan*, and *Spence* did not understand soon enough that they had to abandon attempts to maintain station and concentrate on survival; the judgment necessary for such decisions would, in many cases, require more experience than the commanding officers of the

Hull, *Monaghan*, and *Spence* possessed; and that the need to be prepared to fuel on short notice on the part of the *Spence* may have been a factor in her delay in ballasting.[4]

In the case of the *Hull* and *Monaghan*, the court felt that no offenses had been committed or serious blame incurred by their commanding officers, officers, or crews. In the case of the *Spence*, on the basis of very limited evidence, the court noted: that the commanding officer probably failed to set condition "Affirm," and delayed ballasting until it was too late; that topside ammunition, provisions, and other movable weights were not struck below; but that the commanding officer of the *Spence* was lost with his ship and therefore was not available to testify.[5] Had Jim Andrea survived, his testimony might have introduced evidence that would have explained the loss of the *Spence* in a different light.

In listing the causes of the damage and losses incurred by the fleet, the court included: maneuvering the fleet unknowingly into or near the path of a typhoon under a false sense of security, and a belief that danger did not exist until it was too late; unusual aerological advice based on insufficient data; wishful reasoning in connection with desired operations; a certain amount of delay and maneuvering in the face of the storm and near its track in an effort to fuel destroyers after the storm had struck; a lack of appreciation by subordinate commanders and commanding officers that really dangerous weather conditions existed until the storm had taken charge of the situation, thus delaying until too late the preparations for security that would be expected.[6]

The court went on to state: "The preponderance of responsibility for the above falls on Commander Third Fleet, Admiral William F. Halsey, U.S. Navy. In analyzing the mistakes, errors, and faults included therein, the court classifies them as errors in judgement under stress of war operations and not as offenses. Those pertaining to subordinates . . . are attributed to errors in judgement, or inexperience, or both. The court fully realizes that a certain degree of blame attaches to those in command in all disasters, unless they are manifestly 'Acts of God.' The extent of blame as it applies to Commander Third Fleet or others, is impractical to assess."[7]

The court made ten recommendations:[8]

1. That the Bureau of Ships conduct a design study to improve ventilation systems in CVLs.
2. That as an interim measure, light armor plating be installed in CVL vents and ducts, at hangar deck level, to permit closure when necessary.
3. That all commanders be advised regarding the likelihood of

encountering adverse weather, and particularly typhoons in the Western Pacific.

4. That the Bureau of Ships investigate the design characteristics of present-day destroyers.
5. That steps be taken to assure that commanding officers are fully aware of the stability characteristics of their ships; that adequate watertight integrity must be enforced; and that the effect of free liquid surfaces is understood.
6. That weather ships should be stationed in the area to supplement the present weather system; and that at least two planes daily be designated as weather reconnaissance planes, to cover sectors where unusual weather was suspected.
7. That aerological officers be instructed more thoroughly in the use of single-station observations for forecasting.
8. That older and more experienced aerological officers be assigned to the principal commanders of the Third and Fifth Fleets.
9. That there should be no further proceedings in the case of Lieutenant Commander James A. Marks, U.S. Navy.
10. Recommendation number ten was a simple statement, inviting attention to the fact that since the principal commanders of the Third Fleet were engaged in preparations for imminent war operations, and departed from Ulithi on December 30, they were not constantly available to the court. The matter of any further proceedings or action to be taken was referred to the convening authority.

The official inquiry into the Third Fleet's encounter with the typhoon on 18 December 1944 was finished. The decision as to whether any disciplinary action would be taken concerning the many errors brought to light by the proceedings now rested in the hands of Fleet Admiral Nimitz, Fleet Admiral King, and the Secretary of the Navy.

On 12 January 1945, Lieutenant Howard S. Smith, U.S. Naval Reserve, of the CinCPac staff, addressed a memorandum to the Commander in Chief, U.S. Pacific Fleet. The subject was, "Court of Inquiry to inquire into all the circumstances connected with loss of U.S.S. Hull, U.S.S. Monaghan, and U.S.S. Spence." In three typewritten pages, it summarized the 169-page (plus exhibits) report of the Court of Inquiry, setting forth the gist of the court's opinions and recommendations.[9] While Lieutenant Smith's brief was a masterful job, and carried with it most of the essence of the proceedings, no summary of that length could possibly convey the myriad of details necessary for a full appreciation of all the factors involved. Further, this particular brief contained one paragraph that was inconsistent with the facts in a very vital consideration—namely, the weather warning messages sent by Commander Third Fleet. The paragraph in question is quoted:

> 3. In the afternoon of 17 December, ComTHIRDFlt issued a weather report to the effect that typhoon disturbances of increasing intensity were located about 400 miles to the east of the Fleet, moving NNW at 12–15 K and estimated that it would curve to NE. About 0900 Item, 18 December, ComTHIRDFlt sent a weather report of a typhoon disturbance in 15° N, 130° E, moving NW at 12 K. Again at 1500 Item, a typhoon report was sent out by ComTHIRDFlt giving the center as near the Fleet's position."[10]

By his use of the terms "typhoon disturbance," and "typhoon report," Lieutenant Smith's memorandum conveyed the impression that the Commander Third Fleet issued warnings of the approach of a typhoon in the afternoon of the 17th, and again at 0900 on the 18th. Both Rear Admiral Carney and Commander Kosco had made it clear in their testimony that Commander Third Fleet did not consider the disturbance to be a typhoon until the forenoon of the 18th, and that the report transmitted at 1500 on the 18th was the first message that categorized the storm as a typhoon. Under the circumstances, this was a significant discrepancy. It tended to present the performance of the fleet commander in a more favorable light than the facts justified, by indicating that he had issued messages warning of the typhoon's approach, first 22 hours, and again 4 hours before the storm reached its greatest intensity. In addition, the court's opinion that "the preponderance of responsibility for the storm damage and losses suffered by the Third Fleet attached to Commander Third Fleet, Admiral William F. Halsey, U.S. Navy," was not mentioned. Smith's briefing memo also omitted any note of the fact that for a period of almost nineteen hours, a message from Commander Third Fleet to his subordinate commanders, incorrectly locating the storm center to be more than 400 miles away, when it was known to be about 200 miles closer, was allowed to remain uncorrected.

The discrepancies in Lieutenant Smith's briefing memo are not mentioned to suggest that they were deliberate attempts to becloud the issue of blame. Probably they were the result of Smith's own interpretation, and his sense of what was and what was not important enough to include in the summary. Nor is there any reason to assume that the action taken by the convening authority would have been any different if these inaccuracies had not been present. Fleet Admiral Chester W. Nimitz had a reputation for thoroughness, and it is highly unlikely that he would have failed to read the entire record of the court's proceedings. In addition, there no doubt were other briefing memoranda from other members of the CinCPac staff, one or more of which probably covered Smith's omissions. The action taken by Admiral Nimitz as the convening authority therefore is assumed to have been based on his full understanding of all of the facts in the case. However, the discrepancies noted should serve to demonstrate that even the most trusted and competent subordinate will present to his commander the situation as he sees it. There will be times when his vision will be defective. In such a case, even the hard facts can become distorted.

On 22 January 1945, Admiral Nimitz approved the proceedings, findings, opinions, and recommendations of the court of inquiry. With specific regard to Admiral Halsey's role, Nimitz said:

"The evidence brought forward by the court indicates that the preponderance of responsibility for the storm damage and losses suffered by the Third Fleet attached to Commander, Third Fleet, Admiral William F. Halsey, U.S. Navy. However, the convening authority is of the firm opinion that no question of negligence is involved, but rather, that the mistakes made were errors in judgement committed under stress of war operations and stemming from a commendable desire to meet military commitments. No further action is contemplated or recommended."[11]

With regard to those recommendations for which the implementing actions were clearly within his cognizance, Admiral Nimitz noted in his endorsement: that he intended to see that all flag and commanding officers of the Pacific Fleet were impressed with the need to understand the laws of storms and to give full consideration to adverse weather conditions when they occurred; that he would direct steps to assure that commanding officers were made fully aware of the stability characteristics of their ships, the effect of free surface on stability, and the need to enforce security measures regarding watertight integrity; that weather service in the Western Pacific would be improved by stationing weather ships, establishing automatic weather stations at two proposed locations, and by providing weather reconnaissance aircraft staffed with competent weather observers; and finally, that the task force commanders would be directed to hold conferences for aerological officers to indoctrinate them in single-station weather forecasting.[12]

Concerning those recommendations that were beyond the scope of his authority, Admiral Nimitz recommended: that the Bureau of Naval Personnel be directed to make available a greater number of older and more experienced aerological officers to the higher fleet commands; that the Bureau of Ships be directed to undertake a design study to improve the ventilating systems of the light carriers (CVLs); and that the Bureau of Ships also be directed to investigate the design characteristics of present-day destroyers, with the aim of improving them.[13]

The record of proceedings was forwarded to Fleet Admiral King for his review. On 13 January 1945, Captain Howard Orem, U.S. Navy, of the staff of Commander in Chief, United States Fleet, submitted to Admiral King a briefing memo summarizing the facts, opinions, and recommendations of the court as set forth in an advance copy, received prior to receipt of Admiral Nimitz's endorsement.[14] Copies of Orem's memorandum were routed also to other principal officers on Admiral King's staff, so that they had time to analyze the proceedings and develop proposed actions in advance of receipt of Admiral Nimitz's endorsement. The memorandum consisted of seven typewritten pages, which provided considerably more detail than that prepared for Admiral Nimitz. Further, Orem's version was precisely correct as to the storm warning messages issued by Admiral Halsey, and it did include mention of the inordinate delay in correcting the message of the 17th, which had erroneously reported the location of the storm, and of the court's opinion that the preponderance of responsibility for the fleet's damage and losses rested on Admiral Halsey. On 16 February 1945, comments from his principal staff officers were presented to Admiral King. In general, they concurred with the actions taken by Admiral Nimitz. With regard to the recommendations that the Bureau of Ships initiate a design study with a view to improving destroyer stability, it was noted that BuShips was already investigating the subject, and that therefore no additional directives to the Bureau were necessary "at this time."[15]

On 21 February 1945, after more than a month of review and consideration, Admiral King sent the record of proceedings to the Secretary of the Navy, concurring in the opinion of Admiral Nimitz that "although the preponderance of responsibility for the storm damage and losses suffered attaches to Commander THIRD Fleet, there is no question of negligence involved."[16] King's wording of the remainder of the statement concerning Halsey differed slightly from that used by CinCPac. Nimitz said that Halsey's mistakes "were errors in judgement committed under stress of war operations and stemming from a commendable desire to meet military commitments." King said, "The mistakes made were errors in judgement resulting from insufficient information, committed under stress of war operations, and stemmed from the firm determination to meet military commitments." Noting that Nimitz's plans to improve the weather service in the Western Pacific were logical, and that the Bureau of Ships was already engaged in studies to improve the ventilating systems of small aircraft carriers, Admiral King concurred, "with the proceedings, findings, opinions, and recommendations of the Court of Inquiry and the Convening Authority."[17]

The investigation had been duly considered and acted upon, but serious questions still remained unanswered regarding the continued operation of *Farragut*-class destroyers. The typhoon experience seemed to prove without a doubt that they were only marginally stable. For the remaining ships of Destroyer Squadron One, some positive and constructive response was essential.

CHAPTER 17

Critique

As soon as he had become aware of the full extent of the Third Fleet's damage and its ship and aircraft losses, Admiral Nimitz had set in motion the administrative action required to investigate the circumstances. His overriding short-term concern must have been focused on the need to meet operational commitments. A formal court of inquiry was an absolute necessity, but it had to be tailored precisely to fit the needs of the situation. The investigation would have to look closely at the performance of the top command. By involving the principal commanders in time-consuming administrative proceedings, it could disrupt the Third Fleet's operational readiness. It was essential that it be carefully controlled. One possible course of action was to appoint a court whose senior member was junior to the Third Fleet Commander. To have sought someone senior to Halsey would have run the risk of placing the court beyond the jurisdiction of CinCPac. As long as it remained under his wing, the scope of the investigation was subject to the control of Admiral Nimitz. If he deemed it appropriate, he could instruct the president of the court to ascertain whether or not any offense warranting action by court-martial had been committed, and if not, to pin the responsibility where it belonged, make recommendations to prevent a recurrence, and get on with the business of fighting the war. Regardless of whether or not such a scenario was deliberately envisioned from the beginning, the actual events transpired pretty much in that order. The recommendations that finally were produced by the court probably served to confirm such tentative conclusions as Nimitz may have reached on his own after his conversation with Halsey on Christmas Eve. In any case, the formal court of inquiry did the job as Admiral Nimitz wished it to be done. Appropriate administrative action had been taken, and the major share of responsibility had been placed on the shoulders of the fleet commander.

Five major factors had contributed to the Third Fleet's disastrous experience. The first of these was the strategic concept for the

Western Pacific. It governed the choice of launch points and rendezvous positions and therefore placed the fleet in the general vicinity of the storm. The second was the matter of the low fuel state of the Task Force 38 destroyers. It caused the fueling operations of 17–18 December to take on a sense of urgency that otherwise would have been lacking. The third concerned weather forecasting, with special emphasis on the failure of the fleet commander and his staff to recognize the unmistakable signs of an approaching typhoon. The fourth was the competence of fleet, task force, and task unit commanders, as well as individual ship commanding officers, to deal with extreme weather conditions. Finally, there was the inherent stability of the ships, which had been determined by the design process, under the cognizance of the Bureau of Ships. Clearly, Admiral Halsey exercised varying degrees of control over the first four of these factors. Over the matter of ship design, he had no influence whatsoever.

Concerning the first factor, an earlier chapter summarized the operational and strategic considerations that confronted the third Fleet on 17 and 18 December. The selection of a rendezvous point for the morning of the 18th was restricted by the need to be in a good position to resume strike operations on the 20th, and by the proximity of enemy air fields in the Philippines. The latter limitation applied mostly to the extent of movement to the west. It made sense to place the rendezvous point some arbitrary distance (say 200 miles to the east) from the closest enemy airfield, but there was no limiting factor that would have prevented the selection of a rendezvous point a hundred miles farther to the south, had there been any compelling reason to move it in that direction. We now know that to have done so would have resulted in far less damage and almost certainly no loss of ships. Unfortunately, such a compelling reason was absent from the fleet staff's deliberations. They did not know that the storm was a typhoon, nor did they know where it was.

Concerning the low fuel state of the Task Force 38 escorts, Admiral Carney testified that overriding operational considerations dictated acceptance of the risk of running the destroyers until their need for fuel was critical. The facts raise questions about the logic of that decision.

Additional fighter aircraft had been taken aboard the attack carriers in order to provide a continuous CAP (Combat Air Patrol) over the target area. While this plan required a heavy saturation of fighter cover and offensive strikes during the daylight hours, it called for the presence of only six heckler aircraft and a correspondingly small number of attack missions over Luzon during the night.

Out of a total of 1,671 sorties flown during the three-day period, only fifty-eight were flown at night, with thirty on the night of the 14th, and twenty-eight on the 15th. Of these, the carrier *Independence* provided eighteen each night.[1] The pace of flight operations during the hours of darkness on 14 and 15 December was therefore greatly reduced from that which obtained during daylight. It appears that on either of those nights, fueling the destroyers from the carriers, or from the accompanying battleships would have been feasible. It had been done many times before. The Commander Third Fleet, Commander Task Force 38, and Commanders of Task Groups 38.1, 38.2, and 38.3, all had the authority necessary to arrange and conduct interim fueling for their escorts. Had they done so, the need for fueling on the 17th or 18th would have lost its great sense of urgency. The full attention of the fleet commander then could have been concentrated on avoiding the approaching storm, for even though he did not yet know it was a typhoon, he was attempting to get away from it.

The critically low fuel state of the destroyers therefore did not stem so much from conflicting combat requirements as it did from a deliberate decision not to fuel. This course of action was rationalized by the belief that to refuel would interfere with the accomplishment of the mission.

The court of inquiry did not pursue the question of destroyer fuel reserves. Admiral Halsey was not queried about it at all. Only Admiral Carney was asked whether it was normal for destroyers to have only 15 percent of their fuel on board. His response—that operations did not permit interim fueling or topping off—was undoubtedly made in good faith. The decision not to fuel must have appeared to him (and to the fleet commander) to be the only acceptable alternative. The court might not have agreed with that conclusion had they elicited testimony describing the pattern and the pace of flight operations at night.

In examining the facts concerning weather forecasting, the court appeared to ignore some of the most significant data available for the asking. For example, although there is no mention of the court's awareness of the pattern of barometric readings recorded on the fleet flagship, the record of proceedings includes copies of the *New Jersey*'s deck logs for 17, 18, 19, and 20 December. Barometer readings were an integral part of those logs. We do not know how closely the court examined them. Perhaps they studied them carefully and fully understood their impact on the weather forecasting picture. On the other hand, they were pressed for time, and they may have given them no more than a perfunctory review. They could have asked an expert aerologist, such as Captain Lockhart, to provide an analysis of the barometer's behavior prior to and during the storm. As far as we know, they did not. They could have asked Commander Kosco to review the local weather indicators available to him and to summarize his analysis as a part of his testimony. They did not. They could have introduced the *New Jersey*'s deck log as evidence, and then, as a part of the proceedings, they could have examined the barometric pressures that were recorded for two or three days prior to and during the storm. Again they did not. As far as the record of proceedings is concerned, the court of inquiry did not consider the detailed local weather indicators that provided the basis for forecasting aboard the ships of the Third Fleet.

While aerological officers were assigned to the larger staffs and the attack carriers, every commanding officer, regardless of the size of his ship—from a carrier to a fleet tug—was expected to be able to read local weather signs. The forecasting of the weather, and especially the recognition of the approach of severe weather was, or at least should have been, a responsibility of the line. It should not have been delegated to the staff aerologist. Every ship then was (and no doubt still is) provided with the current issue of the *American Practical Navigator* by Bowditch. In a chapter of that book entitled "Cyclonic Storms," the early indicators of an approaching tropical cyclone are listed and discussed. (A few of these were mentioned in chapter 2 of this book. They are repeated here for ready reference and continuity.) The importance of the barometer as a tool for forecasting is emphasized. These eight typhoon warning signals are provided solely on the basis of barometer readings: (1) An unsteady barometer, sometimes a little higher than usual. (2) Usually after the appearance of cirrus clouds, but sometimes before, a gradual decrease in pressure. (3) Surrounding the storm, a large area throughout which the barometer reads a tenth of an inch or more below average. (4) Restless oscillation of the barometer. (5) Any interruption in the regularity of the diurnal oscillation (the regular rythmic rise and fall that normally occurs in the tropics). (6) A rapid fall in the barometer as the clouds grow thicker and lower and the wind increases. (7) A rate of fall of the barometer of .03 inch or more per hour for three hours or longer. (8) The rate of fall of the barometer indicates the rate of the storm's approach.[2] Bowditch also noted three other important local signs: the existence of a cross swell (Bowditch termed it, "another warning that should never be overlooked"); steadily increasing winds; and rain, usually fine and mistlike in the outer fringes, becoming torrential near the center.[3]

The actual barometer readings, as recorded in the deck logs of the *New Jersey* for the four days preceding as well as the day of the storm, are shown in the accompanying Table 17-I. Even a cursory

Table I. *New Jersey* barometer readings.

Hour	14 Dec	15 Dec	16 Dec	17 Dec	18 Dec
0100	29.83	29.81	29.88	29.88	29.76
0200	29.82	29.85	29.88	29.86	29.70
0300	29.80	29.84	29.87	29.84	29.65
0400	29.78	29.84	29.87	29.82	29.67
0500	29.78	29.84	29.88	29.82	29.67
0600	29.81	29.85	29.88	29.84	29.68
0700	29.83	29.87	29.90	29.83	29.67
0800	29.85	29.89	29.91	29.84	29.60
0900	29.87	29.80	29.95	29.86	29.61
1000	29.87	29.81	29.96	29.85	29.52
1100	29.89	29.81	29.95	29.83	29.47
1200	29.87	29.80	29.93	29.79	29.55
1300	29.85	29.89	29.91	29.73	29.30
1400	29.82	29.86	29.87	29.70	29.23
1500	29.79	29.85	29.87	29.68	29.40
1600	29.78	29.83	29.86	29.70	29.46
1700	29.80	29.83	29.86	29.73	29.54
1800	29.80	29.83	29.86	29.70	29.62
1900	29.83	29.84	29.89	29.75	29.62
2000	29.85	29.85	29.89	29.76	29.74
2100	29.85	29.86	29.91	29.76	29.77
2200	29.86	29.87	29.93	29.76	29.78
2300	29.86	29.87	29.91	29.78	29.80
2400	29.87	29.89	29.90	29.78	29.81

examination of the *New Jersey*'s readings discloses pressure changes similar to several of those described by Bowditch as typical of a tropical cyclone. If the readings for 14 December are taken as a norm, the regular daily diurnal oscillation on the fleet flagship involved highs at about 1000 and 2200, lows at about 0400 and 1600, a pressure range of .08 or .09 inch in six hours, a daily low of 29.78 and a daily high of 29.89. On the 15th, instead of peaking to a maximum at about 1000, as it did the day before, the pressure dropped .09 inch between 0800 and 0900, and remained at about that level through 1200. This appears to have been a definite interruption in the regularity of the diurnal oscillation. On the 16th, the daily low and high readings extended from 29.86 to 29.96, producing an unsteady barometer, somewhat higher than normal. On the 17th, beginning at 1100, the flagship's barometer fell rapidly (.10 inch in two hours). It remained about .10 inch below normal (the corresponding hourly readings for the 14th) for the rest of the day. The drop in pressure from 1100 to 1400 on the 17th totaled .13 inch.

If that amount is reduced by the .04 inch attributable to the regular diurnal oscillation for that period, the remaining .09 inch still equalled the .03 inch per hour cited by Bowditch as indicative of the approach of a tropical cyclone.

Rain squalls were common on the 17th, and the rain finally became constant at first light and then came down in more copious amounts. Wind velocities steadily increased as the storm drew closer. Heavy overcast and black clouds, with some high cirrus, were observed on the 17th. The seas became rough, and then very rough. Admiral Carney's testimony provided early evidence that a cross swell was apparent to him on the 17th. Admiral Halsey also noted the existence of a cross swell that morning.[4]

The action reports and war diaries of other ships of the Third Fleet indicate that there was widespread concern regarding the steadily worsening weather on 17 December. Both Admirals Bogan and Sherman testified that they were aware on that date that a severe cyclonic storm (Sherman labeled it a typhoon) was within dangerous proximity to the fleet. It is also clear now that others, who were not called to testify, were very much aware of the approach of a typhoon. In his action report covering the period 1–24 December 1944, Rear Admiral O. C. Badger, Commander Task Unit 38.2.2, discussed the weather in detail. His analysis provides a convincing example of what kind of forecasting was possible, despite the lack of outside reports: "The first indication of the formation of a typhoon, which might affect the operations of the Third Fleet, was observed at 0600 17 December 1944. The storm center was estimated to be in position 09°40′ N, 131°30′ E, track NNW, speed 9 knots. The *Langley*, a unit of this task group, also reported the storm center at the same estimated position at this time. At 0630 Task Force 38 commenced fueling operations, but high seas with typical typhoon characteristics forced cancellation of exercises."[5]

Badger's report goes on to indicate estimated positions of the storm during the period until 1800 on the 18th. Successive estimates placed it 250–300 miles south-southeast of the *Iowa* at 1422 on the 17th, and 200 miles to the southeast at 0900 on the 18th. At 1400 on the 18th, it was accurately determined by radar to be 38 miles away, bearing 030 degrees.[6] While the two cited estimates showed the center to be at least 100 miles farther away than it actually was, they would have provided a sound basis for determining effective avoiding action. Unfortunately, Rear Admiral Badger was not among those from whom the fleet commander requested weather information, nor was he called to testify before the court of inquiry.

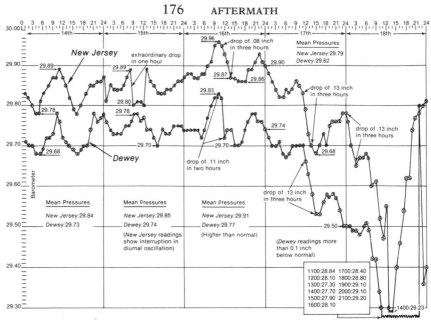

New Jersey vs. *Dewey* barometer readings, 14–18 December 1944.

The local indications of impending disaster were not heeded at the top level of command. Yet the warning signs were there. The question naturally arises as to why the fleet commander and his chief of staff did not appear to appreciate and react to them. Perhaps Admirals Halsey and Carney had placed their complete trust and confidence in Commander Kosco to handle all matters related to the weather, so that they would be free to devote their full attention to strategy and combat operations. Such an assignment of duties was appropriate and logical, but it did not relieve the fleet commander of his ultimate responsibility regarding any threat to the fleet's security. Recognition of the local warning signs of a typhoon did not require the advice of a postgraduate aerologist. The capacity to read the weather is one of the basic requirements of any competent seaman. In this case, preoccupation with combat operations appears to have been the culprit. It is interesting to note that while Halsey and Carney appear to have been unaware of the local weather indicators, in their early analysis of the storm's existence they accepted Kosco's projection of its probable track on the basis of the historical pattern of December typhoon behavior.[7] The possibility that they might eventually be dealing with a typhoon thus appears to have been suggested by the fleet aerologist, and acknowledged, however unwittingly, by the fleet commander and his chief of staff at the very outset.

Since the record seems to indicate that the court did not explore the matter of local weather warning signs, there is a natural inclination to indulge in conjecture as to why. Perhaps the court sensed that the whole business of the Third Fleet staff's weather forecasting performance was a "can of worms." They may have decided that they shouldn't open it up, because to do so would have generated an administrative mess, the cleanup of which would bog down key staff members and interfere with the war effort. Whatever its rationale, the court's inquiry into weather forecasting was shallow and inadequate.

With regard to the matter of the competence of various commanders to deal with the problems of severe weather, the court obtained a fairly comprehensive review of the role played by individual ship commanding officers and a less detailed but adequate summary of the performance of task group and task unit commanders. There were still a number of questions that should have been answered but were never asked. Beginning at 0616 on the 18th, and for almost two hours, the fleet had been maneuvered on courses that quickly brought it into close proximity to the storm center.[8] Yet the court did not ask the task force commander why he had ordered those changes, nor did it ask the fleet commander why he had permitted them to continue. It is obvious now, as it should have been then, that the time spent on course 060° while attempting to fuel made a significant difference. Had that course change not been made, the Third Fleet could have continued on a southerly course at ten knots for the same hour that it actually headed 060° at the same speed. The "difference," as Kosco had called it, would not have been missing it by "two or three miles less,"[9] it would have meant missing it by almost twenty miles more. A matter of twenty miles probably would have made a dramatic difference in the conditions of wind and sea. Perhaps the most significant point that should be made here is the fact that despite the failure of the Third Fleet staff to recognize the local warnings of an approaching typhoon, the staff aerologist made a recommendation at about 0400 on the 18th that the fleet immediately head south. Had prompt action been taken to follow and hold to that recommendation, it is almost certain that no ships would have been lost, and damage would have been reduced significantly. The ultimate deficiency was not one of staff performance, but rather of the competence of command.

In summary, the competence of the fleet and task force commanders, as demonstrated by their performance in the face of typhoon weather, in this particular instance was deficient. There appears to have been no lack of competence on the part of task group or task unit commanders to deal with the problems of severe weather, though they did seem to be insensitive to the relative inexperience of their junior ship captains. The performance of individual ship commanding officers, including those confronted with nearly overwhelming storm conditions, appears to have demonstrated a satisfactory level of competence.

As noted in an earlier chapter, with regard to the inherent stability of the *Farragut*-class destroyers, the Bureau of Ships was established specifically to improve unsatisfactory destroyer design, with special emphasis on problems of stability.[10] Mention also has been made of the fact that the poor stability characteristics of the *Farraguts* were common knowledge within BuShips, and that in 1942 they had dealt with the problem by reducing the number of five-inch guns on those ships from five to four.[11] At the very least, that drastic an action should have made them keenly aware that destroyer stability was a serious concern that required their continuing supervision. The lowest value of maximum righting arm considered safe for the *Farraguts* and all succeeding classes of destroyers had been set by BuShips in 1942 to be 0.9 foot in light service condition.[12] I cannot recall, nor does a search of the records reveal, any communication from any source that informed the commanding officers of destroyers at any time during World War II of the newly established criteria for minimum acceptable stability. It would have been a useful bit of information.

BuShips was aware, from the *Monaghan*'s inclining test of 13 October 1942, that her metacentric height at that time had diminished in two years from about 2.5 feet in light service condition, to 2.0 feet, with a maximum righting arm of 1.05 feet. This was uncomfortably close to the 0.9 foot minimum set by BuShips for all destroyers, but since the forces afloat were generally not aware of that criterion, it is unlikely that the destroyermen aboard the *Monaghan* in October 1942 were very disturbed. Given the differences that always exist between the several ships of a single class, it is not unreasonable to assume that if one *Farragut*-class destroyer had a maximum righting arm of 1.05 feet, then there was at least one other ship of the class for which the corresponding factor was less than that amount. How much less is open to question, but the allowable margin of error was only .15 foot (or 1.8 inches) before the value of the righting arm would have reached the 0.9 foot limit. Even so, the Bureau of Ships considered that the stability of *Farragut*-class destroyers was "critical" and so indicated in its official correspondence. In August of 1944, the chief of that bureau responded to a request from the commanding officer of the *Hull* to modify the ship's ventilation system with this comment: "However, the additional top side weight involved . . . is not considered acceptable in view of the present critical stability of these ships, ..."[13] The BuShips letter was written a full month before receipt of the *Aylwin*'s inclining test data.

The inclining test of the *Aylwin* was made on 24 September 1944. The Navy Yard reported the test results to BuShips by message.[14] The responsible yard personnel must have considered the test data to be deserving of the bureau's immediate consideration and action. This opinion is reinforced by the recollection of Bill Rogers, the *Aylwin*'s skipper, who commented in a recent letter that after the inclining test on 24 September: "My first concern was generated by a shipyard planner, who visited me a day or two later to say that he wanted to check to be sure that we hadn't capsized while alongside the pier. We were all alerted not to use too much rudder on our trial runs, and stability was emphasized en route to WESTPAC."[15] Bill further noted that he never knew whether Captain Mercer thought at the time that the *Aylwin*'s small metacentric height was serious, nor did he ever know what corrective action Mercer or Puget Sound Naval Shipyard initiated, if any. Rogers assumed, as I did, that when inclining tests were conducted by the shipyards, the reports of those tests were subjected to the closest scrutiny and analysis by the Bureau of Ships, and that "they" would take whatever corrective measures were necessary and appropriate. When no such measures materialized, we assumed it was because BuShips deemed it unnecessary. It meant to us that the responsible bureau of the Navy Department had concluded that the ships were still sufficiently stable to allow them to operate safely.

The Bureau of Ships was silent. They provided no reaction to the *Aylwin*'s test. Research of the BuShips files in the National Archives discloses no communication of any kind about *Farragut*-class destroyer stability from September, 1944, until after the typhoon. However, it is most interesting to note that the internal route slip, attached by BuShips to the Puget Sound Naval Shipyard report of the *Aylwin*'s inclining test, shows two handwritten notes by members of the BuShips staff. The first, dated 10/3/44, from R. B. Madden, whose identifying billet number was "814," was addressed to billet number "456," and simply asked a raised-eyebrow kind of question, indicating that two of the *Aylwin*'s inclining test factors looked high. The response, signed "WAK (456)," is undated but presumably was written a day or two later: "This ship has reached the minimum acceptable stability, with a maximum GZ [righting arm] of 0.90' in light service. A policy of strict adherence to complete weight and moment compensation is essential."[16] Obviously, at least one person in BuShips had concluded in early October of 1944 that the *Aylwin* had reached the ragged edge of positive stability. Since the *Farraguts* had been termed by BuShips to have "critical" stability in August of 1944, they must have become "supercritical" on the basis of the *Aylwin*'s test of late September. Normal prudence should have dictated some urgent follow-up action. Preston Mercer's phone call to BuShips on 28 September, expressing concern about the *Dewey*'s stability characteristics during sea trials, should have served to amplify the sound of the alarm bell. Furthermore, it was noted in chapter 1 of this book that the Bureau of Ships had expressed its concern in May, 1944, about the hazards of overloading destroyers.[17] The new data from the *Aylwin* made such overloading even more hazardous for the *Farraguts*. With several ships of Destroyer Squadron One in the process of preparing to sail on 1 October after extensive Navy Yard overhauls, the most vulnerable time for overloading was at hand. Some additional precautionary note from BuShips would have been especially timely. There was no such note. We can only conclude that no one in BuShips saw fit to inform the fleet, type, or unit commanders, or the individual commanding officers of the *Farraguts*, that one of them was on the brink of instability. It was entirely possible that one or more of them had already gone over the edge. The *Hull* and *Monaghan* may have been in that category.

On 23 December 1944, the chief of the Bureau of Ships addressed a memorandum to the Commander in Chief, U.S. Fleet and Chief of Naval Operations, on the subject of "Destroyer and Destroyer-Escort Stability."[18] The memo was attached to a BuShips label marked "URGENT—By messenger to Rear Admiral DeLany." While no mention is made in the memo of the loss of any ships, it obviously was intended to provide information that might be useful to the CNO in understanding why the *Hull*, *Monaghan*, and *Spence* capsized. It included stability curves for those ships, which showed the righting arms for each. It mentioned the establishment "soon after the entry of the United States into the war" of criteria for minimum acceptable stability characteristics for destroyers, and informed the CNO that the lowest acceptable value of maximum righting arm was set at 0.9 foot in light service condition. It noted that, "... this minimum value now obtains in the case of the *Aylwin*. In order to meet the minimum, one 5″ gun and other topside weights were removed from the ships of this particular class."[19] The memo did not indicate that the *Aylwin* was discovered to be at the minimum value on 27 or 28 September 1944, when the Puget Sound

Navy Yard's report was received by BuShips. It also failed to note that the removal of the 5"-gun to meet the minimum took place about two years before, and that there could have been no connection between the removal of the gun and the *Aylwin*'s 1944 inclining test data.[20] At the time the gun was removed, the *Aylwin*'s righting arm must have been somewhere close to the value of 1.05 feet, which obtained in the case of the *Monaghan* in 1942. At best, the BuShips memo to the CNO was confusing. Unfortunately, the court of inquiry raised no questions concerning the BuShips role in the loss of the *Farragut*-class destroyers. The court's recommendations were therefore devoid of any suggestion that BuShips bore some responsibility in the matter, except to indicate that the bureau should undertake a review of destroyer stability. By the time the record of proceedings was forwarded by Admiral King to the Secretary of the Navy, the court's specific mention of destroyer stability had become obscured. It is possible, therefore, that no explanation as to why the *Farragut*s were allowed to go to sea with marginal (or worse) stability, was ever even requested from the Bureau of Ships.

The comment alleged to have been made by Admiral Halsey, that he didn't know whether he or the Bureau of Ships should be court-martialed, but that someone should, went to the heart of the question of blame. It is clear now that despite the court's finding that "the preponderance of responsibility for the storm damage and losses suffered by the Third Fleet attaches to Commander, Third Fleet, Admiral William F. Halsey, U.S. Navy," the losses of the *Hull* and *Monaghan* were attributable, to a significant degree, to their inherent lack of stability. This was a factor over which Admiral Halsey had no control. The Bureau of Ships failed to initiate any positive corrective action, or to impose any restrictions on the operation of *Farragut*-class destroyers in an area where typhoon weather was likely to be encountered, despite the knowledge, from as early as 28 September 1944 that their stability was critically marginal. The Navy Department, therefore, (specifically, the Bureau of Ships) appears to have earned for itself some significant share of the responsibility for the loss of the *Hull* and *Monaghan*. It is also clear that Lieutenant Commanders Jim Marks and Bruce Garrett were blameless for the loss of their ships, and that the court of inquiry should have so indicated.

The following photographs are radar presentations of the typhoon taken from the USS *Wasp*.

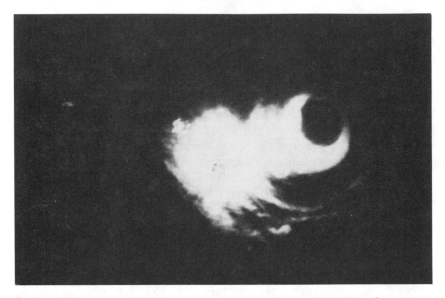

Time: 1100. Approx. ship's position: 14°29.4'N, 127°39'E. True bearing and distance storm center: 077°, 39 miles. Wind direction and force: 336°, 57 knots, gusts to 66 knots. Pressure: 994.5 mbs. (29.37"). Precipitation ceiling of less than 500'. Visibility: 800–1,200 yards. State of sea: very high (20'–40').

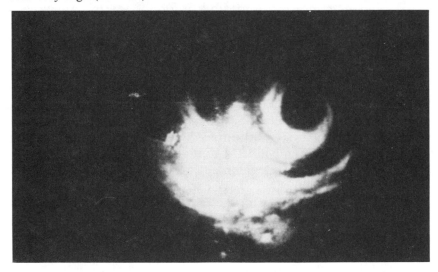

Time: 1130. Approx. ship's position: 14°24.3'N. 127°37.9'E. True bearing and distance storm center: 068°, 38 miles. Wind direction and force: 323°, 68 knots, gusts in excess 80 knots. Pressure. 995.0 mbs. (29.38"). Precipitation ceiling of less than 500'. Visibility: 800–1,200 yards. State of sea: Very high (20'–40').

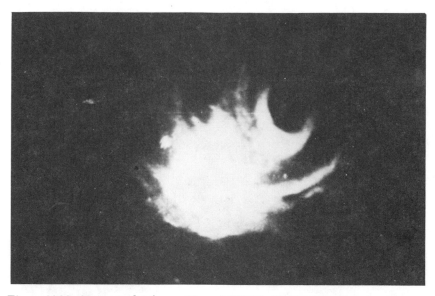

Time: 1200. Approx. ship's position: 14°18′N, 127°34.8′E. True bearing and distance storm center: 055°, 40 miles. Wind direction and force: 315°, 65 knots, gusts in excess 75 knots. Pressure: 996.1 mbs. (29.42″). Precipitation ceiling of less than 500′. Visibility: 600–1,000 yards. State of sea: Very high to mountainous (40′ plus).

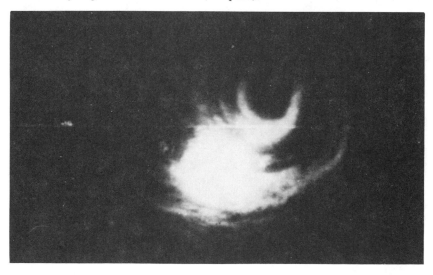

Time: 1230. Approx. ship's position: 14°15′N, 127°39.3′E. True bearing and distance storm center: 042°, 37 miles. Wind direction and force: 280°, 42 knots, gusts in excess 75 knots. Pressure: 993.9 mbs. (29.35″). Precipitation ceiling of less than 500′. Visibility: less than 500 yards. State of sea: Very high to mountainous (40′ plus).

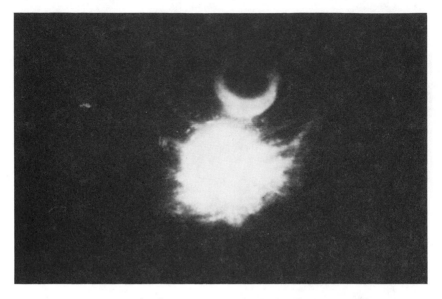

Time: 1300. Approx. ship's position: 14°12′N, 127°44′E. True bearing and distance storm center: 026°, 35 miles. Wind direction and force: 270°, 42 knots, gusts in excess of 75 knots. Pressure: 991.7 mbs. (29.28″). Precipitation ceiling of less than 500′. Visibility: less than 500 yards. State of sea: Very high to mountainous (40′ plus).

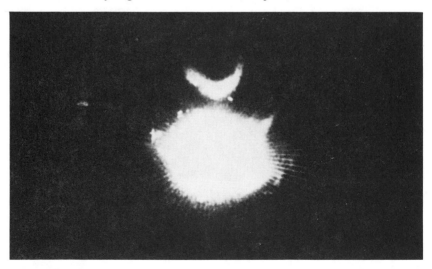

Time: 1340. Approx. ship's position: 14°08′N, 127°51.2′E. True bearing and distance storm center: 005°, 38 miles. Wind direction and force: 270°, 49 knots, gusts in excess of 75 knots. Pressure: 993.2 mbs. (29.33″). Precipitation ceiling of less than 500′. Visibility: 400–800 yards. State of sea: Very high to mountainous (40′ plus).

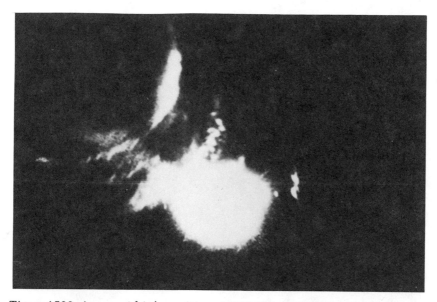

Time: 1530. Approx. ship's position: 13°55.6'N, 128°10.4'E. True bearing and distance storm center: 326°, 81 miles. Wind direction and force: 250°, 41 knots, gusts in excess of 60 knots. Pressure: 1000.1 mbs. (29.53″). Ceiling: 7,000–8,000; patches of clouds at 1,000′. Visibility: 6,000 yards off bow, less than 1,000 yards off stern. State of sea: High (12′–20′).

PART IV

Summary

CHAPTER 18

Conclusion—
The End of the Farraguts

Following the court of inquiry, I concluded that the matter of the typhoon was in the hands of a competent board of senior officers, who would study all of the circumstances and initiate whatever action might be necessary. I assumed that the role of the Bureau of Ships would be one of the subjects examined in the process, and that within two or three months some positive measures would be set in motion to correct the stability of all surviving *Farragut*-class destroyers. My assumption proved to be overly optimistic.

The next six weeks aboard the *Dewey* were spent in a repair status. In addition to the need to construct a new stack, the most critical of our many deficiencies, we had to disassemble and repair our five" gun director, a task normally undertaken only by Navy Yards. The *Dewey*'s own gunnery and fire control personnel accomplished this job, and for weeks the director platform was cluttered with a thousand parts. I wondered if there wouldn't be a few left over, but the whole thing was finally reassembled in good working order. Personnel from the *Prairie*, assisted by the men of the *Dewey*, also conducted extensive repairs to our internal communications circuits, the gyro compass, steering control, and radars. A massive electrical rewiring project also was undertaken. Efforts to repair the anchor windlass continued throughout the entire six-week period, to no avail. We were able to raise the anchor chain off the bottom, but couldn't raise the anchor itself without assistance from the tender. Forced to move away from alongside the *Prairie* every ten days or so to allow Task Force 38 destroyers to receive urgent repair assistance between offensive strike operations, the *Dewey* found herself anchoring close by for two or three days at a time. It then became necessary to drag the anchor when we went back alongside, where the tender's crane could help raise it to its normal housing. It was a frustrating period, but the ship's company and the personnel of the *Prairie* did a magnificent job under very difficult circumstances. We were by no means as combat-ready as we had been prior to the typhoon, but when I reviewed our situation with

Preston Mercer, he agreed with me that we were still able to perform in the capacity of destroyer escort.

Concurrently with the repair of storm damage, we also embarked on an aggressive do-it-yourself campaign to improve stability. With the approval and encouragement of the squadron commander, the ships of DesRon One were stripped of all the excess metal we could find. Aboard the *Dewey*, we conducted daily weight-reduction inspections for more than a week, identifying and marking for removal old electrical cables that were no longer in service, metal boxes and stowage lockers that we could do without, alterations such as the lookout platforms that had been installed at the bridge level by the shipyard, and just about anything else constructed of metal that could be removed without damage to our operational effectiveness. A total topside weight of more than nine tons was removed. Since it was all located fairly high in the ship, we felt that we had improved our stability at least a little bit.

On January 25, Preston Mercer received orders to relieve Captain Jesse G. Coward as Commander Destroyer Squadron Fifty-Four. Jess Coward had been my skipper on the *Sterett* and had initiated the request that resulted in my assignment to command the *Dewey*. On 28 January, I took the *Dewey* alongside the *Remey*, Coward's flagship, to deliver Mercer to his new command, then anchored just a few miles from us. We regretted the loss of Preston Mercer. I considered him to have been an excellent squadron commander and a good friend. I was at the same time delighted to see Jess Coward again and to have him aboard for dinner. He told us of his experience in the Battle of Surigao Straits, a classic action in which his squadron delivered a successful night torpedo attack against the Japanese battleships. The next day I delivered him to Ulithi's airstrip for transportation back to Pearl Harbor, where he joined the staff of Commander Destroyers, Pacific Fleet.

The sojourn in Ulithi at last came to an end, and on 8 February we were more than happy to depart from alongside the *Prairie* (with appropriate expressions of appreciation for their good work) and join Task Group 50.8, the Fifth Fleet's counterpart of Task Group 30.8. We were back with the logistic support group, escorting the oilers again. It was a job we knew well.

The remaining months of the war went by in a hurry. The *Dewey* continued operations with TG 50.8, and proved that she could still perform as an effective destroyer despite her storm damage and primitive repairs. We found that although our new stack was adequate from the engineering standpoint, it created a serious habitability and health problem. It was several feet shorter than the

The *Dewey's* new stack, shorter than the original, frequently filled the pilot house with smoke and rendered it uninhabitable.

original design, and the eddies of air that were caused by the ship's motion frequently created a suction effect that drew the exhaust gases from the stack directly into the pilot house. At times it became uninhabitable, and all of the bridge personnel suffered recurring sore throats, coughing, and inflamed eyes. Nevertheless, we managed to put up with it because there was no alternative. The planners of Service Squadron Ten, to whom we appealed, felt that considerations of stability were so crucial that we couldn't afford to add any more height to the new stack. In the face of that explanation, we decided to live with it as the lesser of two evils.

On 17 February, the oiler *Patuxent*, in company with TG 50.8 and loaded with aviation gasoline, suffered an explosion and fire.[1] We took the *Dewey* alongside to starboard, and with the help of the destroyer escort *Waterman* on her port side, fought the fire. After four hours, with twenty hoses from the *Dewey* and several from the *Waterman* going at full capacity, we had the fires extinguished. By a stroke of sheer good luck, the *Prairie* had given us a brand-new portable 500-gallon-per-minute gasoline handbilly (fire-pump) just before we went to sea. The *Patuxent*'s mishap provided a good chance to test it out. It proved to be a very effective tool.

On 19 February, the oiler *Neches* was detached from TG 50.8 and ordered to proceed to the objective area at Iwo Jima to deliver fuel to the gunfire support ships. In accordance with a prior agreement with the skipper (a wonderful old Norwegian seaman from the merchant service), he immediately requested that the *Dewey* be assigned to escort him. We were delighted to take this more active role, and ended up having a grandstand seat for the flag raising over Mount Suribachi. For the next four days we conducted shore bombardment and fire support missions for the Fourth Marines in the northeast sector of the island.[2] It was a great morale builder for the officers and men of the *Dewey*, although it had its costs. We were hit by a couple of small caliber shells, and six *Dewey* crewman were wounded. Fortunately, none of the injuries were serious.

The shock of our own gunfire during our bombardment further aggravated structural damage caused by the pounding seas on 18 December. We developed cracks in the shell plating in the forward fireroom and soon discovered that we had a dozen broken transverse web frames in the same area. Once again we were ordered back to Ulithi and the repair facilities of the *Prairie*. While there, on 1 March Destroyer Squadron One was written off the records. The *Dewey* became the flagship of Destroyer Division Ten of Destroyer Squadron Five. The *Farragut*, *Aylwin*, *Dale*, and *Macdonough* made up the remainder of the division.

By 4 March we were back in business again with the Fifth Fleet, engaged this time in the Ryukyus Campaign. Kerama Retto became a regular stop for us as we ferried supplies and fuel from Ulithi to Task Force 58. Later in March we had to go back alongside the *Prairie* for repair of still more hull damage caused by the typhoon. By now we had decided that Preston Mercer had been almost clairvoyant in his advice not to go to the aid of the *Tabberer* as she was conducting rescue operations. The storm had seriously damaged

The new stack altered the *Dewey*'s silhouette and led to many queries: "What class ship is that?"

the hull structure in the vicinity of the forward fireroom, and there was little doubt that we would have compounded this damage had we subjected the *Dewey* to additional heavy pounding.

On 25 March Captain Herald F. Stout came aboard as the new division commander, and on the 26th the *Dewey* sailed again to continue her participation in the Ryukyus Campaign.[3]

As the months wore on, we became more and more concerned as to what action was being taken to correct the stability characteristics of the *Farraguts*. In his forwarding endorsement of damage reports from the *Aylwin* and *Dewey*, the Commander Third Fleet, on 3 February 1945, had recommended that immediate consideration be given to alterations and improvements in *Farragut*-class destroyers to increase stability and seaworthiness.[4] On 5 March 1945, the Commander in Chief, Pacific Fleet, concurred in those recommendations and forwarded the basic correspondence to the Chief of Naval Operations.[5] On 22 March 1945, the CNO requested BuShips to forward recommendations to remedy the conditions described in the basic letters.[6] Meanwhile, on 12 March following our discovery of progressive cracking of the *Dewey*'s shell plating and frames in the vicinity of the firerooms, I had originated a second letter to the Commander in Chief, United States Fleet, via the chain of command, describing the damage and requesting corrective action.[7] On 8 April, the new division commander endorsed that letter with these comments: "The apparent lack of stability . . . of this class at full capacity is naturally a source of apprehension. If it is remembered that these ships are stripped to bare essentials for war, it becomes apparent that some further reduction in topside weight is necessary."[8] On 11 May 1945, Commander Destroyer Squadron Five (Captain F. D. McCorkle) appended his endorsement, recommending that, "when ships of this class are again made available for major alterations and repairs, arrangements be made to permanently correct deficiencies disclosed in the basic correspondence."[9] The Commander in Chief, Pacific Fleet concurred in the recommendations. His endorsement was dated 28 May 1945 and included instructions to forward copies of all correspondence to BuShips.[10]

On 27 May 1945, noting the approach of another typhoon season (May through December) and "possible Bureau of Ships plans for alterations to increase stability of *Farragut*-class destroyers," I forwarded to the Commander, Destroyers Pacific Fleet, a comprehensive report of the *Dewey*'s material condition.[11] The division commander (then Captain M. G. Johnson) endorsed the report on 30 May, recommending "availability for complete overhaul of the U.S.S. DEWEY be made as soon as practicable to remedy the defects reported."[12] Commander Destroyer Squadron Five, on 9 June 1945, concurred in Johnson's recommendation.[13]

Meanwhile, the *Macdonough* entered Puget Sound Naval Shipyard, and on 30 March 1945 was given an inclining test. This apparently was intended to be the check on *Farragut*-class stability characteristics, which BuShips had promised Preston Mercer when he reported the *Dewey*'s stability concerns on 27 September 1944. As incredible as it seems today, the bureau finally was going to determine whether or not *Farragut*-class destroyers were stable. It had been more than three months since the *Hull* and *Monaghan* had capsized.

The results of the *Macdonough*'s test were sent to me by Commander Arens, her skipper, on 5 June '45. I found the enclosures fascinating. The Puget Sound Shipyard report indicated that the *Macdonough*'s metacentric height was 1.72 feet, in light service condition.[14] It will be recalled that the *Aylwin*'s metacentric height for the corresponding condition of loading as of 9/27/44 was 1.54 feet, and that this indicated the minimum acceptable level of stability. Armed with that knowledge, and with the loss of the *Hull* and *Monaghan* fresh in mind, Arens now made representations to the shipyard to investigate the rolling characteristics of the *Macdonough* while under way in full load condition.[15] He had determined for himself that his ship's stability suffered a serious reduction. His opinion was shared by his executive officer, Lieutenant Gene LaRocque, who had served in the ship for four years. LaRocque reported on 7 April 1945 that the overhaul just completed had definitely altered the ship's characteristics, and she now was less stable than when she entered the Navy Yard.[16]

The Seattle firm of W. C. Nickum and Sons, Naval Architects and Marine Engineers, was assigned to perform the at-sea test for rolling. Reporting the results of their investigation to the shipyard on 9 April 1945, Mr. G. C. Snyder of that firm commented that the tests showed "a deficiency of stability for safety under the conditions in which this vessel will have to operate."[17] He further concluded that under emergency conditions the *Macdonough*'s range of stability might be exceeded, and that at best the margin of safety was insufficient. The report recommended "corrective measures" before the ship deployed.[18] The Puget Sound Navy Yard forwarded the Nickum and Sons findings to BuShips for action on 11 April.[19] On 17 April, BuShips replied by mailgram to the Navy Yard, the type commander, the *Macdonough*, and others, stating: "Stability MACDONOUGH satisfactory. . . . Bridge inclinometer exaggerates heel when turning. Carefully conducted turning trials other destroyer classes indicate angle heel does not increase materially at speeds over 20 knots. Past behavior MACDONOUGH when turning not affected by recent overhaul."[20]

It isn't difficult to imagine Arens's reaction to the BuShips response. On the basis of his own observations during sea trials, confirmed by the expert opinion of a reputable naval architect, he had indicated that his ship's stability had been reduced. The BuShips reply seemed to tell him that in essence he didn't know what he was talking about. It was a reaction based on opinions formed by persons who had not ridden the ship and whose analysis was conducted in an office more than 3,000 miles away from Puget Sound. Arens also must have wondered how conclusions based on trials conducted on destroyers of other classes could be considered conclusive.

On 2 June 1945, the chief of the Bureau of Ships wrote to the Chief of Naval Operations concerning typhoon damage to the *Aylwin* and *Dewey*.[21] This was his response to the CNO letter of 22 March, requesting BuShips recommendation. The BuShips letter stated that both the *Aylwin* and the *Macdonough* had recently been inclined. It did not mention the fact that the *Aylwin*'s inclining test dated back to more than two months prior to the typhoon. It stated that "both ships meet the Bureau's criterion for minimum acceptable stability," but did not indicate that in the case of the *Aylwin*, her maximum righting arm had been discovered to be at the minimum acceptable value. The 23 December 1944 BuShips memo to CNO had so indicated. The remainder of the letter is quoted verbatim in order to provide the full flavor of the response. Speaking of

Farragut-class ships, it continues: "The ships have met war service conditions successfully, with the exception of this extremely severe storm in which two ships of the class capsized. It is noteworthy, however, that two other ships of the class survived in the same storm. Recognizing the probable demands of war-time service, the Bureau provided considerably better stability characteristics in the design of the DD445 (2,100-ton) and DD692 (2,200-ton) classes of destroyers, unquestionably producing a much higher power of survival in those classes. Yet there are conditions of excessive flooding after war damage, or of extreme storms, which are too much even for these more resistant destroyers, as evidenced by the loss of the *Spence* in the same typhoon. To bring earlier destroyers to a condition even approaching the DD445 and DD692 classes with respect to stability would mean a very drastic reduction in armament. Minor reduction in topside weights would be relatively ineffective. For example, removal of 25 tons from the level of the deck house top, or a correspondingly greater weight from a lower level, would accomplish a reduction in list due to a heavy beam wind approximately equal to a five-knot reduction in wind velocity. Accordingly, the Bureau recommends . . . that no attempt be made to effect drastic changes for the purpose of improving stability. On the other hand, no further impairment of stability of those ships should be permitted, and the forces afloat should be encouraged, on general principles, to effect such minor topside weight removals as can be accomplished without impairing military characteristics."[22] No copies of the BuShips letter were indicated for distribution to anyone. So far as can be determined, the Chief of Naval Operations did not disseminate it to any of the forces afloat.

Mention in the BuShips letter of the fact that the *Aylwin* and *Dewey* survived the storm, while the *Hull* and *Monaghan* did not, apparently was intended to indicate that *Farragut*-class stability was acceptable. It should have been clear after the *Aylwin*'s inclining test in September, 1944, and emphatically certain after the loss of the *Hull* and *Monaghan*, that *Farragut*-class stability was so minimal that it created an unacceptable degree of risk. The fact that BuShips had provided better stability characteristics in the DD445 and DD692 classes seems to have been of little relevance except to emphasize the inadequate stability that had been designed into the *Farraguts*. To suggest by implication that the loss of the *Spence* was proof that even the more stable ships would succumb to "excessive flooding after war damage or of extreme storms,"[23] does not appear now to have been a solid argument. No other 2,100-or 2,200-ton destroyer had been lost in the storm, and the *Spence* probably would not have been lost if she had been tightly buttoned up and ballasted in accordance with existing instructions. Furthermore, no one was suggesting that the *Farraguts* needed to be or should be modified to provide stability equivalent to ships of the DD445 and DD692 classes. All we wanted was sufficient positive margin to provide a reasonable safety factor. To say on the one hand that the removal of 25 tons from the level of the deckhouse would be insignificant, and at the same time encourage the forces afloat to effect minor topside weight removal, appears now to have been entirely inconsistent. Finally, the BuShips recommendation, "that no attempt be made to effect drastic changes for the purpose of improving stability,"[24] appears to have ignored the possibility of the loss of other *Farragut*-class destroyers in typhoon conditions in the future. It was a decidedly negative reaction to a critical situation that needed a positive and supportive approach.

On 5 June 1945, just three days after the Bureau of Ships had responded to the question of *Farragut*-class stability in such a negative fashion, the *Aylwin*, now again operating with the Third Fleet, was caught in a second typhoon. Although she suffered somewhat less severe damage this time, she again rolled excessively and came dangerously close to capsizing. Bill Rogers again reported to the fleet commander, that "with present seakeeping and stability characteristics, the *Farragut*-class destroyers are unable to adequately cope with severe typhoon conditions."[25] Captain Milt Johnson, ComDesDiv Ten, forwarded Bill's report, recommending corrective measures sufficiently drastic to restore the seakeeping qualities and stability of the *Farraguts* so that they could remain effective combatant units even under severe typhoon conditions.[26]

I encountered Preston Mercer a few days after the second typhoon. His greeting to me was, "He did it again!" He was referring to Admiral Halsey, and he went on to say that this time he had informed the fleet commander that he thought they were running into another typhoon. Potter's *Nimitz* (see bibliography) mentions this second typhoon, notes that there was another court of inquiry, again headed by Admiral Hoover, that it placed the preponderance of blame on Admirals Halsey and McCain, and that it almost ruined Halsey's career. Apparently Admirals Nimitz and King felt that Halsey was a national hero of such stature that any punitive action against him would prove contrary to the national interest.[27]

In the meantime, letters were exchanged between the Chief of Naval Operations, the Bureau of Ships, the fleet commanders, and the type commanders concerning displacements and the control of destroyer stability. The BuShips position in all of these was that destroyers were badly overloaded with an accumulation of minor alterations, small items of equipment, spare parts, and excess supplies and provisions, all brought about by ships' personnel. The chief of the Bureau of Ships proposed that this unauthorized overloading be brought under control. CNO, fleet and type commanders all supported BuShips on this point and issued implementing instructions to suppress the flow of small weights introduced on board ships by ships' personnel. As has been indicated earlier, with the possible exception of the *Farragut*, the ships of Destroyer Squadron One (now Five) were not overloaded. With specific reference to *Farragut*-class destroyers, the Commander Destroyers, Pacific Fleet commented: "All ships of this class are under the allowed limit of 2,335 tons. . . . Attention is invited, however, to the concern common to all commanding officers of ships of this class regarding the stability condition of their ships. The loss of the USS HULL (DD350) and the USS MONAGHAN (DD354) has left a lasting impression on the personnel of the sister ships. This is not easily dispelled by quoting inclining experiment data, especially when, during recent overhauls, additional equipment is installed such as ice-cream machines, etc., without any compensatory weight (which can readily be seen by the ship's force) being taken off. It is recommended that another inclining experiment be conducted as early as practicable in order to check the results already obtained on the USS MACDONOUGH (DD351). It should be noted that it is planned to transfer all the ships of this class to the Atlantic Fleet at an early date."[28]

So far as can be determined, BuShips continued to maintain that *Farragut*-class destroyers were stable and that no major alterations to improve stability were practicable. As ComDesPac had noted, the *Farragut*s were all transferred to the Atlantic Fleet a few weeks after V-J Day. The subject of destroyer stability continued to be examined by BuShips, at the urging of the Chief of Naval Operations. However, long before the matter had ever been concluded (if indeed it ever was), my brother skippers from the Class of '38 (and equivalent seniority reservists) and I had been detached and gone to duty elsewhere.

The "Findings and Opinions" of the Third Naval District's Sub Board of Inspection and Survey, following their inspections to determine the disposition to be made of the *Dewey* and *Aylwin* in October, 1945, were typical of the reports made concerning all of the *Farragut*s. They found the vessels "unfit for other than limited service due to . . . [their] stability characteristics and . . . general material condition," and concluded that "the poor stability characteristics of the vessels preclude . . . [their] being altered and equipped for other than limited service."[29] It was recommended that they be sold for scrap. The appraised value of each hulk was estimated to be $4,000! On 19 October 1945, the *Dewey* was decommissioned, and I received a four-line letter stating that, "receipt is acknowledged for the U.S.S. DEWEY (DD349), decommissioned this date." We staged our own little ceremony when her commission pennant was hauled down, but it was a sorry way to end the career of a gallant fighting ship. It was also the end of the *Farragut*-class destroyers. They had added luster to the rich traditions and history of the United States Navy. Those of us who served in them recall that service with pride and nostalgia.

The 5 November 1945 issue of *Time* magazine carried a picture of the destroyers *Farragut*, *Patterson*, and *Dewey* alongside one of New York's East River piers, where Connie Hartigan, the skipper of the *Patterson* (name unknown), and I had left them just a few weeks earlier. The accompanying article described the outstanding war record of the *Patterson* and concluded:

"A faded jack at her bow, her commission pennant and her ragged ensign hanging limply aft, indicated that she was still a ship of the U.S. Navy, but soon these flags would be hauled down and she would be towed off to the boneyard.

"On Navy Day old PAT rested alongside two sisters who were awaiting the same forlorn ending—the heroic *Dewey* and *Farragut*. Across Manhattan, in the North River, the august battleships and carriers and the newer cans of the U.S. Fleet took the applause."[30]

Reflecting on all of these events, the court of inquiry's recommendations and the actions taken to implement them appear to have been well considered and wise. No offenses had been committed by the principal commanders of the Third Fleet, and no punitive measures were necessary or appropriate. Simply placing the major burden of responsibility on Admiral Halsey had been enough. Nothing in this account should detract from his contribution as a great leader when the going was the roughest. There were a number of errors made by subordinate commanders, prior to and during the typhoon. They shared some of Admiral Halsey's responsibility, but it probably would have served no good purpose to single them out and assign specific shares of the blame to them. They knew who they were and where they had failed. They had to live with that knowledge. It seems highly likely that they were more dedicated and concerned during the remainder of their careers because of the lessons learned in the crucible of the typhoon.

With regard to the whole matter of stability, the Navy Department appears to have performed poorly. At least in the matter of *Farragut*-class stability, the Bureau of Ships may have become isolated from the realities of the seagoing Navy. It is possible that they depended too much on theoretical computations and gave too little weight to the observations of those who served in the ships. Considering the gigantic task that confronted them, to supervise a huge shipbuilding program and oversee the shipyard repairs of more than 5,000 naval vessels of all types (more than 3,000 in the Pacific Fleet), it is hardly surprising to learn that the administration of the Bureau of Ships was in some way deficient. When it concerned stability, however, where the very survival of ships was at stake, extraordinary care was indicated. It is clear that in the case of the *Farraguts*, the necessary extraordinary care was lacking. The Chief of Naval Operations could have applied pressure on the Bureau of Ships, but it is likely that the forces afloat did not keep him fully informed. Administrative, as well as task fleet, group, and unit commanders, (and the commanding officers of the ships themselves) missed many opportunities to make strong representations to do something positive about the marginal stability of the *Farragut*-class destroyers. To have allowed the signs of potential trouble that were evident before the storm to be ignored was a symptom of poor leadership at the intermediate level. To have permitted the same negative attitude to prevail after the loss of the *Hull* and *Monaghan*, and in the face of a report by a reputable naval architect that the *Macdonough*'s stability was inadequate, amounted to a serious breakdown in command responsibility at the highest level.

For today's naval officers, and those of the future, there are implications in this narrative that deserve their most serious consideration. In the matter of ship design, stability may no longer be causing a problem, although it would be well to remember that, "In general, there is no ship afloat that cannot be capsized in a seaway."[31] On the other hand, if one considers the seakeeping characteristics of today's destroyers, it is apparent that modern ship design still is sometimes less perfect than we would like it to be. Captain James W. Kehoe's article, "Destroyer Seakeeping: Ours and Theirs," in the November 1973 issue of the U.S. Naval Institute *Proceedings* presents the case very clearly.[32] Unless careful command attention is focused on the problem, the United States Navy could end up with destroyers whose seakeeping qualities would be inferior to those of the Soviet Navy. The forces afloat will have to speak with a loud and authoritative voice to ensure that replacement destroyers coming off the building ways meet their needs. The design process demands the involvement of those unrestricted line officers who will take the ships to sea.

It is also essential that the captains of our ships, as well as our fleet commanders, be competent seamen—always alert to local weather signs, knowledgeable about the laws of storms, and never entirely dependent on satellite communications for their weather forecasting and navigation. General Sir John Hackett's *The Third World War* provides a convincing forecast of the fate of satellites when hostilities again overtake us.[33] It is more important than ever that the basic skills be maintained.

Finally, it seems only fitting that this story should end with a tribute to the 790 officers and men who lost their lives when the Third Fleet encountered the typhoon on 18 December 1944. Peril on the sea overtook them, but they perished with honor, with dignity, and with courage. Those of us who survived pay them homage. They were, after all, our shipmates and our friends.

CHAPTER 19

Epilogue

The information contained in this epilogue did not become available to me until February, 1981, by which time the manuscript for this book was undergoing final editorial review at the Naval Institute Press. Throughout the writing process, the major source of reference material on which to base the narrative has been a copy of the record of proceedings of the court of inquiry, which I obtained from the Navy's Operational Archives in October, 1978. Attached to that copy were forwarding letters from Admiral Nimitz to Admiral King, and from Admiral King to Secretary of the Navy Forrestal, both recommending approval of the court's findings. No return endorsement showing Mr. Forrestal's approval was attached, and so far as my friends at the Operational Archives knew, none had ever been received.

Under the circumstances, since we were aware that the Nimitz and King recommendations had for the most part been implemented, it seemed entirely possible that no formal written concurrence by the Secretary of the Navy had been deemed necessary and that none had been prepared. I reasoned that this was even more likely to have been the case because of the sensitive nature of the court's findings regarding Admiral Halsey's performance. Nevertheless, while I concentrated on other aspects of the story, informal inquiries were set in motion at the National Archives to determine whether a written endorsement by the Secretary of the Navy was in existence. These probings were conducted in low key, but a number of follow-up calls were made over a period of about a year and a half, always with negative results. Finally, however, confirmation that a written endorsement by Mr. Forrestal did in fact exist, was received in the spring of 1980.

By that time my queries had focused on the Central Records Section of the Navy Department's Office of the Judge Advocate General. On 18 June 1980, I addressed a letter to that office, summarizing information that I already had provided by telephone, noting that I was engaged in writing a book about the typhoon, to be published by the Naval Institute Press, and that I needed to know whether Secretary Forrestal had concurred in Admiral King's recommendations regarding the court of inquiry. This letter brought no written response, but in the course of the next few weeks and after several telephone calls in which I was assured that action was being taken on my request, I finally was informed that I would have to deal with another division of the Judge Advocate General's office. It appeared that the Central Records Section did not have the authority to release the records of investigations. I was told that I should contact the Office of the Judge Advocate General (Investigations).

I called that office without delay, and reiterated my request for the Secretary of the Navy's endorsement. Many weeks and several telephone calls later, I was informed that the missing endorsement finally had been located in the National Archives, at Suitland, Maryland, (where I had first made inquiry) and that it consisted of a rubber-stamped approval signed by Mr. Forrestal. The JAG action officer seemed to think that I should be satisfied with that information. When I insisted that I needed a copy of the endorsement, I was instructed to write another letter to JAG, for the record, specifically requesting a copy and indicating the proper identification number of the document, which the action officer provided. I wrote such a request to the Office of the Judge Advocate General (Investigations) on 16 September 1980.

The reply from JAG, dated 5 November 1980, forwarded two documents. The first, dated 5 September 1945, was marked Endorsement #10, and was from the Secretary of the Navy to Admiral Halsey, via the Commander in Chief U.S. Pacific Fleet. It forwarded the record of the court of inquiry to Admiral Halsey for his statement. The second was Endorsement #14, dated 23 November 1945, from the Chief of Naval Operations to the Secretary of the Navy. Its first two paragraphs forwarded the record of proceedings and noted that Admiral Halsey's statement had been reviewed. The third paragraph had been blanked out completely. Paragraph 4 indicated concurrence in Halsey's comment that the weather warning service in both the December, 1944, and the June, 1945, typhoons had been inadequate. The next eleven lines of paragraph 4 had also been blanked out. (I found it hard to believe that the Office of the Judge Advocate General was exercising censorship over declassified matter originated during World War II.) At the bottom of the page, Secretary Forrestal had stamped "Approved," and signed it on 30 November 1945. It was this rubber-stamped approval that the JAG officer had referred to in his conversation with me, and which I had been led to believe (whether deliberately or not), was the only endorsement in existence.

Several things were now clear: there had been a total of at least fourteen endorsements to the record of proceedings of the first court of inquiry (that which dealt with the typhoon of 18 December 1944); someone had considered the material contained in that record to be sufficiently prejudicial to Admiral Halsey as to request that he submit a statement about it; someone in the Office of the Judge Advocate General (Investigations) had seen fit to censor portions of Admiral King's endorsement; and disposition of the record of proceedings of the first court of inquiry had been overtaken by and entangled with the second court of inquiry (which dealt with the typhoon of June 1945).

On 10 November 1980, I wrote again to the Office of the JAG, requesting the full text of the several written endorsements made by Secretary Forrestal, Admiral King, Admiral Nimitz, and Admiral Halsey regarding the first typhoon. I also requested copies of any endorsements concerning the role played by the Bureau of Ships in monitoring the stability of the *Hull*, *Monaghan*, and *Spence*. I noted that my request was considered to be consistent with the terms of the Freedom of Information Act.

On 14 January 1981, having received no reply to my request, I was able to reach the appropriate action officer by telephone. He acknowledged receipt of my letter, and indicated that his office was going to provide me with the requested documents. I asked if I would be given the full text of each. He replied that I would not, that certain portions of the material would be deleted. He then explained that the Freedom of Information Act provided several categories of exceptions that authorized the withholding of information, that determination as to whether the material met the criteria for the exceptions was up to the agency holding it, and that personal privacy would be one of the categories of exception brought into play. He wasn't certain which other categories might also be held applicable as justification for withholding information, but there was a clear indication that the JAG attitude, at least as he interpreted it, was to give me no more information than the law required. He also mentioned that there had been other requests for the same material, and I wondered, in the light of that news, why the existence of the Secretary of the Navy's endorsement had been so difficult to confirm. When I asked whether the other requests had resulted in release of the material, I was told that each request had been handled on a case-by-case basis by another action officer, and that the specific actions taken in each case were not known to him. It also was made clear to me that my letter of 10 November 1980 was not considered to fall within the provisions of the Freedom of Information Act, because it did not conform to the prescribed format for such requests. By this time, I had developed doubts that I ever would receive all of the material to present the full picture of the administrative actions taken to dispose of the first court of inquiry.

I next obtained a copy of the Freedom of Information Act, along with suggested letter formats for use in submitting requests. Using that information, I again wrote a formal request to the Office of the Judge Advocate General (Investigations). I noted that since the matter under investigation by the court of inquiry related entirely to the performance of official duties, the personal privacy exemption did not appear to be applicable, and asked that none of the requested material be withheld. This time, to my utter astonishment, the response was prompt and complete. On 12 February 1981, I received from the Office of the Judge Advocate General (Investigations), the entire record of proceedings of the court of inquiry covering the first typhoon, including all sixteen endorsements in their entirety. The cause of the sudden change from a negative approach to a full and positive response remains unknown.

In any case, the most surprising aspect of this experience was the realization that even now, almost thirty-seven years after the typhoon, there is evidence of a tendency in at least one office of the Navy Department—that of the Judge Advocate General (Investigations)—to withhold the facts. There had been one other major research problem, which for more than a year raised suspicions of a cover-up. I had experienced great difficulty in locating pertinent Bureau of Ships records regarding the stability of *Farragut*-class destroyers. However, after spending several days working with researchers in the archives at Suitland, Maryland, in the fall of 1979, it became apparent that the Bureau of Ships records that were stored there were in a chaotic state of disarray, with hundreds of lineal feet of shelf space filled with boxes of letters, most of them unsorted, uncatalogued, and unorganized. It was an archivist's nightmare, deserving some positive corrective measures. I concluded that the difficulty encountered in locating Bureau of Ships documents was no more deliberately contrived than was the state of their records.

In the preceding chapters it was noted that Admiral King forwarded his recommendations regarding the court of inquiry to the Secretary of the Navy on 21 February 1945. On 14 March 1945, Mr. Forrestal simply forwarded the entire record of proceedings to the

Navy's Judge Advocate General. This was Endorsement #1. The Office of the JAG then forwarded the record to the Chief of the Bureau of Ships for recommendation, via the Chief of Naval Operations, Chief of the Bureau of Medicine and Surgery, and the Chief of Naval Personnel. The next four endorsements established that those people lost in the typhoon were officially *dead*, rather than missing. It should be noted also that the total number of officers and men lost, according to the Chief of Naval Personnel, was 778, or 12 less than the total given in the record of proceedings. It is assumed that 778 is the correct figure.

On 26 May 1945, the Chief of Naval Personnel forwarded the record of proceedings (Endorsement #6) to the Secretary of the Navy (via the Chief of the Bureau of Ships, and the Commander in Chief United States Fleet), noting that his bureau already was assigning the best available aerological officers to the fleet, as the court had recommended. He also questioned whether the opinion of the court of inquiry (that the preponderance of responsibility for the Third Fleet's losses attached to Admiral Halsey) should be considered "a matter of interest" related to that officer's record. In resolving this question, the Chief of Naval Personnel deferred to the Commander in Chief United States Fleet, and suggested that if an affirmative determination should be made, the record of proceedings should be referred to Admiral Halsey for his statement. The record then went to the Chief of the Bureau of Ships for his recommendations.

In Endorsement #7, dated 16 July 1945, the Chief of the Bureau of Ships indicated that action would be taken to modify the ventilation systems and make other design changes in carriers and destroyers, as proposed by the court of inquiry. With regard to the stability of destroyers, he reverted to the language used in his letter of 2 June 1945 to the Chief of Naval Operations, which was discussed in chapter 18 of this book. Repeating many of the thoughts previously expressed in that letter, the Chief of the Bureau of Ships again told the Chief of Naval Operations, (and now also the Secretary of the Navy) that although the *Hull* and *Monaghan* had capsized, two ships of the same class had survived the storm, and that "recent satisfactory inclining experiments for the *Macdonough* (DD352) and *Aylwin* (DD355)," provided "a reasonable check on the stability of the *Hull* and *Monaghan*." I have confirmed with her former commanding officer, Captain Bill Rogers, U.S. Navy (Ret.), that "the recent satisfactory inclining experiment" in the case of the *Aylwin* had to be the one administered at Puget Sound Navy Yard on

24 September 1944, since she never had one after that. I therefore contend that it was not "recent," and while technically it may have been "satisfactory," its allowance for a margin of error was zero. With regard to the inclining test conducted on the *Macdonough*, we already have seen how "satisfactory" her skipper considered her to be after the test had been conducted. The Chief of the Bureau of Ships went on in his endorsement to point out again that the loss of the *Spence* demonstrated that even the new 2,100-and 2,200-ton destroyers, with considerably improved stability characteristics, would find "prohibitive conditions" in extreme storms. Finally, he again concluded that to modify the *Farragut* class to provide stability characteristics even approaching those of the new destroyers would require a drastic reduction in military characteristics. It is my recollection that after her mid-1945 overhaul, one of the *Mahan* class was discovered to be so unstable that her 5-inch battery was reduced from four guns to three. Drastic reductions in military characteristics obviously were necessary when the only alternative was such a narrow margin of stability as to render the ships unsafe. Also, one must ask, if such drastic reductions were permissible for the *Mahan* class, why were they any less acceptable for the *Farragut*s?

The record now made its way to the Commander in Chief United States Fleet. In Endorsement #9, dated 23 August 1945, Admiral King forwarded it to the Secretary of the Navy, recommending that, "In view of a subsequent incident of similar nature in which Admiral Halsey has been concerned," the record be referred to that officer for statement to determine whether there was a matter of interest within the purview of the U.S. Code that related to Admiral Halsey's record.

On 5 September 1945, Secretary Forrestal signed Endorsement #10, forwarding the record of proceedings via the Commander in Chief U.S. Pacific Fleet, to Admiral Halsey for his statement. Admiral Nimitz then passed it on to Admiral Halsey for that purpose. This was Endorsement #11, dated 21 September 1945.

Admiral Halsey signed Endorsement #12 on 29 September 1945, returning the record to the Secretary of the Navy via the Commander in Chief U.S. Pacific Fleet and the Commander in Chief United States Fleet, with the following comments:

    1. Returned.
    2. In view of the fact that another similar incident was apparently the basis for further referring this record to me for statement, I am

compelled to reiterate certain views and recommendations that I have elsewhere expressed in other correspondence.

3. As to further statement concerning the typhoon in the Philippine Sea, 17–22 December 1944, I have no further statement to make; I believe that the facts elicited, and the reasons for decisions, are adequately covered in this record. If the events of a subsequent incident are considered germane to the subject of this record, then I must emphatically state that I attribute both instances to a lack of weather information adequate to enable me to maneuver clear of critical storm areas.

4. I have repeatedly made detailed recommendations for a typhoon warning service which would enable a task fleet commander at sea to conduct his forces to areas of comparative safety. This weather service did not exist in December, 1944, nor was adequate and timely information available to me to completely avoid damage from a typhoon 4–5 June, 1945; in the latter instance positive information as to the location and direction of movement of the typhoon was not available to me from any source until a matter of hours before the typhoon arrived among the fleet forces. And it must be remembered that task fleets cover great areas.

5. Subsequent to the 4–5 June typhoon, the typhoon warning service was greatly improved and approximated the system recommended by me; planes actually located and tracked their centers and good information enabled me to avoid damage on several occasions.

6. I wish to point out that the "law of storms" can enable a single ship or very small unit to make a last-minute evasion and so escape the full devastating force of the center, but with fleets and large forces it may be, and has been, impossible to completely extricate all scattered groups. I also wish to emphasize that typhoon movements are erratic and frequently could not be predicted owing to lack of weather information concerning Empire areas. Forces under my command avoided no less than eleven typhoons without damage during extended operations in the typhoon belt.

7. I have no wish to avoid my proper responsibility in these instances; however, I also wish to state unequivocally that in both the December, 1944, and June, 1945, typhoons the weather warning service did not provide the accurate and timely information necessary to enable me to take timely evasive action. For that inadequacy I can not accept responsibility.

W.F. Halsey

Admiral Nimitz signed Endorsement #13 on 20 October 1945, sending the record (now including Admiral Halsey's statement) back to the Secretary of the Navy, via the Chief of Naval Operations, with but one word: "Forwarded." On 23 November 1945, Admiral King appended his Endorsement #14, addressed to the Secretary of the Navy. It noted that Admiral Halsey's comments had been reviewed in the light of an analysis of the typhoon warning service and the records of the proceedings of the two courts of inquiry. The remainder of the endorsement is summarized in the following verbatim extracts:

> 3. I am of the opinion that the proceedings, findings, opinions and recommendations of the courts of inquiry and of the convening authority . . . are in no way altered and that the primary responsibility for the storm damage and losses . . . attaches to Commander Third Fleet, Admiral William F. Halsey, U.S. Navy.
>
> 4. I concur in the statement of Commander Third Fleet . . . concerning the inadequacy of the weather warning service. . . .
>
> 5. It has been pointed out that the inadequacies in the basic typhoon warning system . . . lay largely in delays in dissemination of information, and it is my opinion that these delays may be properly chargeable to the general conditions then existing. . . .
>
> 6. I note that the steps directed by the Commander in Chief, U.S. Pacific Fleet, in early 1945 produced a great improvement in the warning system prior to the typhoon of June 1945, and still further improvement has been made to date. The lessons learned from the experiences of the Pacific Fleet in these typhoons have been of great value in training and in the problems of ship design, and continuing use of these lessons will be made as appropriate in the future. In view of the lessons learned and the effective corrective measures which have been taken, I consider that the investigations of the typhoons of December 1944 and June 1945 are now completed and I recommend that no further action be taken.
>
> E.J. King

Secretary of the Navy Forrestal stamped the King endorsement "Approved", on 30 November 1945. Endorsements #15 and #16, from the Office of the Judge Advocate General to the Chief of Naval Personnel, and back, were administrative procedures of no consequence. The record of proceedings was finally returned to the Office of the Judge Advocate General on 20 December 1945, almost exactly one year after the date of the first typhoon.

Reflecting on the points discussed in the sixteen endorsements, nothing appears to change the conclusions reached in the earlier chapters of this book. Nowhere in the record of proceedings, or in its review by higher authority, was it ever recognized that adequate warning signs were available to the task fleet commander in the form of local weather indicators that simply were ignored. Admiral Halsey's statement is especially disturbing. Its disjointed, rambling and redundant language, and its defensive tone, seem in themselves to have been enough to cause some concern. In the light of hindsight, it seems highly possible that these were signs of fatigue in a combat leader who badly needed a rest.

With regard to the role played by the Bureau of Ships, the endorsements tend to confirm what was apparent before. The *Aylwin's* inclining test in September 1944 did not set off any alarm bells in Washington. The fact that it did not lulled all of those involved into a false sense of security. Again we see that almost a year after the loss of the *Hull* and *Monaghan*, the Bureau of Ships steadfastly held to the view that *Farragut*-class destroyers were stable. No one ever pointed an accusing finger at, or even raised a question concerning, the role played by the Bureau of Ships in the matter of destroyer stability. It remains an incredible series of events.

There is much about the story of the Third Fleet's encounter with the typhoon of December 1944 that is consistent with the highest traditions of the naval service. The heroic conduct of the sailors of an entire fleet, and the outstanding performance of duty demonstrated by hundreds of officers should be sources of great pride, always. However, there is no way to avoid the conclusion that when it came to the deadly serious and sometimes crucial business of seamanship, involving the struggle of men and ships against the elements, the top leaders of the Third Fleet and their supporting staffs were found wanting, on at least two different occasions. The cost of those shortcomings was more than we ever should have had to pay. Hopefully, the fleet commanders of tomorrow will see to it that it never happens again!

Appendixes

Notes on Stability

(Extracts from Record of Proceedings, Court of Inquiry)

When a ship lists, the center of buoyancy shifts in the direction of the list. In this condition the force of buoyancy acting vertically upward and the force of gravity acting vertically downward through the center of gravity of the ship form a couple tending to return the ship to the upright position. For all moderate angles of

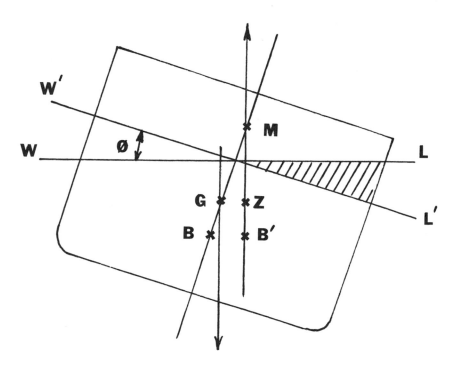

M = transverse metacenter
G = center of gravity
GZ = righting arm
θ = angle of heel
B = center of buoyance—ship upright
B′ = center of buoyance—ship inclined

213

heel (up to about 10°) the verticals through the individual centers of buoyancy intersect the centerline plane of the ship at the same point. This point is called the transverse metacenter (M). The distance between this point and the center of gravity (G) is known as the metacentric height (GM). This is significant in discussions of stability because mathematically, the righting arm, GZ in the figure on page 213, equals GM sin θ, and the moment tending to restore the ship to the upright position is equal to the ship's weight (its displacement) times GZ.

As an initial index of a ship's stability, the metacentric height (GM) is of considerable importance. GM, however, is not a complete index to the stability of a ship in a seaway. The value of GZ is the significant factor. To determine the stability of any ship in a seaway, it is necessary to calculate the righting arm (GZ) for various angles of heel up to the point where GZ becomes zero—the point of vanishing stability.

Third Fleet Task Organization

TG 38.1   *Yorktown**, Wasp, Cowpens, Monterey, Massachusetts, Alabama, New Orleans, San Francisco, Baltimore, Boston, San Diego, Buchanan, Hobby, Welles, Brown, McCord, Haggard, Franks, Halsey Powell, Colahan, Uhlmann, Benham, Cushing, Yarnall, Twining, Stockham, Wedderburn.*

TG 38.2   *Lexington**, Hancock***, Hornet, Cabot, Independence, Iowa, New Jersey****, Wisconsin, Vincennes, Miami, Pasadena, Astoria, San Juan, Dyson, Spence, Owen, Miller, The Sullivans, Stephen Potter, Tingey, Hickox, Hunt, Lewis Hancock, Marshall, Mansfield, DeHaven, Lyman K. Swenson, Collett, Maddox, Blue, Brush, Taussig, Samuel M. Moore.*

TG 38.3   *Essex**, Ticonderoga, San Jacinto, Langley, North Carolina, Washington, South Dakota, Santa Fe, Mobile, Biloxi, Oakland, Thatcher, Clarence K. Bronson, Cotten, Dortch, Gatling, Healy, Cogswell, Caperton, Ingersoll, Knapp, Porterfield, Callaghan, Cassin Young, Preston Laws, Longshaw, Pritchett.*

TG 30.7   *Anzio**, Lawrence C. Taylor, Melvin R. Nawman, Oliver Mitchell, Tabberer, Robert F. Keller.*

TU 30.8.0 *Aylwin**, Jicarilla, Mataco, Tekesta.*

TU 30.8.2 *Nantahala*, Caliente, Aucilla, Chikaskia, Monaghan, Waterman, Bangust.*

TU 30.8.3 *Monongahela*, Neosho, Patuxent, Marias, Thorn, Lake, Crowley.*

TU 30.8.4 *Atascosa*, Mascoma, Cache, Manatee, Dewey, Weaver, Lamons* (*Spence, Hickox* and *Maddox* joined on 17 Dec.)

TU 30.8.12 *Nehenta Bay*, Rudyerd Bay, Wesson, Swearer.*

TU 30.8.14 *Cape Esperance*, Altamaha, Kwajalein, Donaldson, Hull, Hulbert.*

****Fleet Flagship
***Force Flagship
**Group Flagship
*Unit Flagship

APPENDIX C

Nimitz Letter of 13 February 1945

Cincpac File
A2-11
L11-1
Serial
14CL-45
**UNITED STATES PACIFIC FLEET
AND PACIFIC OCEAN AREAS**
HEADQUARTERS OF THE COMMANDER IN CHIEF

13 February 1945

From: Commander in Chief, U.S. Pacific Fleet.
To: PACIFIC FLEET and NAVAL SHORE ACTIVITIES, Pacific Ocean Areas.
Subject: Damage in Typhoon, Lessons of.

1. On 18 December 1944, vessels of the Pacific Fleet, operating in support of the invasion of the Philippines in an area about 300 miles east of Luzon, were caught near the center of a typhoon of extreme violence. Three destroyers, the *Hull*, *Monaghan*, and *Spence*, capsized and went down with practically all hands; serious damage was sustained by the CL *Miami*, the CVLs *Monterey*, *Cowpens*, and *San Jacinto*, the CVEs *Cape Esperance* and *Altamaha*, and the DDs *Aylwin*, *Dewey*, and *Hickox*. Lesser damage was sustained by at least 19 other vessels, from CAs down to DEs. Fires occurred on three carriers when planes were smashed in their hangars; and some 146 planes on various ships were lost or damaged beyond economical repair by the fires, by being smashed up, or by being swept overboard. About 790 officers and men were lost or killed, and 80 were injured. Several surviving destroyers reported rolling 70° or more; and we can only surmise how close this was to capsizing completely for some of them. It was the greatest loss that we have taken in the Pacific without compensatory return since the First Battle of Savo.

2. In the light of hindsight it is easy to see how any of several measures *might* have prevented this catastrophe, but it was far less easy a problem at the time for the men who were out there under the heaviest of conflicting responsibilities. The important thing is for it

216

never to happen again; and hence, while it is impracticable herein
to go into all the factors involved and the experiences undergone,
some of the outstanding lessons will be discussed.

3. Possibly, too much reliance was placed on the analysis broadcast from the Fleet Weather Central, Pearl Harbor. Weather data
was lacking from an area some 240 to 300 miles in diameter (where
the storm was actually centered); and the immediate signs of it in
the operating area were not heeded early enough. Groups of the
Third Fleet tried to avoid the storm center, but neither radically
enough nor to best advantage, since their information as to its
location and path was meager. Fleet damage and losses were ac-
centuated by the efforts of vessels and subordinate commanders to
maintain fleet courses, speeds, and formations during the storm.
Commanding officers failed to realize sufficiently in advance of the
fact that it was necessary for them to give up the attempt, and give
all their attention to saving their ships. There was a lack of appreciation by subordinate commanders and commanding officers that
really dangerous weather conditions existed, until it was too late to
make the preparations for security that might have been helpful.

4. The following conditions were typical during the typhoon:

(a) Visibility zero to a thousand yards.

(b) Ships not merely rolling, but heeled far over continually
    by the force of the wind, thus leaving them very little
    margin for further rolling to leeward.

(c) Water being taken in quantity through ventilators, blower
    intakes, and every topside opening.

(d) Switchboards and electrical machinery of all kinds
    shorted and drowned out, with fires from short circuits.
    Main distribution board in engine room shorted by steam
    moisture when all topside openings were closed to keep
    out water.

(e) Free water up to two or three feet over engines or fireroom
    floor plates, and in many other compartments. It
    apparently all came in from above; there is no evidence of
    ships' seams parting.

(f) Loss of steering control, failure of power and lighting, and
    stoppage of main propulsion plant. Loss of radar and of all
    ability to communicate.

(g) Planes on carriers going adrift, crashing into each other,
    and starting fires.

(h) Wind velocities and seas that carried away masts, stacks,
    boats, davits, and deck structures generally, and made it
    impossible for men to secure gear that had gone adrift, or

to jettison or strike below topside weights when the necessity had become apparent. Men could not even stay up where they would have a chance of getting clear of the ship.

(i) Maneuvering up to the time of sinking, in the attempt to maintain station, by all ships that were lost. *Dewey*, saved by apparently a narrow margin, had given up the attempt.

(j) The storm "taking charge" and making impossible various evasive and security measures which might have been effective at an earlier stage.

(k) Testimony that the ships lost took a long roll to leeward, varying from 50° to 80°, hung there a little while, and then went completely over, floating a short time before going down.

5. The following tabulation does not purport to be the whole story, either for the ships mentioned or for the Fleet as a whole. It does, however, show that some ships, although of the same class as those lost, and undergoing the same punishment from the weather, survived nevertheless. It also indicates some differences in their condition and in the measures taken. Nobody can say, however, how far the outcome was due to these conditions and measures (or lack of them) and how far to blind chance.

6.

Class	All of *Farragut* Class				Both *Fletcher* Class	
	Hull	*Monaghan*	*Dewey*	*Aylwin*	*Spence*	*Hickox*
Outcome	Sunk	Sunk	Survived	Survived	Sunk	Survived
Fuel on hand (app)	70%	76%	?	80%	15%	14%
Water Ballast	No	No	Yes	?	Very little	Fully ballast'd
Fuel to high side	No	No	Yes	Yes	No	?
Cond. "A" taken	Yes	?	Yes	?	No	?
Top weight jettisoned or below	No	?	Yes	?	?	?
Free water in ship	Yes	?	Some	Yes	Yes	Some
Rolled and recovered	70°	?	75°	70°	Hung at 50°, then capsized	70°

7. Various weaknesses were brought to light in our forecasting and dissemination of weather information, in structural details which permitted flooding with consequent loss of power, short circuiting, etc., and in the stability of some our destroyers. Measures to correct these faults are being taken as far as possible. Yet the Commander in Chief, Pacific Fleet wishes to emphasize that to insure safety at sea, the best that science can devise and that naval organization can provide must be regarded only as an aid, and

never as a substitute for the good seamanship, self-reliance, and sense of ultimate responsibility which are the first requisites in a seaman and naval officer.

8. A hundred years ago, a ship's survival depended almost solely on the competence of her master and on his constant alertness to every hint of change in the weather. To be taken aback or caught with full sail on by even a passing squall might mean the loss of spars or canvas; and to come close to the center of a genuine hurricane or typhoon was synonymous with disaster. While to be taken by surprise was thus serious, the facilities for avoiding it were meager. Each master was dependent wholly on himself for detecting the first symptoms of bad weather, for predicting its seriousness and movement, and for taking the appropriate measures, to evade it if possible and to battle through it if it passed near to him. There was no radio by which weather data could be collected from over all the oceans and the resulting forecasts by expert aerologists broadcasted to him and to all afloat. There was no one to tell him that the time had now come to strike his light sails and spars, and snug her down under close reefs or storm trysails. His own barometer, the force and direction of the wind, and the appearance of sea and sky were all that he had for information. Ceaseless vigilance in watching and interpreting signs, plus a philosophy of taking no risk in which there was little to gain and much to be lost, was what enabled him to survive.

9. Seaman of the present day should be better at forecasting weather at sea, independently of the radio, than were their predecessors. The general laws of storms and the weather expectancy for all months of the year in all parts of the world are now more thoroughly understood, more completely catalogued, and more readily available in various publications. An intensive study of typhoons and Western Pacific weather was made over a period of many years by Father Depperman at the Manila observatory, and his conclusions have been embodied in the material available to all aerologists. What Knight and Bowditch have to say on the subject is exactly as true during this war as it was in time of peace or before the days of radio. Familiarity with these authorities is something no captain or navigator can do without. The monthly pilot charts, issued to all ships, give excellent information as to the probable incidence and movements of typhoons. Stress on the foregoing is no belittlement of our aerological centers and weather broadcasts. But just as a navigator is held culpable if he neglects "Log, Lead, and Lookout" through blind faith in his radio fixes, so is the seaman culpable who regards personal weather estimates as obsolete and

assumes that if no radio storm warning has been received, then all is well, and no local weather signs need cause him concern.

10. It is possible that too much reliance is being placed on outside sources for warnings of dangerous weather, and on the ability of our splendid ships to come through anything that wind and wave can do. If this be so, there is need for a revival of the age-old habits of self-reliance and caution in regard to the hazard from storms, and for officers in all echelons of command to take their personal responsibilities in this respect more seriously.

11. The most difficult part of the whole heavy-weather problem is of course the conflict between the military necessity for carrying out an operation as scheduled, and the possibility of damage or loss to our ships in doing so. For this no possible rule can be laid down. The decision must be a matter of "calculated risk" either way. It should be kept in mind, however, that a ship which founders or is badly damaged is a dead loss not only to the current operation but to future ones, that the weather which hinders us may be hindering the enemy equally, and that ships which, to prevent probable damage and possible loss, are allowed to drop behind, or to maneuver independently, may by that very measure be able to rejoin later and be of use in the operation.

12. The safety of a ship against perils from storm, as well as from those of navigation and maneuvering, is always the primary responsibility of her commanding officer; but this responsibility is also shared by his immediate superiors in operational command since by the very fact of such command the individual commanding officer is not free to do at any time what his own judgment might indicate. Obviously no rational captain will permit his ship to be lost fruitlessly through blind obedience to plan or order, since by no chance could that be the intention of his superior. But the degree of a ship's danger is progressive and at the same time indefinite. It is one thing for a commanding officer, acting independently in time of peace, to pick a course and speed which may save him a beating from the weather, and quite another for him, in time of war, to disregard his mission and his orders and leave his station and duty.

13. It is here that the responsibility rests on unit, group, and force commanders, and that their judgment and authority must be exercised. They are of course the ones best qualified to weigh the situation and the relative urgency of safety measures versus carrying on with the job in hand. They frequently guard circuits or possess weather codes not available to all ships; and it goes without saying that any storm warnings or important weather information which they are not sure everybody has received should be re-transmitted

as far as practicable. More than this, they must be conscious of the relative inexperience in seamanship, and particularly hurricane seamanship, of many of their commanding officers, despite their superb fighting qualities. One division commander reports that his captains averaged eight years or less out of the Naval Academy, and this is probably typical.

14. It is most definitely part of the senior officer's responsibility to think in terms of the smallest ship and most inexperienced commanding officer under him. He cannot take them for granted, give them tasks and stations, and assume either that they will be able to keep up and come through any weather that his own big ship can; or that they will be wise enough to gauge the exact moment when their task must be abandoned in order for them to keep afloat. The order for ships to be handled and navigated wholly for their own preservation should be originated early enough by the seniors, and not be necessarily withheld until the juniors request it. The very gallantry and determination of our young commanding officers need to be taken into account here as a danger factor, since their urge to keep on, to keep up, to keep station, and to carry out their mission in the face of any difficulty, may deter them from doing what is actually wisest and most profitable in the long run.

15. Yet if the O.T.C. is to be held responsible for his smaller vessels, he must be kept aware of their conditions, and the onus of this rests on the commanding officers themselves. Each of them must not only do whatever he is free and able to do for his ship's safety, but must also keep his superiors in the chain of command fully informed as to his situation. If there is anything in his ship's particular condition or in the way she is taking the weather that worries him, he should not hesitate to pass the information to his seniors. To let this be regarded as a sign of faintheartedness is to invite disaster, and seniors should indoctrinate their commanding officers accordingly. Going still further, it has been shown that at sea the severity of the weather may develop to a point where, regardless of combat commitments of the high command, the situation will require independent action by a junior without reference to his senior. This becomes mandatory if grave doubts arise in the mind of the junior as to the safety of his vessel, the lives of its crew, and the loss of valuable government property and equipment.

16. The commanders of all echelons in the Pacific Fleet will impress upon their subordinates the necessity for giving full consideration to the adverse weather likely to be encountered in the Western Pacific, particularly the presence of tropical disturbances and the formation and movement of typhoons. In this connection,

each commanding officer should refresh himself on Knight and Bowditch, not only as to the "Laws of Storms", but also to ship-handling in heavy weather. In order to know what outside weather reports are broadcast and what he should be getting, each commanding officer should be familiar with *Radio Weather Aids to Navigation* (H. O. 206), and its confidential supplement H. O. 206-C-S(A). This publication, as well as the Navy *Weather Forecast Code No. 1* (CSP-946) should be on all DDs and DEs, etc. Even more important, a commanding officer should check up on his own ship's system of handling dispatches, to make sure that every incoming dispatch about prospective weather is viewed and understood by himself or some other officer with experience enough to grasp its significance. It should by no chance get buried in files and overlooked. This applies even more strongly to local observations. Preoccupation with the job in hand, or a desire not to disturb the skipper, should never result in disregard of a rapidly falling barometer.

17. Steps must be taken to insure that commanding officers of all vessels, particularly destroyers and smaller craft, are fully aware of the stability characteristics of their ships; that adequate security measures regarding water-tight integrity are enforced; and that effect upon stability of free liquid surfaces is thoroughly understood. For preparing the ship against expected heavy weather, the basic written authorities are:

(a) *Damage Control Book* for ship concerned.
(b) *Ballasting Instructions* issued by the Type Maintenance Administration concerned.
(c) *Notes on Stability of Ships in a Seaway*, (Pacific Fleet Maintenance Confidential Letter No. 7–44).
(d) *Booklet of Inclining Experiment Data* for either ship or class. Issued by BuShips.
(e) *Damage Control Instructions* (FTP 170-B).
(f) "Derangement of Electrical Equipment caused by Ventilation Conditions", *BuShips Bulletin of Information*, No. 12, p. 9.
(g) *Stability and Compartmentation of Ships* (C&R Bulletin No. 14).

18. In conclusion, both seniors and juniors must realize that in bad weather, as in most other situations, safety and fatal hazard are not separated by any sharp boundary line, but shade gradually from one into the other. There is no little red light which is going to flash on and inform commanding officers or higher commanders that from then on there is extreme danger from the weather, and that measures for ships' safety must now take precedence over further

efforts to keep up with the formation or to execute the assigned task. This time will always be a matter of personal judgment. Naturally no commander is going to cut thin the margin between staying afloat and foundering, but he may nevertheless unwittingly pass the danger point even though no ship is yet *in extremis*. Ships that keep on going as long as the severity of wind and sea has not yet come close to capsizing them or breaking them in two, may nevertheless become helpless to avoid these catastrophes later if things get worse. By then they may be unable to steer any heading but in the trough of the sea, or may have their steering control, lighting, communications, and main propulsion disabled, or may be helpless to secure things on deck or to jettison topside weights. The time for taking all measures for a ship's safety is while still able to do so. Nothing is more dangerous than for a seaman to be grudging in taking precautions lest they turn out to have been unnecessary. Safety at sea for a thousand years has depended on exactly the opposite philosophy.

C. W. NIMITZ.

DISTRIBUTION: (5N-45)

Case 2			
List I	A-U.	List VI	J-R.
List II	A-D.	List VII	A-D, Z, AA.
List III	A, D, F, G, K, O.	List VIII	A.
List V	A-K, S-V.	List IX	A.

O. L. Thorne,
Flag Secretary.

Notes

Preface

1. Baldwin, Hanson W., "When the Third Fleet Met the Great Typhoon," *New York Times Magazine*, 16 December 1951, pp. 18–19.

Chapter 1

1. Commander Destroyers Pacific Fleet letter Serial 0990, 20 May 1944.
2. Ibid.

Chapter 2

1. Operational data regarding the ships of Destroyer Squadron One, from 1 October 1944, to 10 December 1944, have been taken from the applicable war diaries of the *Dewey* and other ships involved. They are not footnoted beyond this entry.
2. Commander Wendt had a distinguished naval career and was eventually promoted to the rank of admiral, the only one of Destroyer Squadron One's skippers from that period to attain four stars.
3. Knight, Austin M., Rear Admiral, U.S. Navy, *Modern Seamanship*, pp. 765–66.
4. Bowditch, Nathaniel, LL.D., *The American Practical Navigator*, pp. 281–293.
5. Ibid., p. 292.
6. Ibid.
7. Ibid., p. 276.

Chapter 4

1. Commander in Chief, U.S. Pacific Fleet, Serial 002910, 25 June 1945, p. 9.
2. Ibid.
3. Ibid., pp. 6, 7.
4. Ibid.
5. Ibid., p. 7.
6. Ibid.
7. Ibid.
8. Ibid., p. 11.
9. Ibid., p. 12.
10. Ibid., p. 11.

Chapter 5

1. *New Jersey* deck log, 17 December 1944.
2. *Dewey* deck log, 11 December 1944.
3. Ibid.
4. *New Jersey* deck log, 17 December 1944.
5. Ibid.
6. Adamson and Kosco, *Halsey's Typhoons*, p. 34.
7. *New Jersey* deck log, 17 December 1944.
8. The detailed chronology of events and communications, as they were recorded on 17 and 18 December 1944 by the Third Fleet staff aboard the *New Jersey*, is contained in Commander Third Fleet's report of the typhoon, Serial 00166, dated 25 December 1944.
9. *New Jersey* deck log, 17 December 1944.
10. Bowditch, *The American Practical Navigator*, p. 286.
11. Information relating to rendezvous points, the tracks of the typhoon, both projected and actual, and the tracks of Third Fleet ships, all have been obtained from the track chart marked Enclosure B, *Chronological Summary of Events* (local time), prepared by Chief of Naval Operations, Aerology Section, undated, and filed with the Record of Proceedings of the court of inquiry.
12. Bowditch, *The American Practical Navigator*, p. 289.
13. *Dewey* deck log, 17 December 1944.
14. Bate, David S., letter to the author dated 23 June 1979.
15. Record of Proceedings, court of inquiry, p. 48.
16. *Dewey* deck log, 17 December 1944.
17. *Nehenta Bay* Serial 083, 24 December 1944.
18. Record of Proceedings, court of inquiry, p. 7.
19. *Dewey* deck log, 17 December 1944.
20. Ibid.

Chapter 6

1. Record of Proceedings, court of inquiry, pp. 12, 13.
2. Commander Third Fleet message 170514 December, 1944.
3. Record of Proceedings, court of inquiry, p. 13.
4. Ibid., p. 130.
5. *New Jersey* deck log, 18 December 1944.
6. Record of Proceedings, court of inquiry, p. 14.
7. Ibid.
8. Ibid., pp. 14, 15.
9. Commander Third Fleet Report of Typhoon, Serial 0166, 25 December 1944.
10. *New Jersey* deck log, 18 December 1944.
11. Ibid.
12. Ibid.
13. Ibid.

Chapter 7

1. Adapted from "Typhoon," by Captain C. R. Calhoun, U.S. Navy, as told to John Hubbell, from the January, 1959, *Reader's Digest*, pp. 46–50.
2. *Dewey* deck log, 18 December 1944.
3. Bate, David S., letter to the author, 23 June 1979.
4. *Dewey* deck log, 18 December 1944.
5. Events aboard the *Dewey* on 18 December are set forth in some detail in the Chronological Sequence of Events, marked Enclosure A, and attached to the *Dewey* Report of Damage by Typhoon, Serial 005-44, 26 December 1944.
6. *Dewey* deck log, 18 December 1944.
7. Ibid.
8. Ibid.
9. Ibid.
10. Bate, David S., letter to the author, 23 June 1979.
11. Ibid.
12. *Dewey* deck log, 18 December 1944.
13. In my report of damage by the typhoon, Enclosure A to *Dewey* Serial 005–55, dated 26 December 1944, I commented about Preston Mercer's performance: "The constant steadying influence, sound advice and mature judgement of Commander Destroyer Squadron One were invaluable. It is felt that he, more than any other one person, was responsible for the safe return of the DEWEY."

Chapter 8

1. *Aylwin* deck log, 17 December 1944.
2. Ibid.
3. The narrative of her storm experience is condensed from the *Aylwin's* Report of Storm Damage, Serial 00116, 27 December 1944.
4. Ibid.
5. The narrative of her storm experience is condensed from the *Hull's* Report of Loss, Serial 0025, 1 January 1945.
6. Record of Proceedings, court of inquiry, p. 103.
7. Ibid., p. 97.
8. *Cape Esperance* Report of Damage, Serial 0010, 26 December 1944, p. 8.
9. Ibid.
10. "Turn" and "Corpen" were signals that indicated the method by which formation course was to be changed.
11. Kotsch, William J., Rear Admiral, U.S. Navy (Retired), *Weather for the Mariner*, 2nd ed. (Annapolis: Naval Institute Press, 1977), p. 164.
12. *Hull* Report of Loss, Serial 0025, 1 January 1945.
13. Record of Proceedings, court of inquiry, Exhibit 12.
14. Ibid., p. 38.
15. Ibid.
16. Ibid., Exhibit 12.

17. Ibid., p. 113.
18. McCrane's (*Monaghan*'s senior survivor) statment.
19. Record of Proceedings, court of inquiry, Exhibit 15.
20. Ibid.
21. *Hickox* Report of Storm Damage, Serial 001, 13 January 1945.
22. Ibid.

Chapter 9

1. *Monterey* Action Report, Serial 0036, 22 December 1944. Annex B. p. 1.
2. The narrative of her storm experience is condensed from the *Monterey*'s Action Report, Serial 0036, 22 December 1944.
3. *San Jacinto* Report of Damage, Serial 0062, 24 December 1944.
4. Ibid.
5. Ibid.
6. Ibid.
7. Ibid.
8. *Cowpens* Report of Storm Damage, Serial 0040, 23 December 1944.
9. Ibid.
10. Ibid.
11. Ibid.
12. *Cape Esperance* Report of Damage, Serial 010, 26 December 1944.
13. Ibid.
14. Ibid.
15. Ibid.
16. Ibid.
17. *Altamaha* Action Report, Serial 062, 24 December 1944.
18. Ibid.
19. Ibid.
20. Ibid.
21. Ibid.
22. Ibid.
23. Ibid.

Chapter 10

1. *Dewey* deck log, 19 December 1944.
2. The conversation with Preacher Johnson is also an adaptation from the article, "Typhoon," *Reader's Digest*, January, 1959.
3. Commander Third Fleet message to *Mascoma*, 190435, December, 1944.
4. Commander Destroyer Squadron One message to Commander Third Fleet, 191100, December, 1944.
5. Commander Third Fleet message to *Dewey*, 190345, December, 1944.
6. *Tabberer* message to Commander Third Fleet 181545, December, 1944.
7. *Mascoma* message to Commander Third Fleet 190957, December, 1944.
8. Commander Third Fleet message to Commander in Chief, Pacific Fleet 190222, December, 1944.

9. Commander Third Fleet message to Commander in Chief, Pacific Fleet 191357, December, 1944.

10. *Rudyerd Bay* message to Commander Third Fleet 191943, December, 1944.

11. CTU 30.8.18 message to Commander Third Fleet 200240, December, 1944.

12. Commander Third Fleet message to Commander in Chief, Southwest Pacific 201635, December, 1944.

13. Commander in Chief, Pacific Fleet message to Commander Third Fleet 202147, December, 1944.

14. Commander Third Fleet message to CTG 30.9, 202225, December, 1944.

15. Commander Third Fleet message to Commander in Chief, Pacific Fleet 202332, December, 1944.

16. Commander Third Fleet message to Commander in Chief, Pacific Fleet 210850, December, 1944.

17. Commander in Chief, United States Fleet message to Commander in Chief, Pacific Fleet 211822, December, 1944.

18. Commander in Chief, Pacific Fleet message to Commander in Chief, United States Fleet 230511, December, 1944.

19. Commander in Chief, Pacific Fleet message to Commander in Chief, United States Fleet 241117, December, 1944.

Chapter 11

1. The narrative of her experience in the typhoon is condensed from the *Tabberer*'s Action Report, Serial 002, 24 December 1944; from her report of Rescue of Survivors, Serial 003, 24 December 1944; and from the transcript of a press conference held at Pearl Harbor on January 16, 1945, with Lieutenant Commander Henry L. Plage, USNR, and Lieutenant Robert M. Surdam, USNR, commanding and executive officers, respectively.

2. *Dewey* deck log, 18 December 1944.

3. Ibid.

4. *Benham* Action Report, Serial 071, 26 December 1944.

5. *Tabberer* transcript of press conference with Lieutenant Commander Plage and Lieutenant Surdam, recorded at Pearl Harbor 16 January 1945.

6. Ibid.

7. Record of Proceedings, court of inquiry, Exhibit 13.

8. Commander Third Fleet Report of Typhoon, Serial 00166, 25 December 1944, p. 21.

9. McCrane's (*Monaghan*'s senior survivor) narrative.

10. Ibid.

Chapter 12

1. Commander Third Fleet message to Commander in Chief, Pacific Fleet, 201900, December, 1944.

2. Ibid.

3. Commander in Chief, Pacific Fleet message to *Iowa*, 260045, December, 1944.
4. Record of Proceedings, court of inquiry. Precept, 25 December 1944.
5. Ibid.
6. Ibid.
7. Ibid.
8. Record of Proceedings, court of inquiry, p. 1.
9. Ibid.
10. Ibid.

Chapter 13

1. Record of Proceedings, court of inquiry, pp. 2, 3.
2. Ibid., pp. 4, 5.
3. Ibid., pp. 6–11.
4. Ibid., pp. 72, 73.
5. Ibid., pp. 79, 80.
6. Ibid., pp. 78, 79.
7. Ibid., pp. 65–67.
8. Ibid., pp. 70, 71.
9. Ibid., pp. 68, 69.
10. Ibid., pp. 36–41.
11. Ibid., pp. 57–61.
12. Ibid., pp. 62, 63.
13. Ibid., p. 63.
14. Ibid., pp. 95–101.
15. Research for this book failed to disclose or confirm that any such message had been sent.
16. Record of Proceedings, court of inquiry, pp. 74–77.
17. Ibid., p. 78.

Chapter 14

1. Ibid., p. 11.
2. Ibid., p. 12.
3. Ibid.
4. Ibid., p. 13.
5. Commander Third Fleet message to Commander in Chief, Pacific Fleet and Task Force, Task Group Commanders of the Third Fleet, 170514, December, 1944.
6. Record of Proceedings, court of inquiry, p. 13.
7. Ibid., p. 14.
8. Ibid.
9. Ibid.
10. Ibid., p. 15.
11. Ibid.
12. Ibid.
13. Ibid.

14. Commander Third Fleet message to Third Fleet, 180015, December, 1944.
15. Record of Proceedings, court of inquiry, p. 16.
16. Ibid., pp. 17, 18.
17. Ibid., pp. 107, 108.
18. Ibid., Findings of Fact #29 and Opinion 11 and 12.
19. Ibid., pp. 129–32.
20. Ibid., pp. 132–34.
21. Ibid., p. 135.
22. Ibid., p. 69.
23. Ibid., p. 23.
24. Ibid., p. 25.
25. Ibid., p. 26.

Chapter 15

1. Furer, Julius Augustus, Rear Admiral, U.S. Navy (Retired), *Administration of the Navy Department in World War II*, pp. 218, 219.
2. Record of Proceedings, court of inquiry, p. 83.
3. Ibid., pp. 83, 84.
4. Ibid., p. 85.
5. Ibid., pp. 86, 87.
6. Ibid., pp. 137, 138.

Chapter 16

1. Ibid., pp. 160–66.
2. Ibid., p. 164.
3. Ibid., p. 165.
4. Ibid.
5. Ibid., p. 166.
6. Ibid.
7. Ibid.
8. Ibid., pp. 167, 168.
9. Smith, Howard, Lieutenant, U.S. Naval Reserve, memorandum dated 1 January, 1945.
10. Ibid., p. 1.
11. Commander in Chief, Pacific Fleet, Serial 00306, 22 January 1945.
12. Ibid.
13. Ibid.
14. Orem, Howard, Captain, U.S. Navy, memorandum dated 13 January 1945.
15. Ibid.
16. Commander in Chief, United States Fleet, Serial 00476, 21 February 1945.
17. Ibid.

Chapter 17

1. Commander in Chief, Pacific Fleet, Serial 002910, 25 June 1945, pp. 11, 12.
2. Bowditch, *The American Practical Navigator*, pp. 285, 286.
3. Ibid.
4. Halsey, William F., Fleet Admiral, U.S. Navy, and Bryan, J. III, Lieutenant Commander, U.S. Naval Reserve, *Admiral Halsey's Story*, p. 236.
5. CTU 38.2.2. Action Report dated 6 January 1944.
6. Ibid.
7. Record of Proceedings, court of inquiry, p. 2.
8. Ibid., p. 147.
9. Ibid., p. 15.
10. Furer, Julius Augustus, Rear Admiral, U.S. Navy (Retired), *Administration of the Navy Department in World War II*, pp. 219–21.
11. BuShips memorandum, Subject, *Destroyer and Destroyer Escort Stability*, 23 December 1944.
12. Ibid.
13. BuShips letter file C-DD350/S38–1 (814–638), dated 2 August 1944.
14. Navy Yard Puget Sound message to BuShips, 272359, September, 1944.
15. Rogers, W. K., Captain, U.S. Navy (Retired), letter to the author dated 25 November 1978.
16. Navy Yard Puget Sound message to BuShips 272359, September, 1944.
17. Commander Destroyers, Pacific Fleet letter, Serial 0990, 20 May 1944.
18. BuShips memorandum to Commander in Chief, United States Fleet, 23 December 1944.
19. Ibid.
20. Navy Yard Puget Sound message to BuShips 272359, September, 1944.

Chapter 18

1. *Dewey* War Diary, 17 February 1945.
2. Ibid., 19–25 February 1945.
3. Ibid., 25, 26 March 1945.
4. Commander Third Fleet, Serial 0098, 3 February 1945.
5. Commander in Chief, Pacific Fleet, Serial 005601, 5 March 1945.
6. Chief of Naval Operations, Serial 00131223 (SC) H–49, 22 March 1945.
7. *Dewey* Serial 004, dated 12 March 1945.
8. Commander Destroyers Division Ten Serial 027, 30 May 1945.
9. Commander Destroyer Squadron Five Serial 00142, 11 May 1945.
10. Commander in Chief, Pacific Fleet Serial 006021, 28 May 1945.
11. *Dewey* Serial 012, 27 May 1945.
12. Commander Destroyer Division Ten Serial 027, 30 May 1945.
13. Commander Destroyer Squadron Five Serial 0177, 9 June 1945.
14. Superintendent of Ships, Seattle, undated message to BuShips, reporting 30 March 1945 inclining test of USS *Macdonough*.

15. Assistant to Industrial Manager, U.S. Navy, (Seattle), letter, Serial 20295, 11 April 1945.
16. Executive officer USS *Macdonough* memo, 7 April 1945.
17. W. C. Nickum and Sons letter, 9 April 1945.
18. Ibid.
19. Assistant to Industrial Manager, U.S. Navy (Seattle) letter, Serial 20295, 11 April 1945.
20. BuShips mailgram 172111, April, 1945.
21. BuShips letter Serial 002338, 2 June 1945.
22. Ibid.
23. Ibid.
24. Ibid.
25. *Aylwin* Serial 001, 15 June 1945.
26. Commander Destroyer Division Ten Serial 0037, 27 June 1945.
27. Potter, E. B., *Nimitz*, p. 377.
28. Ship Characteristics Board Memorandum No. 46–45, Enclosure (K).
29. Third Naval District Sub-Board of Inspection and Survey, Report of Material Inspection and Survey of USS *Aylwin* (DD355), 17 October 1945.
30. *Time* Magazine, November 5, 1945 "Old Pat," p. 26.
31. Record of Proceedings, court of inquiry, Exhibit 9–4, p. 4.
32. Kehoe, James W., Jr., Captain, U.S. Navy, *Destroyer Seakeeping: Ours and Theirs*, U.S. Naval Institute *Proceedings*, November, 1973, pp. 26–37.
33. Hackett, Sir John, General, British Army, *The Third World War*, p. 183.

Bibliography

Primary Sources

A. Sources located in the Operational Archives, Naval History Division, Naval Historical Center, Building 220, Washington Navy Yard, Washington, D.C. 20374.

Altamaha Action Report, Serial 004, 27 December 1944.

Aylwin Report of Storm Damage, Serial 00116, 27 December 1944. WW II Action Reports.

Badger, O. C., Rear Admiral, U.S. Navy. Action Report 1–24 December 1944, 6 January 1945.

Benham Action Report, Serial 071, 26 December 1944.

Buchanan Report of Damage and Typhoon Experience, Serial 0495, 22 December 1944.

Cape Esperance Report of Damage, Serial 0010, 26 December 1944.

CinCPac message to ComThirdFlt and others, 202147, December, 1944.

CinCPac message to CominCh, 230511, December, 1944.

CinCPac message to CominCh, 241117, December, 1944.

CinCPac message to *Iowa*, 260045, December, 1944.

ComDesDiv 100 message to ComThirdFlt, 200521, December, 1944.

Commander Destroyers Pacific Fleet letter, Serial 0990, subject, Destroyers—Control of Loading, 20 May 1944.

ComDesRon One message to ComThirdFlt and others, 191100, December, 1944.

CominCH message to CinCPac, 211822, December, 1944.

Commander in Chief, U.S. Pacific Fleet, Serial 00306, 22 January 1945, endorsing proceedings of court of inquiry.

Commander in Chief, United States Fleet, Serial 00476, 21 February 1945, endorsing proceedings of court of inquiry.

Commander in Chief, U.S. Pacific Fleet, Serial 002910, report to Commander in Chief, United States Fleet, 25 June 1945, subject, Operations in Pacific Ocean Areas—December, 1944.

ComThirdFlt message to CinCPac, 170514, December, 1944.

ComThirdFlt message to ThirdFlt 180015, December, 1944.

ComThirdFlt message to CinCPac, 190222, December, 1944.

ComThirdFlt message to *Dewey*, 190345, December, 1944.

ComThirdFlt message to *Mascoma*, 190435, December, 1944.

ComThirdFlt message to CinCPac 191357, December, 1944.

ComThirdFlt message to CinCSWPac and others, 201635, December, 1944.

ComThirdFlt message to CinCPac and others, 201900, December, 1944.

ComThirdFlt message to CTG 30.9, 202225, December, 1944.

ComThirdFlt message to CinCPac 202332, December, 1944.

ComThirdFlt message to CinCPac 210850, December, 1944.

Commander Third Fleet Report of Typhoon, Serial 0166, 25 December 1944.

Cooper, C. S., Commander, U.S. Navy. Report to Commanding Officer, USS *San Jacinto*, of Investigation of Circumstances Surrounding Typhoon Damage, Serial 002, 21 December 1944.

Cowpens Report of Storm Damage, Serial 0040, 23 December 1944.

CTG 30.5 message to CTU 30.5.1, 191211, December, 1944.

CTU 30.8.18 message to ComThirdFlt, 200240, December, 1944.

Dewey message to ComServRon Ten, 200645, December, 1944.

Dewey Report of Damage by Typhoon, Serial 005–44, 25 December 1944.

Dewey War Diary, months of September, October, November, and December, 1944.

Hickox Report of Storm Damage, Serial 001, 13 January 1945.

Hull Report of Loss, Serial 0025, 1 January 1945.

Iowa Action Report, Serial 0132, 31 December 1944.

Nehenta Bay Report of Typhoon Damage, Serial 083, 24 December 1944.

Navy Department Press Release. "USS *Monaghan* Survivors Tell Story." 11 February 1945.

Marks, James A., Lieutenant Commander, U.S. Navy. *Capsizing of USS HULL in Typhoon off Luzon, 18 December 1944*. Film #334.

Mascoma message to ComThirdFlt, 190957, December, 1944.

Monterey message to CominCH and others, 211458, December, 1944.

Monterey Action Report, Serial 0036, 22 December 1944.

Orem, Howard, Captain, U.S. Navy. Memorandum dated 13 January 1945, to Commander in Chief, United States Fleet, summarizing the report of the court of inquiry.

Plage, Henry L., Lieutenant Commander, U.S. Naval Reserve, and Surham, Robert M., Lieutenant, U.S. Naval Reserve, commanding and executive officer respectively, USS *Tabberer*. Radio and Press Conference, Recorded at Pearl Harbor 16 January 1945.

Record of Proceedings of a court of inquiry convened on board the USS *Cascade* by order of the Commander in Chief, U.S. Pacific Fleet, on 26 December 1944.

Smith, Howard S., Lieutenant, U.S. Naval Reserve. Memorandum dated 12 January 1945, to Commander in Chief, U.S. Pacific Fleet, summarizing the Record of Proceedings of the court of inquiry.

Ship Characteristic Board Memorandum 46–45 (undated), Subject, Weight and Stability Control.

San Jacinto Report of Damage, Serial 0062, 24 December 1944.

Tabberer message to CinCPac and others, 181545, December, 1944.

Tabberer Report of Rescue of Survivors, Serial 003, 24 December 1944.
Tabberer Report of Storm Damage, Serial 002, 24 December 1944.

B. Sources located in the National Archives, Washington, D.C.

Deck log, USS *Aylwin* (DD355), month of December, 1944. Record Group 24, "Records of the Bureau of Naval Personnel."

Deck log, USS *Dewey* (DD349), month of December, 1944. Record Group 24, "Records of the Bureau of Naval Personnel."

Deck log, USS *Hull* (DD350), month of October, 1944. Record Group 24, "Records of the Bureau of Naval Personnel."

Deck log, USS *New Jersey* (BB62) month of December, 1944. Record Group 24, "Records of the Bureau of Naval Personnel."

Deck log, USS *Spence* (DD512), month of July, 1944. Record Group 24, "Records of the Bureau of Naval Personnel."

C. Sources located in the National Archives, National Records Center, Suitland, Maryland.

BuShips letter, file C-DD350/S38–1(814–638), dated 2 August 1944, to Commandant, Navy Yard, Puget Sound, and Commanding Officer, USS *Hull*, subject, USS *Hull* (DD350) Ventilation Changes. Record Group 19—General file.

BuShips letter, Serial 002338, to Chief of Naval Operations, dated 2 June 1945, subject, Report of Typhoon Damage to USS *Dewey* (DD349), and USS *Aylwin* (DD355), on 18 December 1944. Record Group 19—General file.

Chief of Naval Operations. Letter Op-23-B-PGB, Serial 00131223(SC)H–47, dated 22 March 1945. Record Group 19—General file.

Commander Destroyer Squadron One. Letter L11, Serial 001, dated 7 January 1945. Record Group 19—General file.

Commander in Chief, U.S. Pacific Fleet, Serial 005601, dated 5 March 1945, (second endorsement to ComDesRon One Serial 001, 7 January 1945). Record Group 19—General file.

Commander Third Fleet, Serial 0098, dated 3 February 1945, (first endorsement to ComDesRon One, Serial 001, 7 January 1945). Record Group 19—General file.

Crisp, P. G., Bureau of C&R. Memorandum dated 7 November 1939, to Admiral A. H. VanKeuren (CC), U.S. Navy, subject: General Comments on Destroyer Overweight and Stability. Record Group 19—General file.

Sub Board of Inspection and Survey, Third Naval District, Report of Material Inspection and Survey of USS *Aylwin* (DD355), 17 October 1945. Record Group 19—General file.

D. Sources located in the personal files of the author. (To be donated to the Naval Historical Center Operational Archives upon publication of this book.)

Aylwin letter, Serial 001, dated 15 June 1945, to Commander in Chief, United States Fleet, subject; Sea and Stability Characteristics of *Farragut*-Class Destroyers under Typhoon Conditions.

Bate, David S. Letters to the author dated 23 June and 14 December 1979.

BuShips mailgram, 172111 April, 1945, to Commander Destroyers Pacific Fleet and others.

Buzick, William A., Jr. Letter to the author dated 15 January 1959.

Commander in Chief, U.S. Pacific Fleet. Endorsement, Serial 006021, dated 28 May 1945, to *Dewey*, Serial 004, dated 12 March 1945.

Commander Destroyer Division Ten. Endorsement, Serial 0020, dated 8 April 1945, to *Dewey*, Serial 004, dated 12 March 1945.

Commander Destroyer Division Ten. Endorsement, Serial 027, dated 30 May 1945, to *Dewey*, Serial 012, dated 27 May 1945.

Commander Destroyer Division Ten. Endorsement, Serial 0037, dated 27 June 1945, to *Aylwin*, Serial 001, dated 15 June 1945.

Commander Destroyers Pacific Fleet Serial 0199, dated 6 July 1945, to Chief of the Bureau of Ships, subject: Cumulative Hull Damage to *Dewey* and Other *Farragut*-Class Destroyers.

Commander Destroyer Squadron One. Serial 001, dated 7 January 1945, to Commander in Chief, United States Fleet, subject: Report of Typhoon Damage to *Dewey* and *Aylwin*.

Commander Destroyer Squadron Five. Endorsement, Serial 00142, dated 11 May 1945, to *Dewey*, Serial 004, dated 12 March 1945.

Commander Destroyer Squadron Five. Endorsement, Serial 0177, dated 9 June 1945, to *Dewey*, Serial 012, dated 27 May 1945.

Commander Third Fleet. Endorsement, dated 1 May 1945, to Commander Destroyer Squadron One. Letter, Serial 07, dated 27 January 1945.

Commander Third Fleet. Endorsement, Serial 0098, dated 3 February 1945, to Commander Destroyer Squadron One, Serial 001, dated 7 January 1945.

Dewey letter, Serial 004, dated 12 March 1945, to Commander in Chief, United States Fleet, subject: Typhoon Damage and Cumulative Hull Damage.

Dewey letter, serial 012, dated 27 May 1945, to Commander Destroyers, Pacific Fleet, subject: Material Condition of *Dewey*.

Executive officer, USS *Macdonough*. Memorandum to commanding officer, dated 7 April 1945, subject: Stability of USS *Macdonough*.

Mercer, Preston V., Captain, U.S. Navy. Personal letter to Fleet Admiral Nimitz, 19 December 1944.

Nickum, W. V. and Sons. Letter to Assistant to Industrial Manager, U.S. Navy, Seattle, 9 April 1945, subject: USS *Macdonough* Stability.

Puget Sound Navy Yard, (Assistant to Industrial Manager, U.S. Navy, Seattle). Letter, Serial 20295, dated 11 April 1945, to Chief of the Bureau of Ships, subject: USS *Macdonough* Stability.

Rogers, W. K., Captain, U.S. Navy (Retired). Letter to Captain George F. Kosco, U.S. Navy (Retired), 17 March 1966.

Rogers, W. K., Captain, U.S. Navy (Retired). Letters to the author, dated 25 November 1978, and 20 February 1979.

Superintendent of Ships, U.S. Navy, Seattle. Undated message to BuShips, reporting results of inclining test of USS *Macdonough* (DD351) on 30 March 1945.

Todd Pacific Shipyards, Inc. Letter to Assistant Industrial Manager, U.S. Navy, Seattle, dated 21 April 1945, subject: Weight Changes—USS *Macdonough*.

Secondary Sources

A. Books

Adamson, Hans Christian, Colonel, U.S. Air Force (Retired) and Kosco, George Francis, Captain, U.S. Navy (Retired). *Halsey's Typhoons*. New York: Crown Publishers, Inc., 1967.

Bowditch, Nathaniel. *The American Practical Navigator*. Washington, D.C.: U.S. Government Printing Office, 1943.

Dictionary of American Naval Fighting Ships, Volumes I, II, III, IV, and VI. Washington: Navy Department, 1959 to 1976.

Furer, Julius Augustus, Rear Admiral, U.S. Navy (Retired). *Administration of the Navy Department in World War II*. Washington, D.C.: Navy Department, 1959.

Hackett, Sir John, General, British Army. *The Third World War, August 1985*. New York: Macmillan Publishing Co., Inc.

Halsey, William F., Fleet Admiral, U.S. Navy, and Bryan, J. III, Lieutenant Commander, U.S. Naval Reserve. *Admiral Halsey's Story*. New York and London: McGraw-Hill Book Company, Inc., 1976.

Knight, Austin M., Rear Admiral, U.S. Navy. *Modern Seamanship*. New York: D. Van Nostrand Company, Inc., 1941.

Manning, G. C., Lieutenant Commander (C.C.), U.S. Navy, and Schumacher, T. L., Lieutenant Commander (C.C.), U.S. Navy. *Principles of Warship Construction and Damage Control*. Annapolis: U.S. Naval Institute, 1935.

Morison, Samuel Eliott, Rear Admiral, U.S. Naval Reserve. *History of United States Naval Operations in World War II: The Liberation of the Philippines*. Boston: Little, Brown & Co., 1959.

Naval Courts and Boards. Washington, D.C.: United States Government Printing Office, 1937.

Potter, E. B. *Nimitz*. Annapolis: Naval Institute Press, 1976.

Roscoe, Theodore. *United States Destroyer Operations in World War II*. Annapolis: U.S. Naval Institute, 1953.

B. Periodicals

Baldwin, Hanson W. "When the Third Fleet Met the Great Typhoon." *New York Times Magazine*, December 16, 1951. ©1951 by the New York Times Company. Reprinted by permission.

Calhoun, C. Raymond, Captain, U.S. Navy, and Hubbel, John. *Typhoon.* *Reader's Digest*, January, 1959.

Kehoe, James W., Jr., Captain, U.S. Navy. *Destroyer Seakeeping: Ours and Theirs*. Annapolis: U.S. Naval Institute *Proceedings*, November, 1973.

"Old Pat," Army and Navy Operations. *Time* Magazine, November 5, 1945.

Index

67, 111; topside damage, 99, repairs, 189; assigned to TG 50.8, 190; topside weight reduction, 190; new stack, 190–92; at Iwo Jima, 192; fights *Patuxent* fire, 192; decommissioned, 199

Essex: hit by Kamikaze, 25
Edsall, Warner B., Commander, USN, ComDesDiv 110: responds to Jim Marks, 71

Factors contributing to disaster, 170–81
Farragut: designated flagship, ComDesDiv Two, 24; Lieutenant Commander C. C. Hartigan, USN, commanding officer, 24
Farragut-class destroyers: history and characteristics, 3, 4; compared to *Fletchers* and *Sumners*, 5; stability described, 133, 169; transferred to Atlantic Fleet, 198
Farrin, James M., Jr., Commander, USN, ServRon Ten assistant maintenance officer: witness at court of inquiry, 135, 156, 157, 158; loss of destroyers, 158
Findings of fact: eighty-four findings, 161
Forrestal, James, Secretary of the Navy: approval of endorsement, 203
Fowler, Oliver, Watertender 1/c, USN, *Dewey*: in charge, after fireroom, 60
Franks: 180730 fuel report, 46
Fueling rendezvous: locations, 34, 129

Gaffney, G. C., Lieutenant (jg), MC, USN, *Spence* medical officer: described by Krauchunas, 79
Garrett, William Bruce, Lieutenant Commander, USN, *Monaghan* commanding officer: description, 24; assumed command, 24; directed ballasting, 76
Gates, Herbert K., Captain, USN, *Cascade* commanding officer: biography, 123
Gibson, Robert C., Lieutenant (jg), USN, *Dewey* engineering officer: description, 11; assumed duties as chief engineer, 25; exercised leadership, 60
Ground, C. L., Seaman 2/c, USNR, *Spence*: on life raft, 80

Guio, Joseph, Jr., Gunner's Mate 3/c, USN, *Monaghan*: advice to McCrane, 77; dies from injuries, 78

Halsey, William F., Admiral, USN, Commander Third Fleet: responsibilities, 25; communications deception, 25; withdraws TF 38, 29; concerned about escorts, 33; suspends fueling, 34; changes rendezvous, 36, 38, 43, reflections concerning, 40; heads west, 44; requests McCain's estimate, 44; cancels rendezvous, 45; directs turn to south, 46; reports to MacArthur, 46; tells CinCPacFlt he is in typhoon, 49; directs search, 49; sets rendezvous for 19th, 49; asks whereabouts of *Spence, Monaghan* and *Waterman*, 100; learns extent of damage, 100; informed of loss of *Spence*, 103; cancels air strikes, 106; reports disaster to Nimitz, 107; searches for survivors, 116; conflicting considerations, 128; testimony, 136–40; "interested party," 140; "preponderance of responsibility," 167; second court of inquiry, 197
Halsey Powell: stands by *Cowpens*, 49
Hancock: hit by Kamikaze, 26
Harrison, S. H. Lieutenant (jg), USNR, *Dewey*: OOD, midwatch, 18 December, 40
Hartigan, Conway C., Lieutenant Commander, USN, *Farragut* commanding officer: description, 22; Herman the chicken, 23
Hean, James H., Commander, USN, TF 38 navigator and tactical officer: testimony, 130
Heater, Seaman 1/c, USNR, *Spence*: on life raft, 80, lost from raft, 116
Herman, the Gilbert Islands chicken: mascot of the *Farragut*, 23
Hickox: attempts to refuel, 34; 180730 fuel report, 46; narrative of typhoon, 80–82; ballasted, 81; control of flooding, 81; rolled to 70 degrees, 81
Hill, Dorwin, Chief Machinists Mate, USN, *Dewey*: loss of lubricating oil, 57, 60
Hill, Harry W., Vice Admiral, USN: mention, 13
Hobson, Buythle E., Machinists Mate 1/c, USN, *Dewey*: remained at his post, 61